THE TRANSLATED JEW

CULTURAL EXPRESSIONS OF WORLD WAR II
INTERWAR PRELUDES, RESPONSES, MEMORY

PHYLLIS LASSNER, SERIES EDITOR

THE TRANSLATED JEW

GERMAN JEWISH CULTURE OUTSIDE THE MARGINS

LESLIE MORRIS

NORTHWESTERN UNIVERSITY PRESS | EVANSTON, ILLINOIS

Northwestern University Press
www.nupress.northwestern.edu

Copyright © 2018 by Northwestern University Press. Published 2018. All rights
reserved.

Printed in the United States of America

10   9   8   7   6   5   4   3   2   1

ISBN 978-0-8101-3763-9 (paper)
ISBN 978-0-8101-3764-6 (cloth)
ISBN 978-0-8101-3765-3 (e-book)

Cataloging-in-Publication data are available from the Library of Congress.

For Shevvy: "*m'illumino d'immenso*"

CONTENTS

ACKNOWLEDGMENTS

This book has taken many years to come to print, and I owe thanks to many people along the way. I am grateful for the support I have received from the Department of German, Scandinavian and Dutch; the Institute for Advanced Study; and the Center for Jewish Studies at the University of Minnesota. A single-semester leave from the College of Liberal Arts made it possible to complete parts of the book. To the following friends and colleagues at the University of Minnesota I owe many thanks: Gary Cohen, Rembert Hüser, Ruth-Ellen Joeres, Amy Kaminsky, Bernard Levinson, Mary Jo Maynes, Rick McCormick, Natan Paradise, Naomi Scheman, Barbara Wolbert, and Jack Zipes. Rabbi Morris Allen has helped me to rethink what it means to live as a Jew within the margins. I am indebted to Jonathan Boyarin for his suggestion of the book's title during a conversation in Durham a number of years ago. Riv-Ellen Prell, a trusted colleague, teacher, and close friend, has been one of the most important intellectual partners for me during my years at the University of Minnesota; I am grateful to her for her astute comments on earlier drafts of the manuscript. Maria Damon has been an ongoing source of inspiration and, in her words, "confabulation," in particular for helping me stage the "Semi(o)text" gatherings in Minneapolis that brought Ben Friedlander, Adeena Karasick, Elliott Malkin, and Alan Sondheim to campus. I am also grateful to Maria for helping me meet the late Anne Blonstein before her death; our correspondence, some of it in the form of *notarikon* poems, is something I will always treasure. Conversations over the years with Kim Leighton have guided my thinking about centers, margins, philosophy, and Jewishness. My sisters Michele Morris-Friedman and Nicole Morris McNeel know what it means to live in translation and outside the margins of Jewishness, and are etched into every page of this book. My nieces Catherine McNeel and Juliette McNeel, bilingual muses, were present in spirit throughout the writing of this book.

In addition, friends and colleagues at the German Studies Association and the Association for Jewish Studies whose insights have been productive for me over the years include Nora Alter, Karyn Ball, Bill Donohue, Amir Eshel, Ben Friedlander, Katja Garloff, Dan Gilfillan, Sander Gilman, Atina Grossmann, Barbara Hahn, Jonathan Hess, Sara Horowitz, Irene Kacandes, Adeena Karasick, Marion Kaplan, Joseph Moser, Todd Presner, Scott Spector, and Liliane Weissberg. To Jay Geller I owe a special debt of gratitude as friend and coeditor of our volume on German Jewish studies, *Three-Way Street: Jews, Germans, and the Transnational*. Karen Remmler has been a close and constant friend and collaborator. I am especially grateful for the input I received from her when she read an earlier draft of this manuscript, and for always urging me to move beyond the margins. Richard Block, trusted friend and confidant, read parts of the manuscript and made invaluable suggestions. I am especially grateful to Don Eric Levine, *il miglior fabbro*, for his insightful comments as I was preparing the manuscript for publication. Martin Hainz has been a steady interlocutor over the years at a number of conferences we have found ourselves at on Czernowitz and Rose Ausländer. I am grateful, as always, for his wry and intelligent commentary, and to Andrei Corbea-Hoisie for our many conversations about Jewish life in Czernowitz. For access to the Ausländer Nachlass in the archives first at the Heinrich Heine Institut in Düsseldorf and later at the Ausländer Stiftung, I remain indebted to Helmut Braun; without his help and support, I would never have written about Rose Ausländer. I am grateful to the Rosenfeld collection in Philadelphia for access to unpublished letters between Marianne Moore and Rose Ausländer. I also want to express my thanks to Daniel Blaufuks, Miklós Mécs, Ulrike Mohr, Shelley Jackson, Elliott Malkin, Daniel Seiple, and the collective of the Berlin Sculpture Park for permission to reprint their images.

Portions of several chapters of this book were first presented as invited lectures. I am grateful to the engaged audiences who helped me to develop my ideas at Dartmouth College, Cornell University, Stanford University, the University of Oregon, Washington University, University of Arkansas, Kenyon College, Arizona State University, University of Florida, Emory University, York University, and the universities of Basel, Graz, Frankfurt, Münster, Freiburg, Lisbon, Munich, Iasi, and the Viadrini Universität in Frankfurt/Oder. I am also indebted to my graduate students at the University of Minnesota, whose insights into many of the texts I discuss in this book were formative.

Grateful acknowledgment is due to the following books and journals in which earlier versions of parts of this book, all of them substantially revised, appeared: "How Jewish Is It? W. G. Sebald and the Question of Contemporary German-Jewish Writing," in *The New German Jewry and the European Context: The Return of the European Diaspora*, ed. Y. Michal Bodemann (New York: Palgrave Macmillan, 2008), 111–28; "Spuren Europas im jüdisch-amerikanischen Schreiben: Alfred Kazin," in *Abschied von Europa: Jüdisches Schreiben zwischen 1930 und 1950*, ed. Alfred Bodenheimer und Barbara Breysach (Munich: Edition text + kritik, 2010), 123–41; "Epistemology of the Hyphen: German-Jewish/-Holocaust Studies," in *Persistent Legacy: The Holocaust and German Studies*, ed. Jennifer M. Kapczysnki and Erin McGlothlin (Rochester, N.Y.: Camden House, 2016), 107–19; "Reading H. G. Adler (Tangentially)," in *H. G. Adler: Life, Literature, Legacy*, ed. Julia Creet, Sara Horowitz, and Amira Dan (Evanston, Ill.: Northwestern University Press, 2016), 375–91; "The Translated J/je/jew/Jude/Juif," in *Trans-lation—trans-nation—trans-formation: Übersetzen und jüdische Kulturen*, ed. Petra Ernst, Hans-Joachim Hahn, Daniel Hoffmann, and Dorothea Salzer (Innsbruck: Studienverlag, 2012), 209–18; "Der modifizierte Jude als Stigmatext," in "Erinnern und Geschlecht," Band II, ed. Meike Penkwitt und Jennifer Moos, special issue, *Freiburger FrauenStudien* 13, no. 20 (2007): 85–101; "Translating Czernowitz: The Non-Place of East Central Europe," *Studies in 20th and 21st Century Literature* 31, no. 1 (2007): 187–205; "Poesie und Verlust: Zur Ästhetik in Rose Ausländers Lyrik," in *Blumenworte welkten: Identität und Fremdheit in Rose Ausländers Lyrik*, ed. Jens Birkmeyer (Bielefeld: Aisthesis Verlag: 2008), 67–76; "*Folg mir nicht nach, mein Bruder*: Rose Ausländers Übertragungen von Gedichten Itsik Mangers," in *Rose Ausländer: Sprachmächtige Zeugin des 20. Jahrhunderts* (Weilerswist: Schriftenreihe der Rose-Ausländer-Gesellschaft, Band 20, 2015), 151–59; and "*Omissions Are Not Accidents*: Rose Ausländer, Marianne Moore und die amerikanische Moderne," ed. Helmut Braun and Walter Engel, in *Gebt unseren Worten nicht / euren Sinn* (Cologne: Schriftenreihe der Rose-Ausländer-Stiftung und des Gerhart-Hauptmann-Hauses, 2001), 97–110.

Phyllis Lassner, editor of the Northwestern University Press series

Cultural Expressions of World War II, deserves special mention for her enthusiastic support of this project. I want to also thank the anonymous readers of Northwestern University Press for their thorough and helpful readings and suggestions about the text. Trevor Perri has been a wonderful editor to work with. Anna Brailovsky and Ann Klefstad were of great help in preparing the manuscript. Thanks as well to Anne Carter for her expert eye on final details. I am indebted to Meyer Weinshel for his help in tracking down Yiddish citations, and to Adelia Chrysler for bibliographic help.

Finally, *The Translated Jew* owes its largest debt of gratitude to Shevvy Craig for thirty-nine years of partnership, four years of marriage, and four shared German shepherd dogs; for reading every page I have ever written; for conversations with me in English, French, German, Italian, and beyond; and for living with me, in translation, always. I dedicate this book to her.

THE TRANSLATED JEW

The Translated J/Je/Juif/Jude/Jew

My mother had a favorite joke that she would tell again and again, in a mixture of English and French. "A cannibal is on an Air France flight. The stewardess asks if he would like to see the menu. 'Non merci, Madame, seuelement la liste des passagers' [No thank you, Madame. Only the passenger list, please]." My mother would be laughing so hard that she could hardly get the punchline out. My mother, who had herself arrived in the United States on a boat from France (and not on an Air France flight) shortly after World War II, loved this joke because it allowed her, through its overtly racist and colonialist prism, to seem French by breezily telling a joke inscribed within French colonial history. "A cannibal is on an Air France flight." Was the joke a gesture of both defiance and allegiance—a declaration, unabashed, of passing, of becoming, through telling the joke, more "French"? Was she in fact like the "très élégant" cannibal, forever passing (as a Hungarian half-Jew in Paris during the war)? Or was the reiteration of the joke a way for my mother to replace and drown out her own story that she never told?

I begin with my mother's joke because it captures both the anxieties and the necessities of translating, as well as the political stakes of being and becoming the "translated Jew" of my title. For if my mother longed to cover her Jewishness with the cloak of Frenchness by obsessively retelling the colonialist joke, the other side to this is that the "cannibal" was forced into his Frenchness. This fraught relationship between Jewishness and translation also marks the genesis of this project. This book has come into being through a long series of encounters with texts, and with my own experience growing up in the United States in a household in which English, French, and Hungarian were spoken; with this childhood multilingual cacophony came a sense that to navigate the complex terrain of what it means to be a Jew in the twentieth century is to simultaneously make one's way, repeatedly, through a morass of languages.

This is what is invoked in the work of Hélène Cixous. In a short autobiographical piece, "My Algériance," Cixous recounts that her German Jewish mother, "in the double grip of Nazi Germany and Vichy Algeria," would never say the word "Jew" out loud in the street in Oran. "All that was left of us was the letter J. J became my first favorite letter: with great energy I said *je*."[1] Stitching together the memory of cultural laceration (as she calls it) in this "stigmatext" of an attempt at autobiography, in which she claims that "all literature is scarry," Cixous carves Jewish subjectivity directly into the scars, or "stigmata," of language and silence: the failure and interruption of speaking the "J"—the word "Jew" cut, wounded, stitched, and substituted as the J that trails off to another sound: the *je* (I).[2]

The Translated Jew: German Jewish Culture outside the Margins begins here: at the interstices of Jewish subjectivity, the place where Cixous articulates the impossibility and also the necessity of "speaking the J." It begins with the multiple meanings of the Jew and the textual forms this multiplicity has taken. Cixous's insistence on thinking and writing "the Jewish" beyond the margins marks my starting place in thinking about the vicissitudes of translation and "the Jewish." The very question of what text is, and what Jewish text is and can be, is at the heart of my project. For Cixous, the Jew has been, and can only be, "translated": speaking and writing "the J," Cixous insists on the multiple processes of translation in which the J is simultaneously the "Jude" and the "Jew" and the "juif," in addition to her mother's suppressed and suffocated sound of the "j/je."

The Translated Jew suggests both a mode of reading that is always, after Benjamin, a reading between the texts and a way of navigating the borders of literary Jewish cultures. It also takes as a point of departure Todd Presner's insistence on the "always already Jewishness" of German culture. In *Mobile Modernity: Jews, Germans, Trains*, Presner dislocates the hyphen between German and Jew in the expression "German-Jewish," turning instead to Derrida's "separatix" to insist that "German modernity is always already German/Jewish modernity. The two are inextricably and fundamentally linked. To reinsert the Jews into 'German culture' would be to imply that they can be truly removed."[3] Presner's extended discussion not only of the entanglement of German and Jewish, but of the ways in which each is "contaminated" by the other and constitutive of the other, finds resonance in *The Translated Jew* in particular in the reflections on self-translation. To return to Cixous and the question she poses of the language of the Jew as signaling multiple family dislocations (France/Germany/Algeria and beyond): as she says in another piece, "a language always speaks several languages at once, and runs with a single word in opposite directions."[4] Writing in another essay in *Stigmata*, Cixous echoes her earlier text on Algeria and its meditation on the J:

> Had I not unthinkingly signed a pact with the letter J among all the letters of the French language, the J, pronounced gee g'it j'y, for Jew in my mother's secret wartime language: he's a J, she would say, to say it without saying it, J the name of the secret, had J not been the name of the most French of all possible letters in the mouth of my German mother—for in German J does not gee, does not jeer, the J winks and wets, it's a yeu, yes, a Jod, pronounced yod, for me J was the alpha and omega of letters, the countersignature in person, the first person.[5]

Cixous gives us a textual case history that documents the multiple ghostings that haunt not only all Jewish writing, but especially the category of German Jewish writing.

I start with Cixous—a German Jewish/Algerian/French refugee writer speaking and not speaking the J/je—to think about the multidirectionality and the polysemy between Jewish and non-Jewish spaces and texts. Cixous's "Algériance" suggests a new way of thinking about affective ties and citizenship, place and the non-place, with the sound of the word "Algériance" linking (and lacerating) Algeria and France, pledging allegiance and forging alliance (in the present progressive, her tense of choice, a sort of eternal present) with the hybrid merged sounds of place, history, and memory.[6] More significantly, to read the German Jewish back into Cixous as writer is to conceptualize, indeed to "translate," a new law of return in the great dispersed imagined community of German Jewry beyond the borders not only of Germany but also of Jewishness. To think of Cixous as a German Jew (or German-J, saying "je") is to imagine German Jewishness as an off-center state of being, of being forever "en passance." The glissando of Cixous's "J" and the silenced "juif" spoken and not spoken by her mother is an apt starting point for approaching the vicissitudes of translation and "the Jewish."

With Cixous as a guidepost, *The Translated Jew: German Jewish Culture outside the Margins* seeks to expand the parameters that have defined what constitutes Jewish text. It also seeks to unmoor the category of German Jewish text from the strictures of a national literature that has, of necessity, needed to delineate its borders. In this, it also takes its cue from Deleuze and Guattari's pivotal essay on Kafka in *Towards a Minor Literature*. Defining a minor literature as that written by a minor voice in a major language, they sketch out the political possibilities of a nomadic, deterritorialized literature "on the run" that has at its core an emphasis on the collective, "machinic" assemblage and not the voice of an individual writing subject.[7] It is no accident that this pivotal piece of literary philosophy has at its center a rumination on the work of Franz Kafka. What Deleuze and Guattari sketch out is a way of thinking about language and ethnicity—specifically, the situation of Kafka, the deterritorialized Czech Jew writing in German—that exists in the "cramped space" of the minor. Their refrain of "being a stranger in one's own language,"[8] of "being a nomad and an immigrant and a gypsy in relation to one's own language," is one of the chords I return to often throughout this book.[9]

The Translated Jew thus echoes the call of Deleuze and Guattari to embrace the "polylingualism in one's own language."[10] It is intentionally free-ranging: it takes as a given the mutability of textuality and of Jewishness, arguing throughout for the capaciousness of Jewish text's inclusions of the polysemic and polylingual. It is an attempt to move farther into the "trans": into the lines between and among translation, transnation, and transformation. It seeks to deterritorialize the question of Jewishness and boundedness (textual and geographical boundedness) as it moves back and forth between Europe and America. *The Translated Jew* does not consider the points of contact between Germany, the United States, and Israel in the textual transmission of Jewishness. There has been a significant body of scholarship on German-Hebrew translation, and even more recently, critical attention to the important work done by Israeli new media and other visual artists who live and work in Berlin.[11] Yet my decision not to include discussion of the important cultural exchange and transmission between German and Hebrew literary and artistic works is both deliberate and strategic: it is part of an attempt to reimagine a post-Holocaust German Jewish aesthetic that does not assign to modern Hebrew (or to the state of Israel) the status created by earlier generations of Germanists, and instead looks to the exchange between Germany and the United States as the primary focal point.

In the chapters that follow, I bring together a disparate set of literary and visual texts in order to create polysemic readings that complicate the relationships among language, place, and meaning in order to expand and "translate" (and not police) the borders of "Jewish" art and literature and the matrix of Jewish history, Jewish memory, Jewish culture, and Jewish urban space. In particular, this book seeks to reconceptualize the very category of German Jewish text and German Jewish subjectivity, especially in what I term the *age of authorial disintegration*. Recent critical work on subjectivity has acknowledged what Emily Apter has termed its "signs of fatigue." Yet more than thirty years after Foucault and Barthes proclaimed their axiomatic death sentences on the author, popular and critical debates are still dominated by a notion of the authenticity of the writing subject, and critical practices have kept the German Jewish author on life support.

The Translated Jew grapples throughout with a set of questions that are at once deeply historical and deeply textual: how does the trace of Jewish history in Germany today shape and mark the complex repatternings of Jewish text? What does it mean to conceptualize Jewish text "outside the margins"—pushing its borders to allow both the Jewishness and the textuality to seep out of the margins, off the page, out of the museum, and outside the closed quarters of the very "center/margin" paradigm that dominates discussions of minority writing? What might it mean to move past a paradigm of boundedness in thinking about the relationship of Jews to other cultures and the relationship of Jewish text to other texts, to think not of boundedness but rather of a "klezmerical" relationship between Jews and other Others?[12] Scholarly work on Jewish literature has long recognized it in such terms—as transnational, multilingual, hybrid. To this I add the category of translation as a fundamental condition of Jewish subjectivity and Jewish text. Translation here is not simply the literary act of moving from one language to another or the cultural transmission that results from moving among texts; rather, it is a "carrying over" of the continual accrual of meaning, metaphor, and sound. In this way, it is marked always in the space "after," in the "post," as an elegiac memory of what comes before, as text that exists always in a state of belatedness.

Yet the discourse about belatedness and mourning keeps the question of Jewishness and translation locked into traumatic structures of language and meaning-making, in which the paradigm of loss and mourning presupposes a similar "lostness" of the translated text, as it relies on a notion of the "original" that is forever irretrievable. This post-lapsarian mode has dominated both literary theory rooted in Derridean conceptions of the ruptures that are constitutive of language and scholarly work on European Jewish culture after the Shoah. *The Translated Jew* instead moves the conversation about Jewishness and translation out of these structures of traumatic loss and mourning, and thinks of the performativity and narrativity of Jewishness and of Jewish text. These performances of writing and reading are enacted in the present as part of encounters between, in, and among Jewish and non-Jewish spaces and texts. These encounters and their role in the accrual and buildup of language are the cornerstone of this project of thinking about Jewishness and translation. To return to Cixous—the continual suppression of the "J" is as much a translation of Jewishness as the repetition of tropes of mourning and loss (shtetl, concentration camp) that have shaped post-Shoah literature.

But let me be more specific about my claims for Jewish text and the translations of Jewishness. Naomi Seidman's *Faithful Renderings: Jewish-Christian Difference and the Politics of Translation* presents an overt challenge to the paradigms of otherness, informed by Anglo-American postcolonial theory, which underlie pivotal work in translation studies. Taking as a point of departure the repression of the heterogeneity within the West that enables it to constitute itself as a unified subject looking at the "other" that is then truly outside, Seidman reminds us of the very particular place of Jews within this cultural imaginary of difference: "Jews become paradoxically central to Western translation in and through the suppression of their difference. Jews are refigured in this conception not only as untranslatable figures—we might say, unconvertible to Christianity—but also as the very site of untranslatability."[13]

Seidman's exploration of Jewish–Christian translation also uncovers what she terms "Christian genealogical anxiety" about the "translational relationship" between Judaism and Christianity, a fixed belief (despite its recent unravelings such as those by Daniel Boyarin and others) in Judaism's role as the "original" to Christianity's "translation." Seidman's book explores precisely the ruptures of this formulation of Jewishness and translation, challenging the formulation of Judaism as Christianity's (reviled) Other.[14] Seidman shifts the focus to include the role of Jews and Jewish text and the inherent narrativity of translation, thus challenging the model of a "universal translatability" and insisting instead on the persistence of translation narrative, translation stories, and translation performance.[15] Taking this one step further, Seidman points to the ways in which translation narratives are temporal, rooted and enacted in time; following Benjamin's mantra about the "Überleben" of the translated text (parsed by Paul de Man in his famous essay about the mistranslations of Benjamin's translation essay into English as "the afterlife"), Seidman thus suggests that the original undergoes a change in its "afterlife"

> because it participates in the movement that is the necessary cor-
> relative of a text being alive. If we call this movement, in the case
> of Jews and their texts, diaspora, and resist as Benjamin does the
> rhetoric of loss, then Jewish culture, as other cultures, emerges
> as a continual translation and transformation, in different lan-
> guages and at different moments in time.[16]

I have lingered on Naomi Seidman's parsing of the translational anxi-eties of Christians toward Jews, and the suggestion in her work of the pervasive translational ambiguity of conversion (of people) that parallels conversion as translation, because what she outlines concerning the re-lationship between Jews and Christians in late antiquity has resonance for thinking about contemporary Jewish culture. The assertion of Jewish culture as existing in a perpetual state of continual translation (analogous to Cixous's state of being forever *en passance*) and thus not marked by the loss ordinarily ascribed to translation—enables us to move past the model of texts being "lost in translation." Thus Seidman's claims (her re-jection of the notion of Jewish translation as "essential" because she sees it instead as rooted in a Derridean sense of undecidability) are vital for the work of literary scholars who aim to break down the intact national, ethnic, and religious structures that have kept Jewish text in its own sort of ghetto.

Furthermore, I want to make a plea for more porous lines between the secular and the religious. As national literature disciplines have gradually absorbed the now-evident transnational mobilities between cultures and national identity, it seems odd that other taxonomies (such as secular and religious) remain unchallenged dichotomies. Yet as a number of new scholarly initiatives in Jewish studies make clear, it is precisely this porousness between culture and nation, the religious and the secular, that opens possibilities for thinking about Jewish text in its various and complex forms. While these borders are being challenged—notably in the substantive debates about the politics of secularism by scholars such as Talal Asad, whose attempt to map an anthropology of the secular carries with it the recognition of the buried traces of "the religious" within secular culture—they often linger as unquestioned assumptions.[17]

In order to consider more fully this porousness between the secular and the religious, and to think about "the translated J," this book explores a range of works, including conventional as well as experimental and conceptual art and poetry, fiction, and visual art. Throughout, it aims to open, expand, and change the very definition of Jewish text. As the subtitle of this book, *German Jewish Culture outside the Margins*, makes clear, it is not only the marginal text to which I turn in the pages that follow, but rather the relationship between center and margin in the first place. This book does not take up the debates about the canon that were so formative three decades ago in literary studies; rather, it makes the claim that it is in the place "outside the margins," that is, outside the paradigm of a center/periphery, that Jewish writing can best be understood.

This book insists upon the always provisional nature of Jewish text. Drawing on Jonathan Boyarin's notion of "thinking in Jewish," a "Jewish" that is a "partial" and "failed translation" for the word "Yiddish,"[18] I explore the idea of the Jewish as always provisional, as always part of a cultural and linguistic operation that has at its source translation—cultural, linguistic, and textual. If anything, this book is dedicated to a process of interrogating "the Jewish" similar to what Boyarin undertakes in *Thinking in Jewish*: to think or read or write in "Jewish" is to already be engaged in the act of translation, and to understand Jewish language as inherently multilingual, transnational, always in a state of becoming. As Boyarin argues, to think "in Jewish" is to retranslate the Yiddish intransitive verb *zikh arayntrakhtn*, literally "to think oneself into something, meaning to consider a matter in depth."[19] He puts forward an idea of Jewishness that insists on the transitivity of Jewish identity: that it is always in process, "ushering in . . . a different Jewish identity through thought."[20]

Historians, literary critics, and cultural studies scholars have in recent years turned their attention to the dynamic interaction between Jews and non-Jews in a variety of geographical and historical encounters (from the early modern period to the present, from the Mediterranean to the United States), stressing how these various groups, previously regarded as heterogeneous and separate, instead demonstrate an interactive encounter that speaks more to the porousness between and among cultures than it does to distinct, separate cultural spheres. Similarly, recent work has explored the complex entanglement of Americanness and Jewishness, an entanglement and interaction that moves in both directions. The American studies scholar Jonathan Freedman, in his recent study *Klezmer America: Jewishness, Ethnicity, Modernity*, suggests a "klezmerical reading" of American Jewish experience: "an experience that stresses the Jews' persistent ability, most evident in their experience in the United States, to engage in a syncretic, hybridizing engagement with a national culture in ways that transform both their own identity and experience and that of the culture at large."[21] To a great extent, this approach within Jewish studies examines more closely the interactions between Jews and non-Jews; recently, work in German Jewish studies has shifted its focus from the impact of non-Jewish culture on Jewish literature, philosophy, and the arts to consider the encounter and impact of Jewish cultural production on the non-Jewish world. As the work of Marc Schell, Werner Sollors, and Hanna Wirth-Nesher makes clear, the field of American literary studies conceptualizes American Jewish writing as transnational, multilingual, hybridized. Wirth-Nesher, in particular, has succinctly demonstrated that while American Jewish writing is by definition multilingual and transnational, the scholarship on American Jewish literature has tended to see it as "one among other European ethnic literatures in the United States, and when read in the framework of Jewish literature, it has been detached from the American literary and cultural forces that have shaped it. Neither of these approaches exclusively can account for the unique contribution of Jewish American writing to the evolution of a transnational, multicultural American literary history."[22]

The Translated Jew also addresses the ongoing debate in the field of Jewish literary studies about what constitutes Jewish literature in the first place. Drawing on Dan Miron's *From Continuity or Contiguity: Toward a New Jewish Literary Thinking*, it seeks to add German Jewish text to Miron's formulation of what constitutes a modern Jewish literary historiography. Miron's model takes Jewish literature beyond the strictly canonical and nationally delineated categories that have sought to order it as part of a historical and cultural continuity. Instead, Miron offers a view of the many strains of "Jewish" writing as "vast, orderly, and somewhat diffuse . . . characterized by dualities, parallelisms, occasional intersections . . . contiguities."[23] In his plea for us to break from the "matrix of Jewish continuity," Miron enjoins us to embrace his notion of "contiguity":

> a kind of a light or diminished contact that would not throw us back into that trip; a contact that avoids all permanencies, is in flux, can be seen as random, and yet is indicative of mobility— free and unfettered—within a space that is vast and open, but then also, in the final analysis, not infinite, because it is circumscribed by a borderline, which can be very fine and barely noticed or deeply and clearly etched. In our case, this is the borderline of Jewishness: not of Judaism as a religious, civilizational, or national entity, "essence," or system, but of the perception of reality through (or also through) the screen of the experience of being "a Jew in the world," to use Buber's phrase—an experience that can be as divergent and multifarious as that of being in love or of being sick.[24]

It is his acknowledgment of the discontinuities, the ruptures and breaks that constitute Jewish literary history, which makes Miron's work so important for rethinking the place of German Jewish text within the matrix of modern European and American cultures. In addition, Miron's wide-ranging definition of Jewishness, Jewish text, and Jewish culture is tied to his articulation of the idea of Jewish literary community as a shared space modeled on contiguity, touching, and the tangential—a space defined by being a "Jew in the world" (*Judesein*). Thus Miron opens up a new way of thinking about the parameters of what constitutes Jewish text, of prying open the spaces of "literary *Judesein*" to see the "strange and wonderful encounters [that] are discreetly and even unconsciously taking place, which the conventional critical imagination would never have dreamt were possible."[25] To be sure, Miron's magical mystery tour of Jewish literary spaces as inhabiting the world of the imaginary itself requires a certain leap of faith. Yet his insights into a way of thinking conceptually about Jewish literary spaces find their way into the various literary and artistic encounters I formulate throughout *The Translated Jew*. Throughout the readings that follow, I draw primarily on his notion of a "tangential" reading to link the disparate authors and artists who populate the pages of *The Translated Jew*.

Similarly, *The Translated Jew* draws on the formative work done by Hana Wirth-Nesher in articulating the fundamentally multilingual nature of Jewish text. In her 2006 work *Call It English: The Languages of Jewish American Literature*, Wirth-Nesher draws on Shmuel Niger's famous claim, in 1941, that "one language has never been enough for the Jewish people." Drawing even more on Niger's claim, Wirth-Nesher points to the ways in which cultures and languages become inscribed, translated, and transmitted even by Jews who are monolingual.[26] Certainly a multilingual poetics has been at play in a number of Jewish cultures (Hebrew/Yiddish poets; Russian/Yiddish poets; German/Yiddish poets) in various locations. Yet while few would dispute the claim of multilingualism as constitutive of Jewish writing and even of Jewish identity, it is the mechanism of translation that I seek to add to this mix.

The emblematic literary text for thinking about the ways in which multiple languages are carried in any single language, and the role of translation in mediating between these modes and languages, is Henry Roth's 1934 modernist novel *Call It Sleep*, in which the English that the child protagonist, David Schearl, hears and translates is a language that carries with it the weight of multiple languages and the weight of living in between multiple languages. *Call It Sleep* is a text that challenges what language is actually being spoken and heard by David Schearl. That mystery is never solved for the reader, who is left in a linguistic maelstrom, unsure who is speaking in what language at any given point in the novel, forever at a loss to distinguish a translated from an eavesdropped conversation. The multilingualism of the book mirrors the experience of the child-narrator as he struggles to interpret the world of his family and the Lower East Side of New York. Roth, who was born in 1906 in the Habsburg crown land of Galicia and immigrated in 1909 to New York, wrote the novel in an English which suggests that it is at the same time a translation from the background murmur of Yiddish, Polish, and Yiddishized English of his own childhood.[27] What we read is the narrator's attempt to translate the Yiddish he hears and in which he thinks into the English of the actual text; at other points in the novel the narrator struggles to decipher the Polish that the adults around him speak so he will not understand what they are saying, into a Yiddish that the reader, however, never hears as Yiddish. With the cascade of languages both spoken and yet only conveyed through translation, the narrator attempts to impose a sort of coherence on the babble of languages that the reader is only dimly aware of. In this way, the narrator draws the reader in as fellow child on this linguistic playground, struggling to decipher and read the world.

If Henry Roth's *Call It Sleep* is the pivotal novel for the early twentieth-century articulation of the dislocated Jewish self wandering amid many languages, the late twentieth-century writer Raymond Federman provides an interesting counterpoint. Federman, an uncategorizable French/American writer, poet, essayist, critic of Samuel Beckett, and most significantly, "self-translator," writes about his "self-translations" in a piece entitled "A Voice within a Voice." Here Federman describes his work as a text in which there is no space "between the two languages. . . . On the contrary, for me French and English always seem to overlap, to want to merge, to want to come together, to want to embrace one another, to mesh one into the other."[28] He goes on to elucidate how he understands translation: "Usually when I finish a novel, . . . I am immediately tempted to write (rewrite, adapt, transform, transact, transcreate) the original into the other language. Even though finished, the book feels unfinished if it does not exist in the other language."[29] Federman's notion of the self-translation is a "transcreation" that becomes a continuation of the original, an "amplification," not an "approximation of the original, nor a duplication, nor a substitute, but truly a continuation of the work."[30] For Federman, the essence of bilingualism is play, a constant state of being attuned to the other, of having "a voice within a voice," a linguistic shadow that cannot be separated from the "self." At the end of "A Voice within a Voice" he writes: "In the totally bilingual book I would like to write, there would be no original language, no original source, no original text—only two languages that would exist, or rather co-exist outside of their origin, in the space of their own playfulness."[31]

Federman's project is also at its heart a deeply Jewish one in its insistence on the impossibility of locating any single textual origin, its commitment to the mutability of text, and the impossibility of separating original from translation. Charles Bernstein, in his preface to a book of essays on Federman, has described him as "our American Jabès, only the rabbis have been subsumed into the bouillabaisse."[32] Federman is, for Bernstein, the poet for whom "the Dark is the ground of his being and his becoming."[33] To inhabit this artistic circle (into which I would also place Paul Celan, W. G. Sebald, Italo Calvino, Fernando Pessoa, Jorge Luis Borges, and Samuel Beckett, self-translators all, and both Jews and non-Jews) means to be cast as one of the translated Jews that are the subject of this book: in other words, as a writer for whom the act of writing is simultaneously an act of translation. For Federman, a child survivor of the "1.5" generation,[34] to write is always to be aware of his own family history of the Holocaust, while acknowledging that it is not the events that count but rather the recounting of the events.[35] Federman thus calls for Jewish writing to "shift its vision and its energy from content to form (from the WHAT to the HOW)."[36]

The Translated Jew also shares some fundamental theoretical underpinnings with Benjamin Schreier's book *The Impossible Jew* (2015), which similarly seeks to dismantle the identitarian foundations of, specifically, Jewish American literary history, rethinking it in order to interrupt what Schreier calls the "reifying procedures that precognitively situate the thinking of difference in often nationalistically, and almost always positivistically, legible populations."[37] In his introduction, Schreier states that his aim in *The Impossible Jew* is, in part, "to help break down the walls of the ghetto in which Jewish literary study these days so often seems to be contained."[38] Schreier's concern is primarily with the ways in which American Jewish literary history has both fitted and not fitted into dominant paradigms at work in the larger field of American literary studies. Like Schreier, I underscore throughout *The Translated Jew* a similar insistence on breaking down a hegemonic view of Jewishness in order to advance the goal of opening up, of ventilating (to use the term Robert

Alter used, famously, in his 1974 piece in *Commentary*)[39] the very category of Jewishness in order to rethink American Jewish literary history.

More than this, *The Translated Jew* seeks to open further the transnational dialogue between European and American literature in order to dislocate, rupture, and point to the contiguous relationship circulating between the United States and Europe. It is the circulation of tropes of Jewishness between the United States and Europe that is at the very center of *The Translated Jew*. While paying close attention to the debates about "figural" vs. real Jews that have taken place over the past several decades, *The Translated Jew* moves the question of Jewishness and the multiple, shifting textual forms it can take in a different direction.[40]

Although Germany has played a formative role in European Jewish modernity, beginning with the *Wissenschaft des Judentums* (academic study of Judaism) to the contemporary reformulations of Jewish identity in a post-1989 Europe, it is in the field of American literary studies, in particular scholarship on American Jewish literature, that the imprint of these debates is most acute. In turning to the literary exchange between the United States and Europe throughout *The Translated Jew*, I also aim to foster interdisciplinary conversations that can help to break up the still-parochial strongholds of national literature departments. To this end, Marc Shell and Werner Sollors's *Multilingual Anthology of American Literature* (2000) serves as my model for a rethinking of the relationship between language, multilingualism, and place.[41] Shell and Sollor define American literature as literature produced in America, regardless of the language in which it is originally written. Thus their project sets out to do for American literature precisely what *The Translated Jew* tries to do for Jewish literature: namely, to rethink what happens when place and language are no longer synonymous. In breaking apart the relationship between language and place, Shell and Sollors have created an opening for rethinking the structures that have defined national and ethnic literatures.

To be sure, the project by Shell and Sollors enables a decoupling of language from place, and opens up a way to think about how to unmoor literature from its linguistic or cultural origins. And certainly, the centrality of Jewish culture to any discussion of multilingualism has been amply demonstrated, from the work done on Al-Andalus in medieval Spain, to the complicated encounters between Hebrew and Arabic in the early twentieth century and, for Habsburg Jewish cultures, on Czernowitz as the emblematic place of Jewish multilingualism. Yet I want to take up what Yasmin Yildiz has called "postmonolingualism," a term that challenges the primacy of the monolingual paradigm but more importantly, helps us to move past a mere celebration of the plurality of languages.[42] Rather than adhering to a binary of monolingualism vs. multilingualism, Yildiz suggests that the "postmonolingual" is one in which mono- and multilingualism are in a productive tension with one another. Yildiz's project, while not focusing primarily on Jewish culture, nonetheless adds an important lens through which we can examine Jewish life in late Habsburg Europe; in particular, her work brings together discourses around multilingual Jewish cultures (her starting point is Kafka in Prague) and the hybrid cultures that resulted from the interactions of German culture with Turkish and Asian texts.[43]

Finally, and also thinking, à la Boyarin, "in Jewish," *The Translated Jew* is haunted throughout by the pivotal German Jew Walter Benjamin, without whom any thinking about Jewishness and modernity would be nugatory.[44] Indeed, Benjamin might serve as perhaps the ultimate translated Jew: conceiving of text and culture always in its most provisional, broken form, teetering at the very edge of multiple moments of danger, he exemplifies a way of thinking, reading, and translating that shows us, as Boyarin has noted, "how to work with fragments of culture without the need to reinvent a fantasized whole."[45] It is the holding together of the shards of history and narrative, language and culture, past and present, that Benjamin has bequeathed to us.

In a frequently cited aphorism in the *Arcades Project*, Benjamin captures the relationship between text and its afterlife, and between past and present, history and text: the heart of the question of translation developed in this book. In this characteristically condensed aphorism that has sparked extensive critical discussion, he writes: "In the fields with which we are concerned, knowledge comes only in lightning flashes. The text is the long roll of thunder that follows."[46] Significantly for *The Translated Jew*, the lightning Benjamin writes about, and that Sigrid Weigel identifies as the "image as a constellation of the what-has-been and the now that come together in a flash," can be understood as seizing the shards of the past that "come together in a flash with the now to form a constellation."[47] If epistemological insight, or knowledge, can only emerge as a lightning flash (*blitzhaft*), then the "long roll of thunder that follows" (*der langnachrollende Donner* in German original) is the movement into the future, carrying the flash of knowledge and insight from the lightning. The poetic formulation of the German, *der langnachrollende Donner*, is the echo that turns back on itself as the word goes on (and on). Rainer Nägele turns to Benjamin's aphorism to suggest a similar relationship between image (lightning) and text (thunder), as he stresses the "tonal" aspects of translation. Nägele cites the Benjamin aphorism to think about the experience of translation as a kind of "echolalia,"[48] as inhabiting multiple languages (and with that, multiple texts) and resisting, always, the process of creating unification and unitary linguistic identity.

This mode of translation as a reading "between" texts, of a reading of correspondences in the interstices that form between multiple texts and multiple languages, is at the center of *The Translated Jew*. In many regards, Nägele and Miron, although not exactly academic soulmates, nonetheless sketch textual approaches that are compatible. They have enabled me to bring together a mode of translation theory, sparked by Benjamin but carried forward by Derrida, with work in the field of Jewish literary studies. Thus, throughout *The Translated Jew*, I posit Jewishness as the sign that is always about to be deciphered, yet is never fully deciphered: Jewishness is, to twist Paul Celan's axiomatic description of the poetic text as being *en route*, as the letter in the bottle that is forever lost at sea, similarly impossible to locate. It is for this reason that *The Translated Jew* begins with Hélène Cixous's articulation of the impossibility of speaking "the J."

The first chapter of this book is devoted to a reevaluation of the dynamics of post-Holocaust aesthetics. Beginning with a discussion of Berlin's Sculpture Park, a provisional exhibition space that has gradually disappeared as it has been bought up by corporate real estate speculators, this first chapter examines the longer history and trajectory of post-Holocaust art and public space in Germany. There has been a great deal of attention since 1989 on the politics of memory spaces in Berlin, with a focus on public art devoted to Jewish memory. Instead of rehearsing what are now familiar debates, I turn instead to a number of projects that have not been at the center of these discussions, as a way to open up and reframe the debate. Examining the spaces of Jewish Berlin, this chapter explores as well the notion of the *eruv*—rabbinically mandated sacred space—in several public art projects. In doing so, it moves the question of Jewish text off the page and outside the margin: it explores public space and Jewishness, and Jewish body and performance art. Focusing on the creation of an *eruv* in Berlin, this chapter reflects on the borders of Jewish art and Jewish sanctified space. An *eruv*, a legal fiction originating in the Talmud that enables Jews to carry objects on the Sabbath, symbolically converts the shared public space within its boundaries into the shared private, sacred space of a community. The simultaneously visible and invisible, legible and illegible lines that demarcate the *eruv* thus serve as a blueprint for the multidirectionality and polysemy between Jewish and non-Jewish spaces and cultural spheres that I explore in the following chapters.

Chapter 2 explores the circulation of Jewishness between America and Europe. Focusing on texts that complicate the relationship between place and language and that break apart and blur the relationship between text and image, this chapter brings together the work of the German writer W. G. Sebald, the bilingual French-American experimental poet Raymond Federman, the mid-century American writer and critic Alfred Kazin, and the contemporary German-Jewish Portuguese visual artist Daniel Blaufuks, all of whose literary and media border-crossings raise linked questions about the nature of Jewishness and the nature of textuality. Reading the work of Sebald, a German-born author and translator who lived his entire adult life in England and who has variously been read as a German writer, a British post-imperial writer, and a Jewish writer, through the lens of Raymond Federman and then the mid-century American Alfred Kazin, this second chapter lays the groundwork for a transnational tapestry of Jewish writing in order to reconfigure the spaces of German Jewish text. Thus, in the section on Kazin, I explore the Europeanness of American Jewish writing as a writing "on the run" that unfolds in the matrix of migration, translation, movement, and encounter. The multidirectional movement of Jews between Europe and America is emblematized by Kazin's own walking through cities (Brooklyn, New York, Cologne), and reflecting on Jews and Jewishness, which consumes Kazin in much of his autobiographical writing. Yet Kazin scholarship has bypassed the multidirectionality of his travels, lauding him as the "native son" he himself claimed he was and as the Jewish writer who categorically resisted inclusion into the canon of American Jewish literature. Kazin, rather uncharacteristically for Jewish literary men of his generation (who tended to embrace the identity of the Anglo-American writer), instead turns his attention obsessively to both Americanness and Jewishness, and equally obsessively ruminates about Europe. This chapter explores the shifting sign of "Europe" in the literary encounters between these key American and German Jewish authors from 1945 to 1950.

In the third chapter, the work of conceptual poets and artists such as Alan Sondheim, Robert Fitterman, Heimrad Bäcker, Adeena Karasick, and Anne Blonstein help us expand the frame of what has constituted Jewish textuality. The role of translation in these works is critical and forces the reader to rethink the status of translated text. For the experimental "codework" of Alan Sondheim, for instance, normative language is called into question as he inserts the languages of digital code. Similarly, the work of the conceptual poet Robert Fitterman forces a rethinking of the relationship between text and image. In his experimental poem entitled "Holocaust Museum," Fitterman gives the reader the captions of photographs from the archives of the United States Holocaust Memorial Museum's online photo archive, yet he withholds the image, breaking the link between caption and image. This suggests similar ruptures between original and translated text. The project by Anne Blonstein, *correspondence with nobody*, which is the subject of the second section of this chapter, is emblematic for the mode of translation that motivates this entire book. Taking Paul Celan's translations into German of Shakespeare's sonnets and subjecting them to the rabbinic exegetical technique of *notarikon*, in which each letter of every word is expanded into a new word, Blonstein creates a new poetic text built on the layers of translation, ultimately transforming the sonnets of Shakespeare into Jewish text through this double filter. In the final section of this chapter, I turn to the debates about indexicality and Holocaust and body art, looking at several performance artists who challenge the primacy of the referent of "Auschwitz."

In the fourth and final chapter, I explore the centrality of translation, in particular self-translation, in the work of the Czernowitz-born poet Rose Ausländer. While the presence of self-translation is vital to understanding the literary and poetic projects of both W. G. Sebald and Raymond Federman, it acquires new twists in the work of Rose Ausländer.

I turn first to the complex palimpsest of meaning-making in Czerno-witz, a former Habsburg city renowned for its multilingual (in particular Yiddish) literary production in the prewar years and which has assumed figurations of Jewishness in the postwar period through the work of Paul Celan and Rose Ausländer. Marked in Paul Celan's *Meridian* speech by a "nervous" finger on a map of a place that no longer exists, Czernowitz carries the trace and the echo of a largely literary and textual past. Exam-ining the layers of repetition and echo in the evocation of Czernowitz as place within the "non-place" of east-central Europe, this chapter sets out to define several new tasks for the literary "translation" of a place whose contours and boundaries have shifted in time, a place that is both heavily remembered and, at the same time, forgotten. Although Ausländer has received considerable acclaim as a German-language "Holocaust" poet, the repetitions and the banality I identify as central to her entire body of work are read alongside the aesthetics of pop, namely the function of repetition and serialism in Andy Warhol's challenge to banality in art. In reading Rose Ausländer as a fundamentally "banal" poet, but one who nonetheless participated in the major articulation of Jewishness as she moved between German and English, between Czernowitz and New York, I recast the work of this acclaimed poet who is emblematic for the translated Jews that make up this book.

In bringing together this disparate set of texts drawn from a range of national literary and artistic traditions, my goal is to cast new light on the very question of Jewish subjectivity and language. In addition, this book undertakes a critical reassessment of the status of German Jewish text. Departing from scholarship that has located German Jewish text as an object that can be defined geographically and historically, my project challenges national literary historiography and redraws the maps by which transnational Jewish culture and identity can — and indeed, must — be read. The central argument of the book concerns the nature and role of translation in the mediation of German Jewish culture. The idea I develop of the "trans-Jewish" and of "translating Jewishness" considers translation not simply as the literary act of moving from one language to another or the cultural transmission that results from mov-ing among texts; rather, translation is a "carrying over" of the continual accrual of meaning, metaphor, and sound. Thus, to translate Jewish memory in Germany is to listen to the constant circulation of memory, postmemory, and text that exceeds the referent of "German" or "Jewish." *The Translated Jew* locates the abrasions, marks, and echoes of "the Jewish" that are always present as trace within German text. In the ruin of German (and German Jewish) history, "Jewish" is the sign that is always implicit, present in its absence; in this way, German writing is always already "Jewish." It is precisely this Jewishness that I seek to uncover and "translate," moving from the particular instance of German Jewish text to think about a new way of doing Jewish studies.

The Translated Jew seeks to complicate the categories of "the German" and "the Jew" and to look at the larger question of Jewish subjectivity at the margins by slipping metaphorically, through multiple acts of translation, within the space of the hyphen that has linked and stabilized the terms "German" and "Jewish" in the descriptor "German-Jewish." In creating new configurations of national literary histories—by breaking the intact diacritical mark of the hyphen—my book undertakes a disciplinary reflection on the alliance between German studies and Jewish studies to suggest a new model for Jewish textual studies. While German thought has provided the primary paradigm for the emergence of European Jewish culture, *The Translated Jew* envisions Jewish studies taken from its Germanic perch in the long aftermath of the *Wissenschaft des Judentums* to occupy a more central, transdisciplinary position within the humanities.

It is indeed one goal of *The Translated Jew* to suggest and enact a mode of reading that opens up new spaces of inquiry between Jewish studies and German studies; at the same time, it recognizes the persistence of established historiographic and textual models for understanding the complex interplay between Jewish and German cultures. Nowhere is this more apparent than in the encounter by the late historian Yosef Haim Yerushalmi with Freud's *Moses and Monotheism*. Yerushalmi conjures Freud's well-known essay, "Analysis Terminable and Interminable," in the title of his book, *Judaism Terminable and Interminable*, aiming to reexamine the "Jewish past which is itself the consequence of a radical break with that past," and thus opening up to scrutiny a wider set of questions about German Jewish culture. Yerushalmi's reflections on the complex modalities of modern Jewish historicism are also an embedded part of the strategy of *The Translated Jew*, calling into question the endurance (or perhaps, to draw on a different critical idiom, the specter) of certain exemplary historical and cultural figures for German Jewish modernity while trying to move past these canonical writers to shed light on the complex interactions of Jewish culture and German culture.

Surprisingly, Yerushalmi does not even mention (or perhaps he simply represses) Freud's essay, which is generally understood to be a summary of both the limitations of psychoanalysis and its potential to create a new space for understanding the unconscious. Most striking is the lack of mention of the one passage in the Freud essay that seems most apposite for the reading of Freud's Jewishness that Yerushalmi enacts in his book: namely, the extended analogy of repression, in which Freud describes how in the process of copying an ancient text the scribe could censor offensive or undesirable passages by crossing them out, so that in the next scribe's copying out of the text, the passage would contain the textual gap.[49] Raising the question of the ethical borders of censorship, textual distortion, omission, or outright falsification, Freud's text suggests how these various modes of textual tampering serve as an analogy for the complex workings of the unconscious. Yet it is precisely the movement of the copied and distorted text into its new and seemingly endless iterations into the future, that is the productive core of Freud's essay.

Yerushalmi parses Freud's Lamarckism as the sense of a pervasive yet elusive Jewishness, writing of the subjective "feeling" expressed by both "committed and alienated modern Jews" of "the enormous weight, the gravitational pull, of the Jewish past, whether it be felt as an anchor or a burden."[50] Yerushalmi goes on to suggest that the Lamarckism of Freud's Vienna was simply "the powerful feeling that, for better or worse, one cannot really cease being Jewish . . . because one's fate in being Jewish was determined long ago by the Fathers, and that often what one feels most deeply and obscurely is a trilling wire in the blood."[51] In invoking the question of time and temporality implicit in Freud's and Yerushalmi's texts, *The Translated Jew* thus situates itself somewhere between spectrality (the hauntedness of these German Jewish figures) and futurity. Amir Eshel recently has described futurity as "the potential of literature to widen the language and to expand the pool of idioms we employ in making sense of what has occurred while imagining whom we may become."[52] Although I have advocated for thinking of Jewish studies, and in particular the case of German Jewish studies, as a possible way to create critical interventions through the "off-centered" modes of reading that it has engendered, the call for a critical Jewish studies demands not only the inclusion of new texts for study, but also new forms of critical writing.

The title of this book, *The Translated Jew: German Jewish Culture outside the Margins*, carries the trace of a satiric yet fiercely antisemitic text from 1893 by the German writer Oskar Panizza, *The Operated Jew*. In Panizza's work, the Jew of the title, Faitel Stern, undergoes a series of bodily operations intended to rid him of his Jewishness and transform him into a blue-eyed, blond German. The experiment ultimately fails, with Stern reverting back to his role as a Jew at the end of the story. *The Operated Jew* must be read as part of the complex tapestry of textual and historical representations of Jewish identity in Germany in modernity. Although *The Translated Jew* does not discuss the topics of medical discourse, Jewish identity, and antisemitism that mark Panizza's *The Operated Jew*, the title of this book draws consciously on it. Furthermore, in its insistence on the fundamental mutability of all texts I am marking as Jewish—whether or not they are by a Jewish author or artist—my book draws, in an interesting way, on this important (yet often ignored) late nineteenth-century tale of Jewish assimilation.

The literary, visual, and digital art projects that are the subject of discussion in the four chapters that follow are all concerned with the questions that, in a sense, animate *The Operated Jew*: How can Jewishness be read and decoded? Is it even possible to separate a German from a Jew? In fact, as Jack Zipes (the translator of the English version of *The Operated Jew*) remarks in an article that appeared in 1980, "the German as operated Jew remains in (both) Germanies today, despite the fact that there is little trace of Jews and what they wanted to realize in their struggle for emancipation and acceptance."[53] For even in Panizza's novella, the non-Jewish German author/doctor merges with the subject/patient of the tale, Faitel Stern. In this way, the imbrication of German and Jew, writer and subject calls to mind the inevitable blurring between translator and author so that, as writers as diverse as Haim Nahman Bialik and Jorge Luis Borges have maintained, the translator becomes coauthor.

Paul Celan, notably, does not translate the line often attributed to the Russian poet Marina Tsvetayeva, "all poets are Jews," at the start of his poem "Und mit dem Buch aus Tarussa" ("And with the Book from Tarussa"), instead veiling it in the Cyrillic script as epigraph. In fact, this epigraph is not a translation but a form of coauthorship, taking another line of a poem by Tsvetayeva that ends with the lines: "in this most Christian of all worlds, / The Poets are Yids!" and in retaining only two words, "Poets" and "Yids,"[54] Celan evokes Tsvetayeva, seemingly citing her but in fact blurring the lines between her poem and his. The incorporation that is at the same time a rewriting (and not translating) of the line from Tsvetayeva is emblematic of the mode of translation that I pursue throughout this book.[55] In this way, not only does the non-Jewish Russian poet Marina Tsvetayeva assert a fundamental Jewishness in the act of writing and of translating poetry, but even more importantly, it is through the act of translation by Celan that this exchange of Jewishness comes into being.

Moving from Cixous's evocations of an imaginary German Jewishness that she claims to inhabit, to the digital media projects in Berlin and New York that explore Jewish spaces through the virtual re-creation of the *eruv*, to a rethinking of the role of Czernowitz in the formation of a modern Jewish poetics, I attend throughout the book to the ways in which Jewishness, and its various textual configurations, shift and move across time and place. Indeed, I am convinced that the various ways that texts move us and in which we move between languages and texts, carries us along with the traces, the translations, and the residue of what is left behind.

If there is anything that *The Translated Jew* insists on, in the many voices that populate its pages, it is the impossibility of an untranslated, untranslatable, or "authentic" Jewishness. Instead, this book is an attempt to think about Jewish texts, visual culture, and Jewish urban space in their broadest and most "unbound" sense. As part of this project, I draw intentionally on what might seem to be a far-flung array of writers, artists, and thinkers. Yet this is precisely my strategy: to work with the traces of these many texts, to read "tangentially" and always on the move, never to come to a resting place in text but instead to wander, nomadically, from text to text. In moving from Hélène Cixous to Walter Benjamin to public art in Berlin to Sebald to Pessoa to Federman to Kazin to Blaufuks, and then from Alan Sondheim to Adeena Karasick to Heimrad Bäcker and Robert Fitterman and Anne Blonstein, with the final nod to Rose Ausländer and Andy Warhol and, finally, Blaufuks again, my aim is not to create a literary or artistic historiography determined by national or ethnic delineations. In bringing together this crowd of writers and artists, I hope to challenge the notion that any one of them can unlock the key to the nature of Jewishness and textuality. Rather, I am purposefully creating a cacophony of voices, and a reading that is fundamentally interstitial—contained within this book's subtitle—in order to explore the border zones of Jewishness, textuality, and translation.

Contained within the margins of this book are the many translated Jews of my childhood and my many literary companions—Jews, non-Jews, the wanna-be Jews and the cannot-ever-be Jews: the trans-Jewish outside the margins.

CHAPTER 1

Translating the Textual/Digital/
/Sacred/Provisional

In a vacant lot in the former militarized Berlin Wall zone that once separated East and West Berlin, a Star of David made out of two traffic yield
signs was partially visible through the overgrown grasses and weeds. (See
figure 1.1.) This area, sixty-two vacant lots on five blocks of urban real
estate that had been in the hands of corporate speculation since the early
2000s, had become a provisional exhibition space for a series of experimental public art projects known as the Sculpture Park (Skulpturenpark
Berlin Zentrum). The park lay on the fault line between east and west,
bordering Kommandantenstrasse, Neue Grünstrasse, and the Seydel-
strasse. Part of the militarized zone once separating East and West Berlin
(1961–89) with bits of the former wall running through the area, the park
was adjacent to the former largely Jewish-owned newspaper and publishing district that once housed the Ullstein, Schocken, and Mosse publishing houses, and the Herrnfeld Theater, the only permanent Yiddish theater in Berlin from 1906 to 1916.[1] Down the street was the Lindenstrasse
synagogue memorial, designed by Zvi Hecker and Eyal Weizmann, in
the courtyard of what was, during the time the Sculpture Park existed, an
insurance company. Dominating the area still is the Axel Springer publishing house, an icon of Cold War Germany and conservative German
politics and press.

In other words, the Sculpture Park was situated on ground that bears
traces of Jewish culture from the Weimar era and has a complex relationship to the American Cold War presence in Germany. It was a site that

Figure 1.1. Miklós Mécs, Star of David. Photo by Leslie Morris.

invites us to think about the many cultural and textual layers that are always present, and which signal the fundamental role that translation must play in our navigation of this historically laden place. The Sculpture Park was provisional and in flux; it also contained the Jewish as trace, as historical layer. Most importantly, the Sculpture Park was the site of the media production that was a formative aspect of Jewish culture in the Weimar era. The piece of land it occupied is replete with excesses of meaning and historical layers; not only does it border the former Jewish-owned Weimar newspaper and publishing district, but it lies across from the government building that now issues passports. The park was a site of industrial ruin in an age of real estate speculation: peripheral, provisional, not legible even in the context of public art in Berlin, which is often found in decaying industrial sites, in warehouses, loading zones, and former freight-train yards. Simultaneously industrial ruin, scrub greenery, and a no-man's-land of a nostalgically evoked East Germany (and before that, prewar Jewish Berlin), the Sculpture Park was there only if you knew where to push in the shaky mesh fence that delineated the space—and if you chose to push the polysemic meanings of the place to see it as both urban and Jewish ruin. (See figure 1.2.)

Figure 1.2. Sculpture Park. Photo by Leslie Morris.

I begin with the art installation of the Star of David yield sign and the larger project of Berlin's Sculpture Park to suggest a way of thinking about "translation" that can take into account the traces of Jewish history in Germany today that are deeply ingrained in the complex repatternings of Jewish culture and text. This installation in the Sculpture Park adds a new dimension to the vast amount of critical and scholarly work that has been devoted to thinking about Jewish memory in Berlin. I hope to resituate the discussion to bring in the layer of translation—in this case, the translation from the spaces of literary texts to those of public art.

The Sculpture Park I have described above no longer exists. The place that I first discovered in the summer of 2007 is now a concrete block of apartment buildings surrounded by a mesh fence, as construction continues. It is still a construction zone, but not one that is conceptualized as simultaneously a space of ephemeral public art. There is no trace of its former use as a provisional exhibition space. In the words of the collective of five artists who founded it in 2006, the KUNSTrePublik e.V., the Sculpture Park "subverts and expands the historical notions of a 'sculpture park.'"[2] It was a site-specific exhibition space in which the historical significance of the site was brought together with the artistic interventions that took place in the park. The elegiac traces of the site, replete with Jewish history from the Weimar era, are now interwoven with the elegiac traces of the Sculpture Park's ephemeral status as exhibition space.

In the pages that follow, I draw on the Sculpture Park and a number of other public art projects in Berlin in order to thicken the description of American Jews and Germany and, even more significantly, to thicken the thinking about the circulation of visual texts in urban culture in what we now conceptualize as a transnational sphere. This thickened thinking (in Jewish) aims to investigate the impact of these new encounters on Jewish text and Jewish culture.

To create a thick description of Jews in Germany is to take into account the shifts of Jewish cultures in a transnational context, the radical shifts in *German* culture and identity, and the complex interplay of interpretation of Jewish spaces of memory. Rather than simply recuperate and celebrate the revitalized Jewish presence in Berlin, a thick (or at least thicker) description of Jews in Germany today can take into account the various spaces of this phenomenon: the spaces of discourse and its many layers; virtual spaces, public art and public discourse; the space of the hyphen in the phrase "German-Jewish"; and the oddly embedded ethnographic project of American Jews studying, in Sander Gilman's provocative formulation, "the German."[3] Rather than describe, celebrate, or critique the new Jewish Berlin for not being Jewish or at least not Jewish *enough*, I attempt thick description in part to shift from what has been, still, a very German optic to one that contains, even with just a sideways glance, Jewish history and Jewish text, making Berlin more Jewish by inserting it into a discourse of Jewish spaces. By thinking about Jewish spaces and architecture in Berlin within a trajectory of Jewish urban space that includes Israel as well as the diaspora, I recast the relationship of Jewish cities and Jewish spaces. If Berlin is indeed to occupy a place on the maps of Jewish geography (as it has begun to, in recent years, with the new practice of American tourists stopping there en route to Israel or back to New York), then its symbolic spaces need to be inserted, or reinserted, into earlier imaginings of the city.

Critical work on the encounter between German and Jew in Berlin after 1989 has largely focused on the elegiac memory projects in public spaces of the city.[4] Significantly, in much of this recent work the state-sponsored structures of historical and cultural memory are more prominent than the shakier edifices that constitute the encounters and mis-encounters of German Jewish history and memory. While contemporary public art projects in Berlin attempt to create a radical eruption of new narrative into history and public spaces of memory, they often monumentalize, reify, and hypostatize the meaning of "place" and, in particular, of Jewish spaces in Berlin today. By examining the role of place in the rhetoric of mourning and loss in Berlin, I suggest that Berlin is a place of mourning but, more significantly, is also a place where the concept of "place" itself is mourned. Thus I take "place" to be elegiac, as the palimpsest of layers of historical and cultural memory in which the trace, the echo, and the displacement of previous texts are what remain.

If the descriptive projects that, to a certain extent, have also been vital in naming and thus claiming this new phenomenon largely recuperate a Jewish presence in Berlin, I instead examine the place of Jewish text in newly configured transnational textual/urban landscapes. By focusing on what I am calling the perimeters of Jewish space, I caution against merely celebrating or describing the new presence of Jews as a way to move past the lament of the artificiality of Jewish life in Germany. Rather, my aim is to reflect on the historical presence of American Jews in postwar Germany, the circulation of memory and postmemory between Germany and the United States, and the intertextual spaces that define Jewish geography in a transnational context.

This chapter investigates Jewish public art and the reconfigurations of Jewish space in Berlin—a city that is saturated with Jewish history, culture, and tourism. There is a large body of scholarship devoted to memory projects in Berlin.[5] Rather than reenter what have now become familiar discussions of the vicissitudes and impossibility of memory and of representation of the Holocaust, I turn first to some lesser-known projects "on the margins" before returning to the Sculpture Park. While there are a number of public art projects that engage Jewish memory and the Holocaust in Berlin that have received considerable attention (e.g., the Stolpersteine; and Stih and Schnock's "Bus Stop" and "Places of Memory—Memorial in the Bayerisches Viertel," or "Orte des Erinnerns—Denkmal im Bayerischen Viertel"), I turn my attention instead to public art projects that forge a historical and geographical link to art projects outside Germany.

Does this renewed circulation of Jewish culture and identity between the United States and Germany mean that we now need a new edition of the old game of Jewish geography, in which American Jews place each other by locating family and communal history on the various maps of American Jewish culture? "Jewish geography" is a speech act that itself performs Jewishness; there is an assertion of a belonging that is simultaneously predicated on not belonging. Additional layers of translation — between Germany and the United States, between public art and Jewish texts — result. These contemporary public art projects carry with them, however, their own historical traces of earlier installations in public spaces of the city. It is to this history that I first turn before exploring the Sculpture Park.

Jewish Geography: Berlin and the Perimeters of Jewish Space

In his 1995 submission to the competition for the Berlin Holocaust memorial, the German conceptual artist Horst Hoheisel proposed, simply, to blow up the Brandenburg Gate and spread the debris over the square. While the proposal never even made it to the second round of the competition, the proposed installation attempted to link art, public spaces of history and memory, ruin, and destruction. Hoheisel's stance as an enfant terrible in his claim that "it's about time" the Brandenburg Gate was blown up marks the attempt not only, as James Young has noted, to remember destruction with destruction, but, even more significantly, to end the circularity and endless repetition about how to capture the interplay between historical memory and the various cultural forms of this memory in Berlin today. The proposed yet failed destruction of the Brandenburg Gate becomes, in the archaeology of public art in Berlin, an absent space of memory and, significantly, an absent space of art in the ongoing production of art that seeks an encounter with the process of mourning and memory.

I begin with Hoheisel's project to suggest how the empty space *not* created — the possibility and eventual refusal of ruin and destruction — is a place replete with the "non-place" of the literary. The proposal to blow up a site that is so heavily marked, and coded with historical, political, cultural, and literary "meaning," a place that despite embodying multiple historical layers nonetheless signifies without ambiguity or allusion, does not, however, destroy the notion of place. Rather, in Hoheisel's project, the referent—the Brandenburg Gate—remains as firmly inscribed in and by the site as it was before. And this is where this proposed installation (and several others by Hoheisel) fail to create a truly radical interruption of new narrative into history and public spaces of memory. Instead, his proposal highlights the overdetermined nature of the site (the Brandenburg Gate), and the installation's exchange of "destruction with destruction" hypostatizes the referent it would supposedly seek to annihilate. In Hoheisel's project there is still a referent, there is still meaning; the proposed destruction, paradoxically, is what redeems and creates meaning. This failure to truly interrupt processes of referentiality and signification that have been circulating in art discourse since the 1960s at once shows the difficulty of the project and makes it that much more problematic, as it creates yet another void between post-Holocaust art and what precedes it. Rather than valorize the exchange of destruction with destruction, I suggest that the survival of the referent in Hoheisel's art works against what has been termed an aesthetics of uncertainty and the allusive as markers of "the literary."[6]

To cultivate an "aesthetics of uncertainty" is one way to formulate a critical response to a post-Holocaust art and discourse that has tended to monumentalize and hypostatize the referent of Auschwitz. It is precisely the weight of public response to the Holocaust in Germany (and in particular in Berlin) that I investigate here. Locating Berlin not as a place of (modernist) certainty and stability or even postmodern indeterminacy, I instead turn to theorists of city spaces such as Michel de Certeau, and to Marc Augé, who has developed the idea of the "non-place."[7] For Augé, the non-places of "supermodernity" are the spaces that "cannot be defined as relational, or historical, or concerned with identity."[8] Augé goes on to define these non-places as being produced by "supermodernity," that is, as spaces that do not absorb or integrate the historical traces of earlier places.[9]

It has become a truism that Berlin is at the very center of a preoccupation with memory and memorializing. The enormous body of work—literary, critical, artistic, journalistic—that has been generated on the topic is itself part of the project of examining the aftereffects of the Holocaust and the various forms that memory, trauma, and the repression of memory have engendered. The preoccupation with commemoration has become the subject of some of these projects, wrapping the relationship between public space and cultural memory in another layer of self-reflexivity. Yet while this discussion suffuses public debate throughout Germany, some vital questions about aesthetics are subsumed in this rhetoric of mourning and loss. Let us look at new ways of thinking about memory projects and public art that enable the inclusion of occluded aesthetic questions.

In his article "Forget Berlin," Lutz Koepnick calls for abandoning the "unmediated application of literary criticism to architectural forms," pleading that in order to address the connections among architectural spaces, urban spaces, and memory and history, German studies must "resist any temptation to read built space in analogy to literary texts and poetic expressions."[10] Yet literary and visual models are not discrete; they exist in a fundamental cross-pollination (and cross-contamination) with each other. It is impossible to think of Weimar Berlin without recognizing how the spaces of *flânerie*, spectacle, spectatorship, and gender performativity which marked that era were inseparable from its literary production. While various artistic representations of the past decade seek to challenge the role of the heroic and the figurative in art and culture and to create in their place a counter-memorial that is both antiheroic and anti-representational, the persistence of memory projects that abound in Berlin leave unanswered questions about the relationships among art, beauty, atrocity, and mourning.

In fact, what creates the difficulty of reading architectural and commemorative spaces in Berlin is the city's connection to the literary conception of space. In other words, it is vital not to abandon the literary so as to privilege analytical and interpretive models of art history and visual studies. It is important rather to rethink the separation between the literary and the visual that Koepnick and others hold out as a straw man. The excess of signification in the form of memory projects in Berlin about the Nazi genocide of the Jews can be enriched by realigning the visual with the literary, by reconstructing these sites of memory as textualized spaces—spaces that even when destroyed are replete with signification, meaning, memory, and interpretation, spaces that reveal how the literary is, as Paul De Man observed, "a moment inherent in all cultural forms."

It is worth noting here that Hoheisel's project to blow up the Brandenburg Gate, while seemingly iconoclastic within the often reverential (and referential) world of Holocaust art, in fact cites a tradition of "blow up" art, in which a full disruption of public space takes place. In the work of artists such as Gordon Matta-Clark, for instance, the public art installation challenges, far more assiduously than does Hoheisel's work, the role of the referent and the relationship between the figurative and the allusive. For instance, in Matta-Clark's *Window Blow-Out* (1976) in the South Bronx, he photographed a building whose windows had been vandalized and broken; Matta-Clark then shot out windows with an air rifle from inside the gallery space that was exhibiting *Window Blow-Out*. In his installation *Splitting* (1974), he cut a house in Englewood, New Jersey, in half. It is important to note that while the destruction takes place in real time, the installation consists of the photographic documentation after the event. The German artist Hans Haacke staged the destruction of a part of the German Pavilion at the Venice Biennale in 1993. Haacke, who is more clearly involved than Hoheisel in the debates about minimalism and the status of referentiality in Germany and the United States (he lives in New York), began his career with his own failed project: an installation in 1971 at the Guggenheim Museum in New York, *Shapolsky et al. Manhattan Real Estate Holdings, a Real Time Social System, as of May 1, 1971*, in which photographs of 142 buildings and vacant lots in New York slum neighborhoods were presented side by side with typewritten sheets, charts, diagrams, and maps detailing real estate transactions. Haacke's insistence on the social conditions of architecture and the deliberate link between institutional power and city spaces emerges, in Fredric Jameson's reading of this art project, as a "solution to certain crucial dilemmas of a left cultural politics based on this heightened awareness of the role of institutions."[11] Matta-Clark's and Haacke's destruction projects theorize Jameson's imperative to link art and the institution. Hoheisel's work undoubtedly has a certain appeal as exemplary of counter-monuments (explored most notably by James Young), but it fails to engage the tradition of public art that conceptualizes and rethinks the borders between art and public space, between history and memory, between site-specific art as an encounter in real time and in discernible physical and institutional space.

Paradoxically, it is in post-Holocaust art that conceptualizes destruction that the figurative and the referent become most prominent, for the coupling of public art and violence has a long history.[12] In fact, W. J. T. Mitchell and others have made the argument that violence is encoded in the very concept and practice of public art, as monuments and memorials veil and repress the violence that led to their creation. The violence thus inherent in public art such as triumphal arches, victory columns, statues, and monuments leads ultimately to a monumentalization of violence itself. Does Hoheisel's proposal to blow up the Brandenburg Gate foreground the violence and destruction that reside within its historical layers, or does it instead, in the scope of its destruction, propose destruction as a cathartic, redemptive force? The destruction of an iconic structure that lingers, in the form of the debris scattered in its square, contrasts with Matta-Clark's installations, such as *Window Blow-Out*, in which the imprint of the destruction is quite minimal.

The force of site-specific destruction art lies in the contradictory relationship between the real time of the destruction and the nature of the space it occupies. As Thomas Crow notes in his discussion of Matta-Clark's *Window Blow-Out*, "Contradiction is the source of its articulateness, so brief duration is a condition of meaning and is presupposed in its founding stipulations."[13] The aesthetics of destruction (and destruction art) are thus predicated on the contradictory relationship between time and place. In a somewhat different vein, Alan Liu develops the idea that the greatest aesthetic potential for "the literary" lies in art that destroys the "eternal now" of the digital/information age. He identifies "the vital task for literary study in the age of advanced creative destruction" as the inquiry into the aesthetic value—the literary—that once was the domain of belles lettres but now resides in the various forms of what he calls "postindustrial knowledge work."[14] Liu heralds this "age of advanced creative destruction" as one in which "art as cultural criticism (and vice versa) must be the history not of things created—the great, auratic artifacts treasured by a conservative or curatorial history—but of things destroyed in the name of creation."[15] He goes on to explain that the most ambitious art will "make history" by performing acts of destruction that will be the "destruction of this eternal now or presence of information."[16]

In a mode analogous to Liu's description of the digital age as an "eternal now," the memory debates in Germany create the sense of an eternal now of discourse. The rhetoric of loss enacted in this *ewige Jetztzeit*, in which the trace and the echo are evoked, underlies the installation that came after Hoheisel's failed proposal to blow up the Brandenburg Gate, *Berlin Gateless: The Brandenburg Gate, an Empty Place (Berlin Torlos: Das Brandenburger Tor ein leerer Ort)* in the Jewish Museum of Berlin. Consisting of photographs that create through computer simulation the fabricated removal of the upper half of the six columns of the gate, *Berlin Gateless* defamiliarizes the Brandenburg Gate, evoking the tension between absence and presence (the missing portions of the columns and the pediment and the quadriga) that has become foundational for a number of counter-monuments.[17] In doing so it creates ruin out of *the* symbol of nineteenth-century German militarism and national unity that became, after 1989, part of the new national spirit of reunification. The simulated destruction of the full gate becomes suggestive as an elegiac reminder of absence and ruin, a reworking of public space and monument that castrates the symbol of German national virility and power.

Memoirs, public art and memorials, literary texts, films, and art installations dedicated to the task of remembering have created their own echo of a cultural ennui that accompanies grieving and mourning after Auschwitz; at the same time, tropes and figurations of loss and grieving, by their repetition, tend themselves to become banal. This is the dilemma posed by the trope of unspeakability, as it hovers between the assertion of the unrepresentability and incommensurability of the Holocaust, and the insistence on new ways of configuring the (im)possibility of representation. Yet the question that Hoheisel's work raises is precisely the relationship between figuration and abstraction, between memory and "fact." By thus marking these repetitions of loss as constituting the "banality of grief," I propose a new way of thinking about the tropes of repetition and circulation, the echoes of grief and mourning that mark remembrance of the Shoah in Germany today (and that circulate between the United States and Germany), and the echo of earlier texts on grieving and banality.

Hoheisel's work challenges the interplay between architecture and monument, the tension between the formed, created monument (or counter-monument) and reworked or "revised" architectural spaces of memory.[18] His installations (both those completed and those that never began) are part of a larger complex of public art projects in Berlin in which buildings (such as the Reichstag, Stadtschloss/Palast der Republik, and Hotel Adlon) are refigured, reconstituted to become yet another sign in the palimpsest city/text of Berlin. While the new dome on the Reichstag or the reworked Stadtschloss/Palast der Republik create, through the various historical and archaeological layers, the palimpsest evoked by Andreas Huyssen, so too does the interplay between the monumental and the destruction of the monument.

Significantly, Hoheisel's one installation about the Brandenburg Gate that did get made referred to Auschwitz. On January 27, 1997, on the anniversary of the liberation of Auschwitz, Hoheisel secured the permission of the city of Berlin to project the genocidal Nazi slogan *Arbeit macht frei* over the Brandenburg Gate with laser light. The installation took place in, and depended on, "real time" that was also the time of a national day of remembrance, and at a specific site. The projection of *Arbeit macht frei* for a night, in "real time," alters the Brandenburg Gate, reconfiguring it as a Holocaust monument and creating a palimpsest of the layers of the violence and trauma inherent in all national histories; additionally, the photograph that documents the actual event serves to underscore the palimpsest nature of the monument across space and time. Yet while the idea and the execution are undeniably clever, *Arbeit macht frei* falls short first of confronting the interesting questions about public art that site-specific art has raised since its inception in American minimalism in the 1960s and, second, of reworking the hold of modernist art on the referent, which minimalist and post-minimalist art of the 1960s made into the new foundation.

The critical literature within German studies on post-Holocaust artists (such as Hoheisel, Stih and Schnock, Libera, and others) has created a critical context in which these works are valued as interventions into the ongoing exploration of memory and history in Germany today.[19] Yet just as the trope of destruction that Hoheisel draws on is found both in German and American art (think of Hans Haacke's 1993 destruction of a portion of the German Pavilion at the Venice Biennale), so too the disruption of public space by the projection of images onto sites did not begin in the late 1990s with Hoheisel but stretches back to early minimalist interventions from the 1960s.

Arbeit macht frei calls to mind the projection pieces done in the 1970s by the Polish artist Krzysztof Wodiczko, in which public spaces become, literally, the screen memory of the past and the lens through which the spectator can enter into history and the public sphere more generally. For Wodiczko, this takes the form of exploring "the ideology of public space": "I am interested in how architecture in the so-called 'public domain' operates culturally. I am not about revolutionary messages on walls. I want to analyze the relationship between the human body, the body of someone who lives here, and the social body and the body of the architectural and spatial forms around that body."[20] Wodiczko's early work often projects body parts—hands, arms, ears, eyes—onto institutional structures ranging from MIT to the School of Architecture at the Technical University in Halifax. By doing so, the structure—institutional or monumental—is revealed as a space where the city-dweller can superimpose critical reflections and thoughts on the form of the monument.

In an interesting way, these projections are superimposed "projections" of the spectators' own thoughts about the site. Additionally, Wodiczko aims to fragment the otherwise intact, monumental structure in order to "reassemble on the surfaces of the buildings according to what these surfaces and parts of buildings suggested to me."[21] In Germany, Wodiczko projected a pair of "corporate hands" at the top of the Stuttgart main train station, and illuminated the Mercedes Benz sign on top of the tower. (Unfortunately, shortage of funding prevented Wodiczko from adding a pair of guest worker's hands to the projection.) He also, famously, in 1983 during the heated public debates about American missile sites during the national election campaign, projected Pershing missiles onto the Victory Column in the Schlossplatz in Stuttgart. In a similar pairing of neoclassicism and missiles, in 1985 he projected missiles onto Nelson's Column in Trafalgar Square; during the work on this projection, Wodiczko improvised an image of a swastika on the pediment of the South Africa House in Trafalgar Square in support of anti-apartheid groups (after two hours, the police intervened and halted the projection).

Wodiczko's and Hoheisel's projections merge the temporal and the spatial, creating the kind of modern sculpture that Rosalind Krauss claims merges the possibility of an art of time (for Lessing, poetry) with an art of space (the visual arts).[22] In Hoheisel's *Arbeit macht frei* projection, however, it is unclear whether the project opens up debate about the very notion of public art, whose central question is, or at any rate should be, the viability of the idea of private art. As an art installation that seeks to re-create and restage destruction but in a new key, it inevitably reifies the referent in the process of creating art. Thus the work presents an interesting test case of what it is that gets lost, in aesthetic and literary terms, when art as destruction becomes realized, when the figurative dominates and obscures the allusive. This is also the case with Hans Haacke's installation *Der Bevölkerung*, in which he constructed in dirt and grass the inscription in the Lichthof of the newly rebuilt Reichstag: the words "To the People" ("Der Bevölkerung"), which then projected upward and became superimposed on the inscription "To the German People" ("Dem deutschen Volk").

As with all projections onto public sites, the photograph that documents the event of the projection not only has a documentary purpose, but is also a trace of the spectacle of the event. In the case of Wodiczko's projection of the swastika onto the South Africa House, the artist stated afterwards: "Many people told me that even though they hadn't seen the actual projection (i.e., they had only seen media images of it), somehow when they look at the pediment the swastika is seen as missing, as a kind of afterimage."[23] Significantly, Wodiczko, who did the first and best-known projections onto public spaces, raises the question of public art in relation to public practices of the historical avant-garde by asking whether these works are not merely "liberal urban decoration."[24]

That site work depends on documentation—and on photographic documentation in particular—is self-evident. This interdependence of event and documentation is at the center of Shimon Attie's *Writing on the Wall* installation, done in Berlin's Scheunenviertel, or Jewish quarter, in the early 1990s. Attie projected photographs of Jewish life from the 1920s and 1930s onto the spaces of the Scheunenviertel that were beginning to emerge as a rebuilt Jewish district soon after the fall of the Berlin Wall. Significantly, not all the photos of the past were actually from the Scheunenviertel or even from Berlin, thus boldly dispensing with any notion of historical "accuracy" or "documentation" that might be seen to compete with the installation's status as art object.[25] What the installation does do, however, is create from the contemporary Scheunenviertel—which has become a tourist destination on the Jewish tours of Berlin—a place of both photographic memory, however forged or inaccurate, and contemporary mourning. It foregrounds that Jewish "life," seen in photographs of the time when the Scheunenviertel was marked as a Jewish place, is as much an illusion as the newly fabricated tourist quarter, thus causing a rethinking of the elegiac lost spaces of Jewish history that are now mourned in Berlin.

While there has been critical attention focused on the iconic images of Jewish faces and Jewish city-dwellers that suddenly erupted on the still-unrenovated facades of the Scheunenviertel buildings in 1993, I shift the optic from iconic Weimar-era Jewishness to examine the architectural spaces which are equally iconic—as ruins from East Germany. Scholarly work on Attie has focused largely on the interplay between presence and absence, between Jewish life and Jewish death, mourning, and commemoration. Yet turning to his work now, several decades after German reunification, what is striking is that the buildings he photographed in the early 1990s were ravaged, still in ruins. What does it mean to project these photos onto buildings that in the early 1990s are themselves palimpsests of places and of lives, in that period shortly after German reunification that Andreas Huyssen has aptly referred to as one of "urban tabula rasa fantasies"?[26] Read this way, the installation does not simply project an elegiac, lost absence of Jewish life onto the present as it grapples with the spectral presence of the past (Huyssen, Ladd), but rather forces a rethinking of what constitutes both elegiac and public space that can move from the historical (Weimar era) to a present that is equally infused with a historical past (East Germany). By superimposing the elegiac (Jewish life from the Weimar era) onto the now-elegiac spaces of Berlin that in the 1990s were becoming retextualized as memory spaces of Berlin, Attie recasts and forces a rethinking of what constitutes elegiac spaces and images in the first place. Looking at *Writing on the Wall* ten years after its installation, the rupture between the "real" and the "originary" in contemporary Berlin splinters and refracts, with the "originary" now taking on new dimensions as containing echoes and layers not only of iconic images of eastern European Jewish culture in Berlin in the 1920s and '30s, but also of the architectural ruins of East Germany and the nascent efforts, in the early 1990s, to absorb them.

Site-specific art reverses the modernist paradigm of the autonomy of art, in which art is marked by "indifference" to the site and is thus transportable, placeless, and nomadic; the photographic documentation of the event dismantles this opposition, creating an additional layer of the elegiac, as the lived experience of the installation moves into the spectral realm of memory and "Nachträglichkeit" (afterwardsness). In distinguishing site-specific art from modernist works, Miwon Kwon notes that "site specific works used to be obstinate about 'presence,' even if they were materially ephemeral, and adamant about immobility, even in the face of disappearance or destruction."[27] In site-specific installations, the site and the work are synonymous: the space of art becomes a "real" place, not a tabula rasa, and depends on the presence of the viewer—in this case, the city-dweller and the tourist—for its completion. Site-specific art opposes the idealism of modernism in which the art object was seen to have fixed and transhistorical meaning, as not belonging to any one place.

A 1999 site-specific installation very much on the margins, *Trabihenge* suggests a very different sort of cultural translation than Attie's project. On June 21, 1999, a group of artists staged a reworking of Stonehenge made entirely out of old blue Trabant automobiles (Trabis) in a field outside of Berlin, just off the B-101 Autobahn, placed in as precise relation to the sun as Stonehenge itself. It was an elegiac recasting of the dolmens and menhirs of ancient Britain, as well as an ironic gesture to the nostalgia for the lost East Germany that had begun to take on new proportions about a decade after the fall of the Berlin Wall. This installation was a highly effective part of exhibitions and discussions about *Ostalgie* (such as Andreas Ludwig's "Open Depot" museum in Eisenhüttenstadt, in which objects from everyday life were donated by residents and put on display). The opening of the work consisted of a celebration of the solstice that lasted until the "first light of the next morning" (in the poetic phrasing of the *Berliner Zeitung*). The artists, calling themselves *Landschaftsmonumentalisten* (Landscape Monumentalists), declared their sculpture to be a sign of the temporal, merging the landscape outside Berlin with the ancient "time" of Stonehenge. (See figure 1.3.)

Trabihenge does more than simply critique the temporal in its evocation of both Stonehenge and East Germany; rather, it shows the fault line between sculpture and monument identified by Rosalind Krauss in her analysis of Rodin's *Balzac* sculpture, in which she understands the monument as the "negative condition" of sculpture—"a kind of sitelessness, or homelessness, an absolute loss of place."[28] In other words, according to Krauss, modernist sculpture is essentially nomadic and de-

Figure 1.3. *Trabihenge.*

pends upon this loss of site, "producing the monument as abstraction, the monument as pure marker or base, functionally placeless and largely self-referential."[29] Krauss uses the example of Stonehenge in particular to cite how post-1960s critics of minimal and pop art drew on older, "timeless" historical precedents (such as Stonehenge) to legitimate minimalist sculpture as a mediation between the "extreme" past and present. *Trabihenge* is also part of a coded system of road art that cites most notably the public art installation *Cadillac Ranch* (1974) in Amarillo, Texas, in which ten used Cadillacs were buried partway in the ground, at an angle corresponding to that of the Great Pyramid of Giza in Egypt. The installation in Germany takes as a given the sudden, the unexpected, the placement of "art" in the non-place of the highway, or what Krauss terms the "not-landscape." Sculpture, she argues, has since the 1960s "entered a categorical no-man's-land: it was what was on or in front of a building that was not a building, or what was in the landscape that was not the landscape."[30] It is allusive, expressive of the aesthetics of uncertainty, and it is about time and the non-place, non-sculpture, of the literary.

The *Eruv*: Real, Digital, and Imaginary Jewish Spaces

It is to the fundamentally open interpretive practice of Jewish "textual reasoning" that I now turn in order to rethink the status of Jewish text (including visual and urban texts in the production of Jewish memory in Germany) and the circulation of text and memory in different national and historical spaces. The role of urban space in this is crucial; while modern Jewish historians have generally treated the city as a kind of backdrop to events in Jewish history, Jennifer Cousineau has stressed that "the urban context for the actions of Jews has played a central role in the making of those historical events and processes."[31] Berlin is part of this matrix of Jewish urban spaces.

Anthropologists of Jewish culture and Jewish demographics have long observed that Jewish identity comes into being when Jews live in close proximity to each other. While urban space is always "shared space," Jewish culture in the United States in the postwar period emerged as a distinctive culture in part because of the large groupings of Jews in urban and suburban spaces. As Berlin emerges as a city with a visible Jewish population, and as a newly found tourist destination for American Jews, the question of Jewish space takes on new considerations. Jewish tourism in Germany and eastern Europe has created a newly refigured eastern Europe, with new points on the map that include Prague, Krakow, Theresienstadt, Auschwitz, and also Poland, with Berlin increasingly now a stop on the way to Prague or Poland.[32] Berlin is thus refigured within the new matrix of Jewish geography, through tourism and new conceptions of Europe, and also, significantly, through the presence of American Jews in Berlin.

While urban Jewish space in Berlin has been canonized within the maps of former Jewish life in Berlin (Scheunenviertel), displaced to official memory sites about the Holocaust (Peter Eisenman's Memorial to the Murdered Jews of Europe), and reinscribed into new tourist maps of Jewish places, there is a distinctive urban Jewish spatial practice that is, significantly, absent in Germany today: the *eruv*. An *eruv*, a "legal fiction" originating in the Talmud that enables Jews to carry objects on the Sabbath, is a practice that developed in rabbinic times of making public city spaces "private," thus circumventing the prohibition against the carrying of objects outside of the home. An *eruv* allows carrying on the Sabbath by symbolically converting the shared public space within its boundaries into the shared private space of a community. The *eruv* reestablishes the Temple, in conceptual, abstract form, by drawing a line, with wire, around city spaces and making the public space of the city analogous to private interior space. The *eruv* domesticates nondomestic, public space, making the public private, blurring the distinctions between the two;

significantly, as Charlotte Fonrobert has argued, the *eruv* has particular resonance for diasporic cultural politics, because it embodies territorialism that does not lay claim to control over that territory; it is, as Fonrobert states, a model of "territoriality without sovereignty."[33]

There is currently no *eruv* in Germany, yet there are countless architectural and city-spaces devoted to Jewish culture; historically, there were *eruvin* in Frankfurt and Hamburg and smaller cities and towns.[34] While the historical absence of *eruvin* in Germany is an expression of the acculturation of Jews there, the very idea of creating an *eruv* on German soil evokes, in the popular imagination after the Holocaust, concentration camps, ghettos, and other spaces of Jewish enclosure. (In fact, critics of the London *eruv* point to the poles and wires of the *eruv* as bearing associations with the camps as restricted spaces of Jewish history.) In 2008, the Lauder Foundation had begun the process of establishing an *eruv* in Berlin's Prenzlauer Berg, with the idea of linking the Rykestrasse synagogue with the newly built yeshiva in the Brunnenstrasse on the border between Mitte and Prenzlauerberg. Yet the possibility of an *eruv* in Berlin demands more than the municipal reworking of public space: it would necessitate a rethinking and reordering of the borders of Jewish art and Jewish sanctified space. It would mean visually marked Jews walking in invisibly marked city spaces; most importantly, it would shift the Jewish center from the Scheunenviertel to a part of Mitte that is not a tourist draw.[35]

I draw on the concept of the *eruv* in order to show the complex fault lines of Jewishness and its remappings. I am thinking of the *eruv* as a conceptual, imaginary, provisional, and contingent Jewish space, as an instance of transnational Jewish geography, where meaning and signification are "carried over" (*über/setzen*), one that serves as a blueprint to excavate and read the layers of Jewish memory in contemporary Berlin. In doing so, what I propose is a thick description of the conceptual possibility of the *eruv* for the Jewish spaces of Berlin that would adhere to Clifford Geertz's definition, in which the details are part of "interworked systems of construable signs . . . within which they can be intelligibly . . . described."[36]

The simultaneously visible and invisible/legible and illegible lines that demarcate the *eruv* serve as a blueprint for the multidirectionality and the polysemy between Jewish and non-Jewish spaces and cultural spheres. In exploring critical art projects that work within a matrix of Jewish history, Jewish memory, Jewish culture, and Jewish space, and that insist on the circulation and encounter between Jewish and non-Jewish spaces—the movement in and out of Jewish demarcated space and the shifting readings of these spaces—I propose to expand the borders of what might count as "Jewish" art.

The *eruv* creates the fiction of Jewish legal space yet at the same time legally demarcates Jewish space. It needs to blend into the existing cityscape, yet be definable enough to pass rabbinic inspection. To the untrained eye it is unmarked, yet made visible in part to the outsider by the sight of the visibly marked (Orthodox) Jews walking within its boundaries. Most significantly, the *eruv* symbolically changes urban space, presenting methodological problems for historians of material culture, since the perimeter of the *eruv* is simultaneously part of the fabric of the city, a "ritual reconstitution of a lost place, framed as law and embodied as a book."[37]

In a recent article on the new "Jewish" quarter in Munich, Manuel Herz critiques German Jewish urban space more generally as fundamentally "anti-*eruv*"—as spatial configurations that have "a maximum of Jewishness in a minimum of physical space." The *eruv*, in contrast, disperses Jewish space, erasing the borders between private and public realms. Critiquing the visibly expressive "Jewish architecture" of Germany (with Libeskind's Jewish Museum in Berlin as the most obvious example) for its "visible reinforcement" of the Federal Republic's public stance of remembering Jews, Herz sees the Jewish architect as the "court's fool" who "unwittingly annuls, with the building of dramatic synagogues and museums, the critical potential of architecture within society, to integrate it into the established discourse and to normalize it."[38] Seeking to transform Jewish spaces in Berlin beyond these state-sanctioned memory sites, Herz turns to the *eruv* as a possible future site of lived Jewishness. He argues that the physical presence of Jews in Germany today is ideologically "anti-*eruv* and anti-Diaspora," despite the fact that German Jews represent the diasporic condition par excellence.[39] For Herz, the "anti-eruv" model of Jewish spaces in Germany has had a profound impact not only on Jewish architecture and Jewish communities in Germany, but even more significantly for the political establishment that regulates Jewish memory in Germany today.[40]

For Herz, the illustration of this "anti-*eruv*" model of city planning is the Munich Jewish community center, in which Jewish institutional structures (synagogue, Jewish elementary school, community school, café, bookstore, museum) are concentrated into one city square—"a minimum of physical space with a maximum of Jewishness. The architecture, which is supposed to express the equal rights and secured standing of Jews in Germany, performs a vital official and state-certified function: it is the litmus test for the allegedly healthy German Jewish relationship, for the well-being of the Jews in Germany. It is the fool's architecture as an institutionalized experiment resulting from a mutual dependence."[41] If the ostensible radicality of the architecture and Jewish spaces in Berlin—Libeskind, Eisenmann, and so on—only reinforces the underlying power/authority of a conservative government, in which the (Jewish) architect is indeed the court fool, the antidote to dramatic synagogues and visible Jewish buildings would be for an *eruv* to be developed, in which "instead of a small number of key buildings containing Jewish functions in a centralized space, a decentralized and commonplace Jewish presence in the shape of kosher butchers or mezuzahs on doorframes would spread throughout the city, thereby establishing a minimum of Jewishness in a maximum of space."[42]

The *eruv*—both a real *eruv* or the one still provisional and in blueprint—points to what is there but not there. It is a demarcation that, paradoxically, marks nothing. In this way, it illustrates philosopher Charles Sanders Peirce's definition of the indexical sign, which has a directly causal connection to the referent, as in the case of a pointing finger: "The index asserts nothing: it only says 'there!'" Critical work (by Rosalind Krauss, Marianne Doane, et al.) in visual studies has renewed attention to the indexical powers of the image, and the index can also help us to shift the discussion about Jewish (and post-Holocaust) art in Germany past the referent of Auschwitz. Rather than establish Auschwitz as referential icon, the indexical opens the interpretive field with which we might speak about Jewish art and Jewish space.[43] If the icon always foregrounds the ontological status of the object to which it bears relation, the indexical tells us only that there is something "there" to look at, foregrounding the act of looking, deprivileging the object, and keeping open the interpretive field of the spectator.[44]

The indexical is a textual strategy that suggests the forever contingent—

in the case of Jewish text, it enables thinking about a place of art (and Jewishness) that must by definition always be provisional. Thus it is not the evidence of the real to which the indexical *might* point; instead, the indexical can open up interstitial spaces of meaning and signification. It is in the interstitial and precarious interpretive space that the indexical opens a space in which to reflect on Jewish memory, Jewish space, and the "aleph" that begins the textualizing of Auschwitz: Auschwitz—the aleph-schwitz, the first letter, an open letter, a glottal stop that is silenced, the point where language and signification end.

This matrix of icon, index, and sites of Jewish remembrance is at the center of the work of the new media artist Elliott Malkin, whose installations explore the links between digital and sanctified space. In 2005 Malkin created a digital graffiti installation on the Lower East Side of Manhattan entitled *eRuv: A Street History in Semacode*, pasting digital semacode—an optical pattern that allows the viewer to access a web page by scanning it with a mobile phone—along the now-absent former border of the Lower East Side *eruv*, one of whose borders was the 3rd Avenue elevated train. (See figure 1.4.)

Each location along the *eruv* corresponds to a semacode ID. The duration of the installation was as long as the posted semacodes were still intact and readable from the cell phones, so there was a gradual decay, with the decay of the city space, of the installation. Camera phone users could receive archival photos of the former *eruv* at that location, creating a historical reconstruction mapped back onto the original space. As Malkin explains, "The train line, dismantled in 1955, was more than just a means of transport; it was part of an important religious boundary—an eruv—for a Hasidic community on the old Lower East Side."[45] More than Shimon Attie's elegiac re-creation of lost, absent Jewish space, Malkin's *eRuv* project digitally maps the no longer existent *eruv* (and 3rd Avenue elevated train) back into the contemporary space of the city, highlighting these as virtual, imaginary spaces.

While an *eruv* is typically constructed with poles, wires, and also city structures such as walls and gates, Malkin's most recent project, *Modern Orthodox*, uses a combination of low-power lasers, Wi-Fi surveillance cameras, and graffiti in order to designate sacred volumes of space in urban areas. Malkin explains: "In *Modern Orthodox*, I built an eruv out of laser beams and wifi surveillance cameras, instead of wires, so that the

Figure 1.4. Elliott Malkin, *Semacode*. Courtesy of Elliott Malkin, eRuv Project.

integrity of the eruv can be monitored from a remote location. One of the reasons I am interested in the eruv is that it is essentially an ancient virtual space, one that exists in the minds of those who respect it. Non-observers who live within the eruv either cannot, or choose not, to see it."[46] In 2006 Malkin unveiled *Cemetery 2.0*, which he describes as a concept for networked devices that connects burial sites to online memorials for the deceased. The prototype links the gravestone of Hyman Victor, his great-grandfather, to his surviving internet presence. Visitors to the physical memorial can view related memorials on the device display, while visitors to any of the online memorials will recognize that their browsing is associated directly with the actual burial site. Central to Malkin's exploration of the links between religious practice, mourning, and technology is a reflection on contained Jewish space and the complex ways in which meaning and Jewish memory are disseminated, digitally.

Malkin's exploration of the ways in which religion and technology combine to inform the construction of memorial sites has resonance for thinking about memorial sites more generally. We can think, too, about how archival and photo collections both demarcate and open up the spaces between private and public, historical and personal memory, seeping across the borders of the visible and the invisible, marked and unmarked, pointing—like the *eruv*—to the ongoing process of seeing and containing Jewish life.

Susan Hiller's *The J. Street Project* similarly draws on the indexical nature of signs pointing backward in time to the lost, former presence of Jews. First shown at the Jewish Museum in New York in November 2008, *The J. Street Project* consists of over 300 photographs of street signs in Germany that have the name "Juden" in them. The project is a serialist compilation of images that is described in the catalog and other museum promotional material as evoking the absence of Jews through the presence of the street signs. Hiller has explained that her use of the phrase "J. Street" recalls, with bitter irony, the loss of Jewish communities by using the type of classification terminology that the Nazis employed to destructive ends. The serialized images were hung in a seven-foot grid on a white wall, and as the catalog states, they

> suggest the everydayness, and something more, in these thoroughfares in cities, suburbs, towns, and, perhaps most surprisingly, rustic roads and woodland paths. The signs recorded by Hiller now function as inadequate memorials to destroyed communities, some marking locations where Jews had lived segregated from public and municipal life, as far back as the eleventh century.[47]

Near this grid of photos, the curators hung a large-scale, starkly simplified map of Germany and a list of the locations of each street. In an adjacent gallery, a 67-minute single-channel video projection showed all 303 photographic sites, edited to reveal the texture and pace of ordinary life. As Hiller explains, "on each street, my camera recorded incidental and transient details: weather, shoppers, landscape, building, children, cars, cows. It's their everyday matter-of-factness that makes the photographs unsettling. They convey an uncanny resonance by revealing connections between some very ordinary contemporary locations, history, and remembrance, as the street signs repeatedly name what's missing from all these places."[48]

The tension between the photographs of the signs showing a repetition of absence and the very present (in memory and in documentation of the Nazi period) historical marker of the "J" used by the Nazis to mark, in red ink, the identity papers of Jews, opens up a new discursive space for thinking (and translating) the J of Hiller's *J. Street Project*. Hiller's abbreviation of "J. "for "Jew" or "Jewish" is, as Jörg Heiser has described it, a "semiological cipher" and also, significantly, one that is entirely in English, despite the fact that the entire project was photographed in Germany.[49] Thus Hiller's *J. Street Project*, photographed on German soil by an American Jewish artist and shown at the Jewish Museum in New York, is yet another project which demands that we read it as part of a complex translation of Jewish culture and history as it moves back and forth between Germany and the United States.

Under a "Judenstrasse" sign, another sign denotes the street's Nazi-era name, Kinkelstrasse, named for a nineteenth-century German nationalist writer admired by the Nazis; the city restored the name to its original "Judenstrasse" in 2002. Interestingly, the city chose to match the new sign with one saying "Kinkelstraße" written in Fraktur (a traditional German typeface often used until World War II), with a red slash through the old sign and Christmas lights around the whole thing. The use of Fraktur in the two signs bridges the historical rupture that the placement of the new sign in 2002 would otherwise suggest. The type style used for the defunct Nazi-era name links past and present, suggesting historical continuity with the Nazi era rather than claiming a mastery of it, yet at the same time rupturing that continuity by inserting the red slash through the name and street numbers below. Street signs in East Berlin that were renamed after 1989 were, characteristically, crossed out in black; the red in this image serves to distinguish this street renaming from that other visible moment of the change in demarcations of German public space under National Socialism, while it also enables the viewer to see the name that is being erased.

Although Hiller's *J. Street Project* is not to be confused with the Washington-based, pro-peace, pro-Israel PAC named "J Street," the artist does assert the broader political impact of the project in the catalog by suggesting links between the traumatic history of the Jews of Europe with political violence more generally: "But the present is a summation of everything that precedes it and each photograph will be seen in the context of everything that happens afterwards. In that way, *The J. Street*

Project has allowed me to reflect not only on one unique, incurable, traumatic absence, but also on more recent attempts to destroy minority cultures and erase their presence."[50]

But none of this is what is actually interesting about Hiller's project. While it echoes earlier work (such as that by Attie) which evokes the spectral presence of Jewish life in contemporary Berlin by focusing on the tension between absence and presence, Hiller's project, in its monotonous, serialized repetition of images located in the everyday (and largely in southern Germany, in rural settings and small towns), suggests the tedium of invoking Jewish memory. More significantly, however, the linking of word and image situates this project less within the trajectory of Holocaust art commemorating Jewish absence in Germany than in the emergence of the linguistic turn in conceptual art and word art, in which the insertion of written text (slogans, street signs, sentences) into the work of art makes the viewer an active, engaged reader. To understand Hiller's project we need to see it as an elegiac commentary about Jewish absence in Germany but also as part of a longer trajectory of art (both Jewish and non-Jewish) that destabilized the relationship between word and image. In a similar way, the site-specific public art projects by Horst Hoheisel, Stih and Schnock, and Shimon Attie discussed earlier in this chapter, which have been read almost exclusively as post-Holocaust German explorations of Jewish trauma and memory, need instead to be placed within the larger historical context of American pop art and minimalism (Warhol, Wodiczko, Matta-Clark) that both theorize and enact the destruction of "place" and "site." Critical work on German post-Holocaust installation art has not provided this comparative and historical perspective.

To this end, it is also important to note that Hiller's earlier work is reminiscent of the work of Lawrence Weiner and other word artists. In addition to *The J. Street Project*, she contributed a sound art installation for the Fifth Berlin Biennale in the Sculpture Park. Especially interesting is the title: *The J. Street Project* invokes and veils at the same time, asserting Jewishness and yet paying tribute to the injunction against referentiality. Hiller collapses all the sites and place names within the larger marker of the J—the elided "Jewish" that recalls Cixous—that mark the innate indexicality of the "J" as the first sign of the Jewish. In this way, the "J" signs work against the logic of the *eruv*. Pointing solely to absence, the signs evoke a nostalgic moment; yet in rural places, where Jews once lived, they do so as signs of the pre-urban, premodern Jewish life in Germany.

As these many projects about Jewish space suggest, the difficulty of finding interpretive and real spaces for Jewish life in Germany after the Shoah is part of a lively debate about place and ethnic identity. Manuel Herz's call to transform Jewish spaces in Berlin by turning to the *eruv* as a possible future site of lived Jewishness is an important intervention in the very public displays of Jewish culture in Germany. Yet my call to rein-scribe the *eruv* in our contemporary maps of Jewish Berlin is not a sugges-tion to create a more or less "authentic" Jewishness in the ruins of history. Rather, it is a way of thinking about contemporary Jewish urban space and historical spaces of memory that allows Jewish space—embodied in the *eruv*—to move from its original meaning in Talmudic text to the complex ordering of the private, public, and sanctified spaces of urban Jewish culture.

Berlin's Sculpture Park: A Tree Grows in Berlin

Like the simultaneously visible and invisible, legible and illegible lines that demarcate the *eruv* currently proposed for Berlin, the shaky mesh fence of the Sculpture Park signaled the multidirectionality and poly-semy characterizing the spaces between Jewish and non-Jewish sites in Berlin. It was an industrial ruin in an age of real-estate speculation: the experience of the vacant lot was accompanied by the knowledge that it would soon be gone. The site was peripheral, provisional, dispersed, not legible even as public art in Berlin, and thus offered an alternative way of thinking about the traces of Jewish culture and the now-commodified Jewishness circulating in other parts of the city. This aesthetic of the vacant lot can link the traces of East Germany (the *Mauerstreife*, or the border strip of where the wall had been) with those of Jewish Berlin. (See figure 1.5.)

There are countless other exhibition and gallery spaces in Berlin oc-cupying former sites of industrial decay, warehouses, and loading zones, such as the Nolan Judin Gallery, located on the site of a former freight-train yard near the Hauptbahnhof and the Hamburger Bahnhof mu-seum. This district was incorporated into the Art Forum in 2009, and the city of Berlin has drafted plans for urban renewal in that area. Yet the

Figure 1.5. Fence to Sculpture Park. Photo by Leslie Morris.

Sculpture Park, as exhibition space that was on borrowed land and on borrowed time, bears a different relationship to exhibiting and installing art. In many respects, it exemplifies W. J. T. Mitchell's conception of the relationship between place and sculpture. Responding to his question, "'What does sculpture want?'—that is, both what it desires or longs for, and what it *lacks*"—Mitchell writes that

> sculpture wants a place, a site, a location both literally and figu-
> ratively. . . . like the naked human body which is its first model,
> it is both a homeless wanderer, an exile from the Edenic utopia
> where it was the genius of the place, and itself the home that it
> can never completely abandon. Sculpture wants a place to be
> *and* to be a place.[51]

The ephemeral quality of the Berlin Sculpture Park only heightened the desire for place that Mitchell locates as central to sculpture. Finally, since the Sculpture Park always exhibited art amid threats of the park's imminent extinction, and documentation of the installations was placed on the wire fence at the park's periphery, it calls to mind Robert Smithson's theory of "non-sites," a three-dimensional representation of the actual site.

Critical work on ruins and memory in the fields of geography and urban studies has consistently pointed to the ways in which urban and industrial ruins do not merely evoke the past. Rather, as Tim Edensor notes in his study of industrial ruins in Britain, "they contain a still and seemingly quiescent present, and they also suggest forebodings, pointing to future erasure and subsequently, the reproduction, of space, thus conveying a sense of the transience of all spaces."[52] As site-specific land art, almost all of the installations in the Sculpture Park engaged with the materiality of these vacant lots as spaces of vegetation as well as real-estate speculation. Perched on the edge of several districts, the Sculpture Park was replete with the excess of meaning and the collision of historical layers that bordered the park. Existing as a ruin as well as a no-man's-land of a nostalgically evoked East Germany and, before that, prewar Jewish Berlin, the Sculpture Park was there if you knew it was there and if, after pushing past the shaky fence encircling it, the viewer was able to push the polysemic meanings of the place, to see it as a ruin and as a space for exhibiting art. The polysemy of Sculpture Park is tied as well to involuntary memory, as Benjamin evokes that term: an intrusion of memory (involuntary memory always intrudes, unexpectedly) on the border of regulated space, beginning with the provisional fence that surrounds the park and which often serves, without the spectator realizing it, as the first "textual entry" into the park. Like the invisible fences that demarcate the space of the *eruv*, the fragile fence of Sculpture Park is the indexical announcement that the uncertain, provisional space we are witnessing is, somehow, "there," that there is a regulatory function at work that will shape our entry into this space/text. (See figure 1.6.)

Miklós Mécs's Star of David, made from two yield signs, was part of the 2007 Sculpture Park installation *Parcella*. It was barely visible in the wild underbrush, and as the summer progressed it became more and more difficult to see. During the same period as Mécs's installation of the Jewish star, Folke Köbberling and Martin Kaltwasser's piece, *Turn it one more time*, excavated three sites in the park and literally turned over—dug up—the site's historic and archaeological foundations.[53] The

Figure 1.6. Fence to Sculpture Park. Photo by Leslie Morris.

excavations mirrored the form of the viewing platforms that once existed in West Germany along the Berlin Wall. Rather than leading upwards and to a view of "the east," the excavations by Kaltwasser and Köbberling led downwards, like an archaeological dig, and offered a new view into the history of the site. The holes uncovered former building foundations, cellars, toilets, coal furnaces, and more. The stairway going down did not only represent a symbol of historical significance; in their words, it "provided an experiential path." It invited visitors to observe the site's intrinsic, biological processes. Viewers were brought eye-level with the ground where the territorial appropriation by wild plants could be observed. This overwhelming presence of flora presented the natural potentials of the place—which typically lay beyond the interests of its potential developers. On the park's billboard, the artists recorded the diverse array of plants that they encountered.

The Sculpture Park's most striking contribution to the genre of land art can be seen in Ulrike Mohr's 2008 installations, *Green Remains (Restgrün)* and *New Neighbors (Neue Nachbarn)*, which were part of the Fifth Berlin Biennale and the Sculpture Park's 2008 exhibit "Spekulationen." In *New Neighbors*, Mohr transplanted trees that had been growing on the roof of the Palace of the Republic as it was awaiting demolition; these trees were the spontaneous vegetation that resulted from a seedbed inadvertently created by a mix of bitumen, polystyrene, and concrete. Quickly, moss, lichen, and various grasses and trees germinated. On April 4, 2006, demolition work on the Palace was stopped for one day and the roof's scrubby, self-seeded trees were identified botanically, labeled, and dug out, and at the precise moment when the Palace of the Republic was demolished, they were replanted in the Sculpture Park in exactly the same position in relation to each other that they had occupied on the roof of the Palace.[54] For this installation Mohr marked the trees transplanted to the Sculpture Park with Palace of the Republic medallions and small plastic botanical classifications pushed into the ground. Otherwise, "the trees quietly and symbiotically blended in with their new neighbors, wild trees and vegetation, who similarly sprouted from cracks after the fall of the Wall."[55] (See figures 1.7, 1.8, and 1.9.)

To find several trees that had germinated and grown spontaneously on the roof of the Palace of the Republic is itself extraordinary. Noteworthy too is the historical trajectory of this building that chronicled an iconic ar-

Figure 1.7. Trees on top of the Palace of the Republic. Photo by Ulrike Mohr; courtesy of Ulrike Mohr. Copyright © 2008 Artists Rights Society (ARS), New York / VG BildKunst, Bonn (Germany).

Figure 1.8. Transporting trees. Photo by
Ulrike Mohr; courtesy of Ulrike Mohr.
Copyright © 2008 Artists Rights Society
(ARS), New York / VG BildKunst, Bonn
(Germany).

chitecture whch has been destroyed and rebuilt several times. Originally
built in the fifteenth century, the palace served as the main residence for
Prussian kings and emperors from 1701 until 1918 as the Royal Palace
(Stadtschloss). Heavily damaged by Allied airstrikes in 1945, the Royal
Palace was demolished in 1950 by the East Germans and was rebuilt as
the Palace of the Republic, with the newly refurbished space opening in
1976. It was a combination of cultural center and parliament building
in East Germany. With the fall of the Berlin Wall in 1989, the fate of
this iconic East German building was hotly contested until it finally was
demolished in 2006, the point at which Mohr spotted the trees growing on the roof. Significantly, the rebuilt space, called the Humboldt
Forum, will chronicle Germany's short-lived yet genocidal colonialist
history in Africa in a space that reconstructs the original baroque archi-

Figure 1.9. Tree signs. Photo by Ulrike Mohr; courtesy of Ulrike Mohr. Copyright ©
2008 Artists Rights Society (ARS), New York / VG BildKunst, Bonn (Germany).

tecture of the Royal Palace. Thus the visual replacement of the Palace of
the Republic creates an architectural pardoning, or amnesia, of the postwar period, substituting one genocide for another. Although Mohr's tree
project began before the final fate of the rebuilt palace was determined,
it nonetheless must be read as a layer in the complex historical archaeology of the place.

Ulrike Mohr's discovery of the trees on the roof of the Palace of the Republic is tied to an earlier installation entitled *Measures at Normal Null*
(*Maßnahme am Normalnull Berlins: Eine Rechenaufgabe mit offenem
Ende/Berlin Seit 2004*). In this work, Mohr calculated the median point
between the highest and lowest publicly accessible places in Berlin, and
redefined the median as "Normal Null" (the usual orientation being sea
level), thus placing a large part of the city into the negative, minus zone.
Mohr's concentration on systems of position and location refers as much
to sociology as geography: these projects ask, for instance, "what is my
position in this system; what is my place in the ranking, provided I appear there at all; where are the gaps in my network; am I inside or outside
again?"[56] It was during the process of photographing these buildings that
Mohr discovered the trees on the roof of the palace.

Mohr's next project was to transplant the five trees that had originally grown on the roof of the Palace of the Republic to the roof of the New National Gallery (Neue Nationalgalerie; the Mies van der Rohe-designed museum of modern art in former West Berlin), with the constellation and placement of the trees corresponding to the corner points of Mies van der Rohe's main hall, thus establishing a new link between east and west. The Prussian Cultural Ministry forbade it, but Mohr was able to create a documentary exhibit of the trees in the main hall of the National Gallery. Mohr had planned to keep the trees permanently in the Sculpture Park, but because of new building regulations she had to uproot the trees after the Biennale in fall 2008; they were transplanted to a tree nursery in Berlin. (See figures 1.10 and 1.11.)

Finally, Mohr proposed an installation, *Exile*, in which the self-seeded, uprooted and transplanted trees, now conceptualized as "Palace Tree Refugees" (*Palastbaumflüchtlinge*), would be transported to the Villa Aurora, the former home of the German Jewish émigré writer Lion Feuchtwanger, in Pacific Palisades, California. Funding and other practical considerations forced her to abandon this project. In the plans for

Figure 1.10. Mohr, New National Gallery. Photo by Ulrike Mohr; courtesy of Ulrike Mohr. Copyright © 2008 Artists Rights Society (ARS), New York / VG BildKunst, Bonn (Germany).

Figure 1.11. Mohr, *Baumdepot*. Photo by Ulrike Mohr; courtesy of Ulrike Mohr. Copyright © 2008 Artists Rights Society (ARS), New York / VG BildKunst, Bonn (Germany).

the project, Mohr writes, "I plan to bring the trees into exile and to give them a sort of ID card, to create a 'genetic fingerprint.' As unique as they are, they should be replanted in open nature and be able to spread."[57] In proposing to plant the trees in Los Angeles, Mohr created a bridge of exile between Los Angeles and Berlin; the proposal also stresses the artificiality of Los Angeles and the fact that the city is encroached on by the desert. As Mohr writes: "bit by bit, in a city where the house numbers on gridline streets reach into four figures and where pumas and rattlesnakes live in the parks and where garbage dumps are transformed into green spaces, perhaps it's not a utopian idea to bring the post-socialist Palast trees to 'paradise.'"[58]

Mohr planned to build modules in order to transport the five "Palace Tree Refugees" to exile in Los Angeles. In her notes for the project, Mohr states that for the transport the trees "would be placed in autonomous boxes, and would be given water and would have light, and would be climate controlled. The size of the boxes would conform to the specific growth form of the trees. The trees are on average ten years old, at any rate much smaller than they would have been if they had been able to grow in dirt. With the collaboration of trained people, modules shall be developed that will have the necessary materials such as wood, Styrofoam, water, and electricity-generated solar panels, etc."[59]

A Los Angeles exile for the "Palace Tree Refugees," which would be brought not only to Los Angeles but, more specifically, to the former home of Feuchtwanger, evokes the trees as exilic German Jews, truly "rootless cosmopolitans." For Mohr, Los Angeles is a site of German Jewish refugee history, but it is also a city that is in flux between nature and culture, city and desert; it is a place of land art and site-specificity, a place of rampant and fast growth, a place with a scarcity of water resources that has the most stringent regulations for importing living plants. Into this landscape of deprivation, immigration, urban entanglement, and German Jewish history, Mohr wanted to place the "Palace Tree Refugees."

Why is this project of interest for a discussion of Jewish culture in Germany? Does it delineate Jewish space, German space, American space of the refugee? I am far less interested in whether the status of Mohr's project is "Jewish" art; more interesting, it seems to me, is that Mohr's installations and (failed) proposals, in which vegetation erupts in the entanglement between Jewish and German spaces, suggest the rhizomatic spread of Jewish to German to Jewish, and they insist that the German is always already Jewish. Seeking to transport the "Palace Tree Refugees" from former East Berlin to the heavily marked Jewish spaces of the former Berlin Wall zone, with a stop at the modernist mecca of the Mies van der Rohe museum (occupying another border zone between east and west) and then to Feuchtwanger's exile residence in Los Angeles, Mohr uproots dominant ways of thinking about Jewish spaces and public art in a city that is replete with debate about Jews and the public sphere.

Like the exhibit by Susan Hiller and the *eruv* digital art installations of the new media artist Elliott Malkin, which has the potential to stretch the boundaries of sacred Jewish space to encompass texts more broadly, Mohr's project forces us to contemplate Jewishness in a major metropolis (Berlin, Los Angeles) in the age of digital media that is in a complex dialogue with New York, Tel Aviv, and Los Angeles, and which plays a vital role in the shaping of new Jewish life in cities to the east of Berlin — Krakow, Vienna, Budapest, Vilna — as these cities have been emerging from their own complex historical and cultural ruin. Yet unlike Herz, with his call for a more dispersed *eruv*-like Jewish space in Germany, my call to reinscribe the *eruv* in our contemporary maps of Berlin is not to create a more "authentic" Jewishness, whatever that would mean. And like the *eruv* projects, Mohr's refugee trees, which are rootless cosmopolitans in their own right, are not attempting to reroot any notion of authentic Jewishness in the ruins of German Jewish history. Rather, all of these projects open up a way to reimagine German Jewish urban space, history, and memory, and to move from the reification of Auschwitz to the spaces—semiotic, discursive, and indexical—that lie beyond the aleph of Auschwitz.

CHAPTER 2

Reading Tangentially

The public art projects discussed in the previous chapter—from Ulrike
Mohr's refugee trees to Elliott Malkin's *eRuv* project—suggest playful, at
times ironic art practices that conceptualize the inextricably diasporic,
exilic, and Jewish nature of place, travel, and the transnational. This
chapter deals with several literary works that, similarly, translate the Jewish in their interrogation of the very nature of the literary text. Certainly,
in the past decade there has been significant scholarly discussion about
the parameters of what we might understand as Jewish transnational writing. This has shifted our understanding of the relationship between Jewish American and European literature. If the earlier studies focused on
exile writing, thus creating a relationship between Europe as locus of
trauma and America as place of refuge, more contemporary work has
enabled the complex encounter between European Jewish refugees and
American culture to unfold.

In this chapter, I set out to enact tangential readings that open up
an exploration of the Europeanness of and within American and Anglo-
American Jewish writings. In seeking to offer new ways of thinking about
Jewish literature, I move away from categorizing Jewish text as that written by a person who identifies as (or is identified as) Jewish, to instead
explore literary encounters, textual correspondences, and the complex
mechanism of translation that are all constitutive of the category of "Jewish writing." To be sure, Jewish writing is, and has always been, and will
likely always be transnational; as a multilingual, diasporic literature that

unfolds in the matrix of migration, translation, movement, and encounter, it has never and cannot be circumscribed into any narrow national framework. By bringing together a range of texts I insist on mobility among texts. Dan Miron describes this sort of textual mobility as "airy," enabling us to read contacts where they have not yet been detected, enabling us to see "that within the space of literary *Judesein* (being a Jew in the world), strange and wonderful encounters are discreetly and even unconsciously taking place, which the conventional critical imagination would never have dreamt were possible."[1]

This chapter examines several case studies of writers who foreground, in various ways, the process of translation. In the work of both the postwar German writer W. G. Sebald and the bilingual French-American writer Raymond Federman, the role of author/translator (and, in Federman's case, self-translator) is paramount. Federman and the American Jewish writer Alfred Kazin create complex works that mediate between the United States and Europe, and the work of the German-Jewish Portuguese artist Daniel Blaufuks reflects on Sebald and Georges Perec. Finally, Sebald, Federman, Kazin, and Blaufuks all open up a space for thinking about the relationship between text and image. In bringing together writers who do not usually occupy the same critical spaces—reading in the mode that Dan Miron has coined "tangential" or "contiguous"—I hope to open up readings of Sebald, Federman, Kazin, and Blaufuks to suggest the multidirectional movement between the J and the Jew and the Jude and the Juif: in other words, reading these three writers tangentially, as part of a multidirectional matrix, is one more way of thinking about the complex relationship between Jewish writing and translation.

To bring together Sebald, Federman, Kazin, and Blaufuks as part of a contiguous Jewish literary history is also to reconfigure the landscape of German Jewish text after 1945, which is forever shifting and provisional. The standard historiography of postwar German literature is one in which figurative rubble dominates—the rubble of language, signification, epistemology, nationhood, and edifice in its broadest sense. Yet at the same time, the narrative of postwar German-speaking Jewish writing has been rooted in a notion of textual causality and continuity, as it struggles to assert an existence out of the ruins of history. To read in this way is to recast the causal structures that have defined and delimited German Jewish literary subjectivity, and instead to read tangentially, allowing for a more oblique contact or "airy touching" between a range of literary and visual texts.

At the very center of the works by Sebald, Federman, Kazin, and Blaufuks is the question of how literary and aesthetic form can represent the Holocaust. These are all texts that grapple with the fundamental impossibility of narration and of textuality. Thus Federman states in his manifesto about Holocaust writing and the Jewish writer that "it is NOT through content but form, NOT with numbers or statistics but fiction and poetry that we will eventually come to terms with the Holocaust and its consequences."[2] In this way, this writer who, despite his following among certain literary circles, remains on the margins of the canon of Holocaust literature, raises some of the most vital questions about the meaning of Holocaust experience and its translation into the written text.

In what follows, I suggest some ways of approaching Sebald, Federman, Kazin, and Blaufuks as writers and artists who are all fundamentally concerned with the question of aesthetic form. Kazin is the most canonical of the three writers, although Sebald is part of a certain canon in both Germany and the United States. The marginal figure here is Federman—an experimental writer and academic whose Ph.D. thesis and subsequent critical work on Samuel Beckett certainly shaped his own literary works. In contrast to W. G. Sebald, however, who has been published and read by mainstream American presses in translation, Federman's work remains obscure to the general reading public. Turning to the contemporary German-Jewish Portuguese video and media artist Daniel Blaufuks, whose work mediates between literary texts (Sebald, Perec, Kafka) and the visual, this chapter also pushes the literary outside the margins as it rethinks the status of the visual.

In breaking out of previous models of literary approaches to traumatic personal history, all of these writers and artists suggest new ways of conceptualizing Jewish writing.

German Jewish Writing in the Age of Authorial Disintegration

In 2002 the recently deceased German writer W. G. Sebald received a posthumous "special award" among the annual Jewish book prizes given by the American Koret Foundation, for his 2001 novel *Austerlitz*. Despite the fact that Sebald received this "special award" and not the annual award for fiction, no conversation ensued about how, or if, Sebald might or should be considered a Jewish writer and *Austerlitz* a Jewish novel. There was no discussion about the slipperiness of the very category of "Jewish writing."[3]

So how Jewish is it? I begin with Sebald's Koret award not to concur with nor dispute the Jewishness (or Germanness) of Sebald and his novel.[4] Rather, the award offers a way to examine the larger issue of Jewish writing in Germany and to pose the following set of questions: Is German writing now, in the post-Holocaust age, shaped by ruin and the rubble of German (and German Jewish) history? Is this an age in which the trace of Jewishness is omnipresent, always "Jewish"? Is German Jewish writing now marked *not* by the hyphen between German and Jew in the descriptor "German-Jewish" (a diacritical mark that keeps intact the myth of a German Jewish symbiosis), but rather by the interplay among texts that results from translation—translation, literally, between languages, but also the translation of Jewish culture in Germany today? Does the "Jewishness" of Sebald's texts consist in the encounters (or rather, the missed encounters) between the presumably non-Jewish, largely autobiographical narrator and the various Jewish characters? Is Jewishness a figuration in Sebald's texts, a narrative condition staged as an encounter (between German narrator and Jewish interlocutor) in the context of travel, migration, and exile in which the Jewish figure is the cosmopolitan, the flâneur, the emigré who traverses city and national spaces? Is it the diasporic quality of Sebald's writing, where language and place are no longer linked, that enables the text to be seen as Jewish? What is the relationship between Jewish text and text as ruin that is evoked in Sebald's work, and which has emerged as a dominant trope of contemporary German Jewish culture? And, finally: What is the place of Jewishness within the transnational Europe that has emerged since the 1990s and which has, in part, sparked various cultural imaginations of community? Does the translation of Jewishness into these new figurations of imagined communities help to create an imagined transnational community?

I pose this series of questions in order to move beyond the critical impasses into which German Jewish studies and post-Holocaust studies of German culture have led: the impasse of identity debates ("How German is it?" and "How Jewish is it?") and the impasse of debates about representation in art and atrocity.[5] Finally, this book attempts to move beyond the impasse of having exhausted ourselves in thinking about the parameters of grief, mourning, loss, the interplay between presence and absence, between German and Jew, the reappearance of the past in the present, the exhausted tropes of testimony, witnessing, belatedness, trauma, postmemory, and even that of ennui itself. Rather than exhausting memory yet again, I approach these questions first with a return to Roland Barthes's paradigmatic reflections on the text: "that neutral, composite, oblique space where our subject slips away, the negative where all identity is lost."[6] It is precisely in Barthes's "oblique space where our subject slips away" that I propose we situate Sebald as "translated Jew" as well as translations of Jewishness in the post-Shoah world, exploring the space of the diacritical mark of the "German-Jewish" as a possible "oblique space where our subject slips away." By invoking Barthes, I seek to open up and break the hyphen that keeps intact the referent of "the German" and "the Jewish," in order to contemplate German Jewish writing in the age of authorial disintegration. In other words, I propose that we think about Sebald as a "Jewish" author while at the same time dismantling the category of "the author."

Sebald, whose texts place the vicissitudes of ruin—architectural, narrative, visual, epistemological—at their center, has played a significant role in the past several years in reshaping the contours of the public debates in the United States about Jewishness, Germanness, and cultural and historical memory; yet at the same time his work highlights some of the divides of these debates between Germany and the United States. As countless critics have now made clear, a large part of the appeal of Sebald for the Anglo-American reading public is that he crafts a notion of the narrator/author as a nomad wandering, post-traumatically, in the rubble and ruin of critical reflections that have piled up, as Benjamin suggests, "Trümmer auf Trümmer" ("wreckage upon wreckage"), in the aftermath of the Holocaust.[7] While many German critics see his work as antiquated reflections of a hopelessly neo-romantic European nostalgia and sentimentality, the Anglo-American press has praised the allusive, elegiac, fragmentary, ruminative, and diasporic qualities of his writing. Oddly, for the German reading public Sebald is figured as antiquated, archaic, and in this regard, intensely German; for the American reader, Sebald's rumination on the German past makes him somehow legibly

"Jewish."[8] Sebald is, for some American critics, a quintessentially German author steeped in the German modernist narrative tradition, writing novels that express a Hegelian dialectic between prose and poetry that defines the conceptual narrative framework of the nineteenth-century European novel.[9] With countless references in his works to high modernist authors such as Kafka, Proust, Rilke, and Nabokov, Sebald expresses for some critics an affinity with the narrative forays of European modernism, embracing in particular the dominant strand of German modernism, remaining thus first and foremost a *German* author. Others challenge the postmodern quality of the nomadic, exilic narrative voice and structure, arguing for the fundamentally modernist relationship to place and text found within Sebald's work.[10]

Rather than entering the impasse of our age's version of the battle between the ancients and the moderns (i.e., modernism versus postmodernism), I propose to cast some of these questions in a slightly different form—with the aim of reconsidering the larger question of the role of text and authorship, in particular Jewish text and Jewish authorship, in the production of contemporary Jewish identity in Germany. The twin questions of "How Jewish is it?" and its absent echo "How German is it?" enable reflection not only on why Sebald has dominated the critical field in the past few years, but more significantly, why this interest stretches from Germany to the Anglophone world in a way that is unprecedented for a German author in the postwar period.[11] The appearance of Sebald's work in English has shifted the terms that have dominated discussions of post-1945 history, memory, and narrative, and has shifted the very terrain of national literatures as it blurs, intentionally, the lines between German literature written abroad and literature written in German on "English soil." In the case of W. G. Sebald, the place of literary production— simultaneously the place of immigration—becomes the defining mark of the national, not the language in which the text is written.[12]

Yet does Sebald's writing presence in England enable the reading public to construct Sebald—or, more precisely, the translation of Jewish memory in his texts—as simultaneously a German and a British writer? More significantly, does the blurring of national identity and the space of literary production carry with it the marks of "Jewishness" that create the slide from German to—surprisingly—Jew? Reading Sebald, not only in the wake of the Koret award but, more significantly, after the publication of Günter Grass's *Crab Walk* (*Krebsgang*, 2002, trans. 2004) and Sebald's own *Airwar and Literature*, what becomes clear is that his work has become inseparable from the recent debates about German victimhood and suffering that were circulating in Germany and the United States. Public debate about memory and history after 1945 has been, to a very large extent, shaped by public discourse in both Germany and the United States, creating a litany of discourse/events that usually begins with the 1980 airing of the miniseries *Holocaust* on West German television, and then moves to the fuller recitation: Bitburg; Historians' Debate; Jenninger affair; Wilkomirski; and so on.[13] There is a certain estrangement in the sound of this recitation, since it is no longer the event that is recalled, but the now seemingly endless chain of associations. There is, as well, an acoustic memory that has been created—not of the event (rallies, loudspeakers, the sound of Hitler's voice), but of the recitation of the events, a litany that creates a metonymic slide from one event to the next, linking them in cultural memory, in which the discussion of memory becomes a stand-in for memory itself. Thus the memory in Germany of the Holocaust is a speech act that consecrates the order of public events that mark turning points in the discussion. The debate ignited by Grass and by the publication of Sebald's *Airwar and Literature* (and which intensified with the popular and critical acclaim of his work that came immediately after his untimely death in 2001) grows out of and is then absorbed into this litany.[14]

Post-Holocaust literary and aesthetic studies were marked in the 1980s and 1990s by intense inquiry into the nature of representation and text (Berel Lang, Saul Friedländer, Dominic LaCapra, Hayden White, James Young) and by work on trauma and loss (Cathy Caruth, LaCapra);[15] the critical discussion sparked by Sebald incorporates these strands of literary and critical inquiry, yet at the same time the circuitous narrative structure and the vital interplay between text and image in Sebald's work demand a rethinking of aesthetic and literary categories that have created critical impasses in post-Holocaust discourse. Sebald's work has generated considerable scholarly attention to the role of the visual in post-Holocaust literature. Rather than privileging analytical and interpretive models in visual studies over the literary, I propose reading Sebald's visual narratives in order to realign the visual with the literary, thus reconstructing sites of memory in these works as textualized spaces that reveal how the literary is, as Paul De Man observed, "a moment inherent in all cultural forms." In fact, I argue, Sebald's texts prevent the reader from creating legibility of the links between the literary and the visual, since he constantly disrupts the possibility of legibility, creating instead both correspondences and dissonances not only between image and text but also intertextually, among texts.

In this, Sebald is in the company of writers such as Umberto Eco, Raymond Federman, Georges Perec, Italo Calvino, Fernando Pessoa, and Jorge Luis Borges, whose texts always exceed the category of the literary to become blueprints for literary theory and philosophy. In Sebald's work it is the figurations of ruin, which have become a central organizing principle of current German Jewish discourse, in which the lines between history and narrative, between German and Jew, become blurred; in the rubble of this new narrative world, epistemological certainty and literary and cultural "legibility" also lie in rubble. Sebald presents topographies of destruction, ruin, rubble, spaces the narrator and others move through and dwell in, actual ruin, "fields of rubble," transformed buildings that exist in metonymic relationship to each other. Yet it is not only that there are ruins scattered throughout the texts, spaces where the encounter between the narrator and the (often) Jewish traveler are staged, but that Sebald conceptualizes and creates narrative ruin. Here he is, in many ways, at his most German, continuing the postwar German and Austrian literary rumination on Adorno's most famous and contested dictum that to write poetry after Auschwitz is barbaric, and suggesting the ruin of coherent or unified historiography,[16] and thus following in the footsteps of mostly non-Jewish writers such as Peter Handke, Ingeborg Bachmann, Max Frisch, Christa Wolf, Günter Grass, Uwe Timm, and Peter Weiss, as he weaves the autobiographical with the historical, both repressing and uncovering the traces of atrocity, violence, and trauma.

Yet even in the context of this very German reflection since 1945 (and since 1989) on the viability of representation and of historiography, Sebald's work moves in a new direction. Not only does he place ruin at the very center of his project, but also, more significantly, translation as act and as idea is embedded in the texts as a layer in this archaeology of narrative ruin. In this, not his fellow Germans but rather writers such as Calvino, Eco, Borges, Federman, and Pessoa become significant, all of whom have explored the intimate ties between place and text and translation. With the "turn to translation" of many late twentieth-century studies of culture and with much scholarly work that has been devoted to examining both the "task" and the after-tasks of the translator in the post-Benjamin age, Sebald's preoccupation with ruin raises the question of what it means to "translate" Jewish memory and to create Jewish text. To read Sebald now—in English, after his death, and in the wake of his "special award"—is to be engaged with a process of translating Jewish memory from and back to Germany today, translating the memory of Jewishness to a present-day Germany marked by its absence.[17]

Translation occupies a major place in Sebald's work: the significance of the translation of Sebald's texts between German and English, the fact that Sebald founded an institute for translation studies at the University of East Anglia, and even the extended encounter between the narrator and Michael Hamburger—the Celan translator—in the *Rings of Saturn.* Yet I conceive of translation not simply as the literary act of moving from one language to another or as the cultural transmission that results from moving among texts; translation is a "carrying over" (as the Greek root implies) not only of meaning but of the continual accrual of meaning, metaphor, and sound. "Translation," as I am bringing it to bear on Sebald's work, is a consideration of the mediation between aesthetic form (that is, between text and image) and between German and American culture, identifying forms of art and literature that cross over between these two separate but linked cultural spheres, establishing a new critical voice that can mediate between German and Jewish American culture. Thus, to translate Jewish memory in Germany, or German Jewish memory in the United States, is to think about and listen to the constant circulation of memory, postmemory, and text beyond the borders of either the German or the Jewish. The work of the non-Jewish German writer W. G. Sebald bears the abrasions, marks (Jewish stigmata), and echoes of "the Jewish" that are always present as trace within all German texts. In this way, Jewishness is the sign that is always implicit, present in its absence, returning over and over again. The "translation of Jewish memory" that Sebald's texts enact is thus one layer in the palimpsest of memory texts circulating between Germany and the United States. It fundamentally rethinks the status of Jewish text, creating from the material a more diasporic notion of text that takes into consideration the way in which texts traverse spatial, historical, and personal memory.

As part of the task of "translating Jewishness" into Sebald and thus asserting the diasporic quality in his writing, I propose yet another experiment: reading this non-Jewish, German-born writer, whose texts were written in German but who lived most of his adult life in England, *not* as a German writer (who nonetheless sparks a very German debate about the Allied bombings and the role of German victims), but rather as a British post-imperialist writer, one who takes his place as much among writers such as Hanif Kareishi, Kazuo Ishiguro, and Pico Iyer as beside Günter Grass and Uwe Timm.[18] And yet, perhaps what is at stake is not whether Sebald is to be characterized as a German or a British author, but instead whether the very category of "British fiction" or any national literature (or, to push it further, Jewish writing) is itself in ruin in the post-imperial era. If Sebald's work can, in fact, be read as post-imperial British fiction, then what are the implications of this for German history, German culture, and the ongoing debates about German and Jewish memory? Does the "Jewishness" conferred upon Sebald (or his texts) place him as a kind of extraterritorial? Does this make a European pastiche out of Sebald's texts, a pan-post-everything (postcolonial, post-imperial, post-modern, post-German)? Is it the diasporic quality of his writing, where language and place are no longer linked, that enables the text to be seen as "Jewish"? These are the questions that the Sebald phenomenon raises.

Sebald's preoccupation with travel, airplanes and airports, movement, railroad stations, and suitcases and knapsacks suggests the narrators' encounters and mis-encounters with Jewish Germans rooted in literary tropes of the flâneur, the wanderer, the cosmopolitan, the extraterritorial—in other words, the Jew who inhabits multiple urban spaces, moving between them and between layers of historical and cultural memory. Sebald's preoccupation in *Rings of Saturn* (*Die Ringe des Saturn*, 1995; trans. 1998), for instance, is with travel, movement, and memory. The novel opens with the narrator describing how he ends up in a hospital in Norwich "in a state of almost total immobility," a year to the day after he completed a walking tour of the county of Suffolk—walking for hours in the day, confronted, as we learn in the opening paragraph, "with the traces of destruction, reaching far back into the past, that were evident even in that remote place." It is in the confinement of his hospital room, where he experiences—like Gregor Samsa, to whom he compares himself—a bewildering relationship between the enclosure of the room and the once-familiar spaces beyond it, that the narrator begins to write what follows (or rather, to conceive of it: "It was then that I began in my thoughts to write these pages").[19] After another year, he assembles the notes written in the hospital and writes the text. The illness—"a state of almost total immobility," of stasis, of ceasing to move through space and time—signals the end to the narrator traversing the eastern coast of Britain and with that, British history and memory. Writing as illness; writing as sign of trauma and its belatedness, as the narrator writes the account one year to the day later; writing that carries with it the belatedness of other texts, that is, Kafka; reflection as pathology of modernity; traces of destruction highlighting the acute subjectivity of the author: all of these place Sebald as much in the German tradition (post-Kafka) as it does in the domain of British post-imperial writing.

The narrator's flight from Amsterdam to Norwich highlights this question of movement and travel, and suggests Sebald's affinity with global networks of travel that have been at the center of British post-imperial writing. Sebald's description of Schiphol airport in Amsterdam echoes, for instance, the work of the Indian British writer Pico Iyer. Sebald starts the passage on Schiphol by noting the "strangely muted" atmosphere of the airport, making it seem as if one were "already a good way beyond this world. As if they were under sedation or moving through time stretched and expanded, the passengers wandered the halls or, standing still on the escalators, were delivered to their various destinations on high or underground."[20] Sebald continues, embedding a line from Hamlet's famous soliloquy on death: "The airport, filled with a murmuring whisper, seemed to me that morning like an anteroom of that undiscovered country from whose bourn no traveler returns."[21] Pico Iyer, in fact, cites precisely this passage from Sebald (citing Hamlet) in *The Global Soul*, linking the "bright and sterile spaces" of the airport, "a terminal zone," to the hospital, where "one by one people disappear as their names or departures are called out."[22]

In *The Emigrants* (*Die Ausgewanderten*, 1992; trans. 1996), the narrator's identity—always murky, unclear—merges, as it does later in *Austerlitz* (2001), with the stories of the emigrants whose lives he uncovers, layer by layer, in England. While critics have argued that Sebald eclipses and elides the Holocaust in *The Emigrants*, speaking of it only obliquely and in code, it is there as frame, as spectral presence, as displaced and belated memory, and as a sort of "origin" for these tales. It is also, at times, literally incorporated into the mouth of the narrator, who recounts the story of the four emigrants within the embedded story. In both *Austerlitz* and *The Emigrants* the narrative is punctuated with the repetition of "said Austerlitz," or "said Ferber," thus blurring the lines between interlocutors, between transmitted and narrated memory, between the present moment in England and the German past.

The acoustic effect of the repetition of "said Austerlitz" and "said Ferber" frames the structure of narrative and translation that is central to all of Sebald's texts; it links the act of translation to the acts of bearing witness, giving testimony, and storytelling, and to the elegiac nature of translation as a process of loss and recovery. Furthermore, this key narrative technique demands a focus on the role of the acoustic in Sebald's work. This shift to the acoustic might suggest new ways of approaching Sebald's work beyond the extensive scholarship that focuses on the primacy of the visual in his novels.

The confusion and blurring of the narrator's recounting with the narrative told to him by the Jewish figure (Austerlitz, Ferber) suggests that Sebald is bringing back to life the storyteller that Benjamin, in his pivotal essay, "The Storyteller," lamented had ceased to be a force in the twentieth century. Benjamin's scrutiny of the art of "experience that is passed on from mouth to mouth" has bearing on Sebald's narrative technique in both *Austerlitz* and *The Emigrants*.[23] Benjamin asserts, furthermore, that

> storytelling is always the art of repeating stories, and this art is lost when the stories are no longer retained. It is lost because there is no more weaving and spinning to go on while they are being listened to. The more self-forgetful the listener is, the more deeply what he listens to is imprinted upon his memory. When the rhythm of work has seized him, he listens to the tales in such a way that the gift of retelling them comes to him all by itself.[24]

By turning to Benjamin's own focus on the acts of listening to and repetition of the sound of the story being told, I add the acoustic to the process of translation that Sebald's work embodies.

Yet translation is not only part of the narrative structure of repetition in the text; drawing on Carol Jacob's insight that Benjamin's essay on translation itself performs an act of translation, I claim that Sebald's texts can be similarly read as performances of translation, as they continually unsettle words and meanings from prior contexts.[25] The blurring between narrator and Jewish figure is analogous to Benjamin's insistence on the translation's great ability to defamiliarize the original language, rendering the familiar "original" language foreign and unknown. In a late fragment found in the Benjamin estate, "La Traduction—le Pour et le Contre," Benjamin evokes precisely this sense of the unfamiliar and the unknown ("Das Unerkannte").[26] The dialogue, possibly originally intended for radio broadcast in France, begins with the first speaker recounting how he found a French translation of a German philosophical text in the bookstalls on the Seine. Only identifying the text as one by Nietzsche later in the fragment, the speaker goes on to express his surprise that the passages which had most occupied him in the past, in this text, were not to be found in the French translation. When asked by the other speaker if this means he simply did not find the passages, the other speaker responds that he found them, but that he had the feeling that the passages were as unable to recognize (*erkennen*) him as he was unable to recognize them. Concurring with the other speaker that the Nietzsche translator was highly regarded, the first speaker explains that what was disorienting to him was not a deficiency in the translation but rather "something which may even have been its merit, that the horizon and the world around the translated text had itself been substituted, had become French."[27]

This fragment serves to open up several interpretive lines for reading Sebald. First, it is significant that the speaker (not Benjamin, but certainly in this text a heteronymous stand-in for him) comes upon the translation by chance. The encounter with the translated text is evoked as analogous to the face-to-face encounter, as the speaker describes the act of looking for the missing passages as one in which he peers into the face (*als ich ihnen ins Gesicht sah*) of the passages, discovering their mutual illegibility (of face, of text).[28] The fragment, itself a found object, bears the mark of this illegibility. Similarly, Sebald's texts are comprised of a narrator's re-creation of a transmitted conversation and, often, testimony, thus repeatedly highlighting that the text we are reading has been collected, often by chance, and reconstructed from the ruins of memory and forgetting.[29]

The presence of the narrator, and behind that, Sebald the author, generates this testimony and witnessing. While critics have generally read the encounter (or mis-encounter) between the narrator and his various Jewish figures as one that probes the relationship between the German Jewish past and the present in a landscape of ruin, I want to call attention to Sebald's own presence in the text—as well as in the translation of the text—as author and, at the same time, as translator, poet, collector, storyteller, émigré, and, finally, as "Jew." The tendency in the scholarship on Sebald to read an autobiographical presence hovering behind the narrator, and the narrator's ramblings then as a pseudonymous screen for Sebald himself, has led to charges that Sebald "appropriates" Jewishness. I propose abandoning the assumption of authenticity of experience and identity that underlies this charge of appropriation, and, in the wake of Foucault's and Barthes's axiomatic reflections on the status of the author, to focus on the more significant question of authorship.

Instead of approaching the narrator as a thinly veiled W. G. Sebald, and the narrative as the German-born writer's journey to recapture a lost Germanness that includes the loss of the Jewish, let us think of Sebald's texts as creating heteronyms that are reminiscent of the work of the Portuguese modernist writer Fernando Pessoa. Pessoa's best-known work, *The Book of Disquiet*, situates the author Fernando Pessoa behind what he terms the "semi-heteronym" Bernardo Soares, whom Pessoa called "a mutilation of my own personality." Pessoa's *Book of Disquiet*, his collection of poems, and his collected writings have been referred to as "a trunk full of people," texts that express what Agamben has termed a radical de-subjectification, in which the text is comprised of meditations by a heteronymous author who is not a stand-in for Pessoa. As Chris Daniels explains, "A heteronym is a fictional writer that may or may not reflect or refract some aspect of the personality and desires of the inventing writer, who isn't trying very hard, if at all, to hide the fact that the heteronym is fictive."[30]

Pessoa's heteronyms offer a new way of reading Sebald that can potentially eclipse the problem of "authenticity" and authorship that plagues not only much critical work on Jewish culture in Germany, but more generally, discussions of art after Auschwitz. Heteronymity as literary practice and ethos provides, too, a way out of the circular debates about the ethics of authorship sparked by recent literary and memoir scandals such as Wilkomirski, Demidenko, and Yasusada. As Bill Freind explains in his article on the Yasusada controversy, "heteronymity offers a means of both acknowledging the continued desire of many readers for the presence of an author behind a work of literature while simultaneously calling attention to the fictive status of that presence. Rather than serving to limit or control the text, the heteronymic author instead becomes part of it and thus can be read and interpreted."[31] In the debates following the Wilkomirski affair and the newly translated poems by Yasusada that were revealed as fakes, it became apparent that public and critical discourse about the "authentic" writing subject are being enacted in the critical vacuum after Foucault and Barthes's pivotal texts on the author. These two texts offer a substantive framework for the turn to heteronymity that I propose as a new way of reading Sebald and a new way of thinking about German Jewish subjectivity today.

Roland Barthes, for instance, prefaces his *Roland Barthes by Roland Barthes* with the following command about this autobiography, placed just underneath the title on the frontispiece: "It must all be considered as if spoken by a character in a novel." Later in the text, he goes on to explain, "I do not say: 'I am going to describe myself' but: 'I am writing a text, and I call it R.B.'"[32] The desire for a nostalgic conception of the writing subject before Foucault and Barthes also sidesteps the debates in public art about the status of the referent. Perhaps more productive than the moral outcries following the revelations of Wilkomirski or Yasusada would be Pessoa's fragment about translation, written in English, in which he muses on the trilogy that remains to be written: a History of Translation, a History of Plagiarisms, and a History of Parodies: "A translation is only a plagiarism in the author's name . . . a translation is a serious parody in an other language."[33] In a more serious vein, Marjorie Perloff reflects on Foucault's importance in contemplating the impact of these literary hoaxes: "Foucault's central position, which has come to be de rigueur in the academy, is that it is the culture that constructs or writes the author, not vice-versa."[34]

To turn to Foucault and Barthes means, of necessity, to enter into the debate about the ethical dimensions of writing; yet my turn to the heteronym is an attempt to pose a set of questions regarding what it might mean to create and disassemble narrative voices that are distinct from that of the author. One of Pessoa's heteronyms, for instance, writes, "Strictly speaking, Fernando Pessoa does not exist."[35] Outdoing even Barthes, Pessoa here proclaims the death or nonexistence of the author by the author's own alter ego. In writing about the genesis of his seventy-two heteronyms, Pessoa explains his desire to create a "fictitious world, to surround myself with friends and acquaintances that never existed."[36] In a letter to one of his heteronyms, Adolfo Casais Monteiro, he goes on to explain his penchant for heteronymity as his tendency toward "depersonalization": "Today I have no personality: I've divided all my humanness among the various authors whom I've served as literary executor. Today I'm the meeting-place of a small humanity that belongs only to me."[37]

Pessoa's reflections in his *Book of Disquiet* wander and meander, with a common thread of the presence of art, the question of text and authorship, and, indirectly, the aesthetic question of translation. Throughout these reflections, however, Pessoa returns, again and again, to a stance of anti-subjectivity or what he termed extreme depersonalization, producing reflections in which the narrative standpoint is consistently obliterated, erased. For instance, he writes in one passage of the "vagabond words that desert me as soon as they're written, wandering on their own over slopes and meadows of images, along avenues of concepts, down footpaths of confusion . . . these pages are the scribbles of my intellectual self-unawareness. I trace them in a stupor of feeling whatever I feel, like a cat in the sun, and I sometimes reread them with a vague, belated astonishment, as when I remember something I forgot ages ago.[38]

Later in this passage, Pessoa, or rather his "semi heteronym" Soares, claims with a characteristic crypticness that is itself a play with encryption: "I sphinxly discern myself."[39] In other words, the writing subject—in this case, not Pessoa but his beloved heteronym Bernardo Soares—is engaged in the Sisyphean task not of revealing or unraveling identity, thought, feeling, but rather the impossible, and always failed ("sphinxly") attempt to discern the self.

Pessoa's reflections on art, authorship, and translation find resonance in the narrative structure of Sebald's works. Yet let me make a brief detour—very Sebaldian—from Pessoa to the work of the late-twentieth-century bilingual writer Raymond Federman. Federman, a writer, poet, and literary critic who wrote three books on Beckett, is an interesting counterpoint to Sebald. In fact, Federman as a self-described "self-translator" has a similar relationship to his original texts and their retranslations as does Sebald. In *Double or Nothing* (1998), subtitled "a real fictitious discourse," Federman undertakes the project of writing his autobiography. The first section, entitled "This Is Not the Beginning," echoes Magritte's painted words "Ceci n'est pas une pipe" ("This Is Not a Pipe") that are simultaneously true and not true: the pipe is not a real pipe, but rather a representation of a pipe in a painting. Similarly, Federman's prologue to his book, "This Is Not a Beginning," is a beginning, but it is not clear what might follow. This first section consists of long, nomadic sentences that each meander for longer than a page, with some of the words in boldface, suggesting that they are key words, or guideposts for the reader; the boldface words are interjections, or "interpellations,"[40] puncturing the narrative as if they are the whispered corrections to it from the child whose story is being narrated. These boldfaced words si-multaneously derail the reader and provide vital missing information.

The project, we are told in the first sentence, is that "a rather stubborn and determined middle-aged man" has decided to "record for posterity, exactly as it happened, word by word and step by step, the story of another man."[41] We quickly realize that the middle-aged Federman has undertaken the task of recording "word by word, step by step" the tale of his own immigration from Poland to the United States at the age of nine. The "word by word, step by step" approach suggests a writing that is si-multaneously a performance of lived experience, making of the written narrative a re-creation of real life that is lived in real time.

Federman has written that the only possible Holocaust narrative is one that is filled with breaks, ruptures, one that does not permit the possibility of a "healing" from writing. This is like the work of another "1.5" gen-eration French writer, Georges Perec, whose entire body of work seems intended to confound the boundaries of language, translation, and text. His best-known project was the novel *La Disparition* (*A Void*), in which he wrote the entire novel without using the letter "e." In Perec's 1975 novel *W, or the Memory of Childhood* there is, in an analogous mode in Federman's work, an extended rumination on the "x":

> the sign of multiplication and of sorting (the x-axis), the sign of the mathematical unknown, and, finally, the starting point for a geometrical fantasy, whose basic figure is the double V, and whose complex convolutions trace out the major symbols of the

story of my childhood: two V's joined tip to tip make the shape of an X; by extending the branches of the X by perpendicular segments of equal length, you obtain a swastika (卐), which itself can be easily decomposed, by a rotation of 90 degrees of one of its ⁄ segments on its lower arm, into the sign ⁄⁄.[42]

Similarly, the entire project of *Double or Nothing* is a play of words — but not only words. It is the word/text as image that is also at work throughout *Double or Nothing*. Each time Federman refers to his immediate family members, all four of whom were gassed to death in Auschwitz, he inserts four X marks—X X X X—thus marking and not marking, a game of tic-tac-toe minus the O. The withholding of the key to his traumatic history—the murder in Auschwitz of his father, mother, and sisters, and his own miraculous survival due to his mother pushing him into a closet as the police were arriving—by using the "X X X X" to substitute for the names of his family members is also linked to his deliberate splitting of narrative voices, and the creation of multiple selves who are at work narrating. Susan Suleiman describes this in psychoanalytic terms, drawing on D. W. Winnicott to elucidate the way in which Federman engaged in the "restorative function of play" as a way to work through his childhood Holocaust trauma. Suleiman teases out the paradoxical nature of Federman's work, looking at it less as a sign of the poetic (in its assertion of ambiguity and veiled meanings) than as the "unstable or split identity that is the consequence of traumatic experience."[43]

Suleiman has written extensively of Federman's use of the rhetorical figure of preterition, of "saying while not saying." In particular, Suleiman notes that the four X marks that recur in all of Federman's work "are emblematic of the figure of preterition, in that they indicate both presence and absence, both the lost objects and their 'exing out,' their erasure."[44] In what has been described as a "pulverized" narrative, the visual play at work throughout *Double or Nothing* consists of the many pages of concrete poetry interspersed with the narrative, the visual games that come and go throughout the work, the constant rupturing of narrative so that gleaning the story is an act of courage on the part of a reader willing to wade through the morass of symbols and images on the page. And yet despite the brokenness, the pulverized, the episodic and nomadic quality of Federman's writing, it carries and, indeed, even conveys the weight of his traumatic past.

In Federman's novel *SHHH: The Story of a Childhood* (2010), the many voices that erupt and challenge the central narrator's attempt to tell and digress from the central story of his survival recall not only Perec and Beckett, but also Pessoa's heteronyms. Federman's *SHHH* is an extended homage to Samuel Beckett (whose epitaph from *The Expelled* graces the start of Federman's work: "I don't know why I told this story. / I could just as well have told another"), and is simultaneously memoir and novel mixed in one; as Davis Schneiderman enjoins us in the introduction to *SHHH*: "hear the nothingness that the character of Raymond Federman worked so long to finally unwrite."[45] The text begins with Federman recounting the day of July 16, 1942, when the French police came to their apartment building and rounded up his parents and two sisters. His mother had pushed him into a closet on the staircase, with her final word/sound to him, "shhh." Explaining that the title of the book, *SHHH*, is the last word he heard his mother utter, it is at the same time "not my mother's last word. It was the first word of the book my mother knew I would write some day."[46]

Federman as self-translator is also Federman who hears his mother's command to not talk and, by extension, to not write about it. In *SHHH* he describes the silence of the day and night he spent in the closet after his family was taken, followed by the silence and solitude of the early years after he came to the United States: "During the first years of my exile when my native tongue was slowly fading in me, while another strange tongue was painfully taking shape in my mouth."[47] That translation and multilingualism are constitutive of Federman's life (and, simultaneously, his body of writing) is a topic returned to throughout *SHHH*: "It took many years for me to understand what my mother meant with her *shhh*. I can still hear that word in my ear. But I always hear it in French: *chut*. To write *shhh* falsifies what my mother meant. But since I am writing this version of my childhood in English, I have to practice hearing *shhh*."[48] Throughout, Federman insists that what he is writing is "pure fiction" because he has forgotten his entire childhood. "It has been blocked in me. So I've to reinvent it, reconstruct it."[49] Federman's interlocutor constantly interrupts the narrative, addressing him as "Federman" and challenging him to tell the story and admonishing him, at one point, "Federman, one of these days you're going to get lost in your own stories, and you won't know how to get back to the real world."[50] The narrator responds, with characteristic wryness, "Besides as I've often said, the real world, it's a nice place to visit, but I wouldn't want to live there permanently."[51]

Like Federman's multiple narrative voices that clash and collide within his texts, Sebald too creates a series of narrative subjects that in many respects function like Pessoa's heteronyms, through what Agamben has called, in reference to Pessoa, "three different subjectifications/desubjectifications" that ultimately enact a "radical desubjectification" of the primary narrative presences in the texts.[52] The mystery of the narrator, a figure always loosely based on W. G. Sebald himself, but not purely autobiographical, becomes part of the mystery of the narrative he recounts and attempts to reconstruct; ultimately, this mystery calls to mind, again, the blurring between fiction and reality in the work of Federman, and returns us to the puzzle of how to read Sebald as writer: German? British? Jewish?

This is particularly acute in the final section of *The Emigrants*, when the Jewish figure — Max Aurach in the original German, Max Ferber in the English translation — tells the narrator that he has not left Manchester for twenty-two years.[53] The first line of the story provides the echo for this, creating a doubling effect between the two figures: "Until my twenty-second year I had never been further away from home than a five- or six-hour train journey."[54] Like the painter Ferber, who continually undoes the images on his canvases, the narrator, at the end of the story (now winter 1990/91) "not infrequently" unravels what he has written to date about the account of Max Ferber, as he is cast into a crisis not only about the act of writing about Ferber, but more generally "about the whole questionable business of writing."[55] The text he has been working on — presumably, but not necessarily, the one we have been reading to this point — consists of hundreds of pages of scribble, "in pencil and ballpoint. By far the greater part had been crossed out, discarded, or obliterated by additions. Even what I had ultimately salvaged as a 'final' version seemed to me a thing of shreds and patches, utterly botched."[56] By reading *The Emigrants* as a text comprised of heteronyms, we can read the narrator's expression of literary impotence at the end of the Max Ferber chapter not as an exploration of the limits of and failure of writing to capture the experience of the Shoah, but rather as Sebald's acknowledgment of his role as storyteller and collector (of the photographs and images that are found in the text).

This written version that is a condensed and "botched" translation/transmission of Aurach's life story, again mirroring Aurach's "botched" paintings, is also a translation/transcription from the English conversations between the narrator and Aurach and the German in which it is written down. When the narrator tracks down Aurach and spends "three days and nights" in conversation (a conversation "in which many more things were said than I shall be able to write down here"), we learn, for the first time, that Ferber has not spoken German since his departure from Munich in 1939 and has in fact lost his native tongue, thus suggesting traumatic loss as the basis of Ferber's loss of the German language:[57] "It survives in me as no more than an echo, a muted and incomprehensible murmur. It may have something to do with this loss of language, this oblivion, Ferber went on, that my memories reach no further back than my ninth or eighth year, and that I recall little of the Munich years after 1933 other than processions, marches, and parades."[58] The German text for the phrase "the loss of language, this oblivion [*diese Einbuße oder Verschüttung der Sprache*]" evokes language as entrapped — as in a bombed-out building — not spoken, banned from its natural environment, impoverished, language amid the rubble and in a process of decay. English phrases and expressions are scattered throughout the German original, suggesting this very notion of decay; like the photographs and images that interrupt the narrative, the eruption of English within the German text creates a layer of textual abrasion that sometimes interrupts, sometimes simply recasts the narrative. In this way, the presumed English that Ferber and the narrator speak, in the German original text, always calls the Germanness and the idea of the original of the text into question, suggesting instead that the German text is itself a translation of the transmitted, putatively English dialogue between Ferber and the German-born narrator.

While the English translation absorbs and erases the foreignness of English of the German text, what we do not hear, however, in the German version, are the accents of Ferber and the narrator, the inflections that would be present in the English they speak. Thus we are reminded of the near-impossibility of the translation of sound and of the acoustic layers of speech, perhaps the aura of speech. The auratic sound of Ferber's (Aurach's) lost, muted German that no doubt finds its echo in his accent in English is as much a layer of ruin as the photographs that punctuate the text. Finally, one has to ask whether the images in the English edition are also translated, or whether they stand as echo and trace of the original. As trace of the original, are the images the auratic in the text, that is, the authentic original which cannot be translated?

The figure in the original German of *The Emigrants*, Max Aurach, is generally taken to be based on the German-Jewish British painter Frank Auerbach who, like Sebald, was born in Germany and became a British citizen after the war.[59] The migration of sound and meaning of the name Auerbach to Aurach, and then to Ferber in the English translation, suggests a number of readings. First, the collapse of the name Auerbach to Aurach suggests the trace and spectral presence of the iconic name Auerbach, which is laden with traces of German cultural and intellectual history and also British art.[60] But the English translation of *Die Ausgewanderten* migrates even further, replacing the already "translated" and collapsed name Aurach with the name Ferber, itself a pun on the vocation of the figure Max Aurach/Ferber, a painter who obsessively paints over and thus erases, Penelope-like, and at the same time creates new layers of painting on his own canvases.[61]

The puzzling switch from Aurach to Ferber in the English translation has been explained, in an article in the *Guardian* shortly before Sebald's death, as a result of Auerbach's refusal to allow his paintings to appear in the English edition. Aurach's name carries the echo of Benjamin's notion of the aura, while Aurach himself, as painter, continually fails to produce the original work of art, producing instead repetitions that are erased. Aurach, whose name suggests the trace and the aura of the German émigré and with that, a spectral presence of German *Bildung*, a figure whose life story is "botched" by a narrator we never "know," inhabits a Manchester that is an "immigrant city,"[62] a city of industrial ruin, and a place of British, German, and Jewish memory. Recounting how he has never returned to Germany, Aurach tells the narrator: "To me, you see, Germany is a country frozen in the past, destroyed, a curiously extraterritorial place, inhabited by people whose faces are both lovely and dreadful."[63]

Returning to his room in the Midland Hotel in Manchester, after having visited Aurach/Ferber, who is in the hospital for pulmonary emphysema (and who now finds it "next to impossible to use his voice"), the narrator wanders back through the streets of Manchester to the Midland, a once-glorious nineteenth-century hotel that is "now on the brink of ruin," where one "rarely encounters either a hotel guest or one of the chambermaids or waiters who prowl about like sleepwalkers."[64] The narrator suddenly feels as if he were in a hotel "somewhere in Poland," in a hotel room described as sepulchral ("the old-fashioned interior put me curiously in mind of a faded wine-red velvet lining, the inside of a jewelry box or violin case") and, in this state which evokes death, enters into a reverie sparked by the sound of a concert (it is not clear he is really hearing it—"the sound came from so far away") that triggers the memory of seeing, "one by one," the photographs from an exhibition in Frankfurt he had seen the year before of the "Litzmanstadt ghetto." Here the most significant linguistic displacement in *The Emigrants* is found, the one that most clearly situates the entire story as one that hinges on translation and the echo. Using the Germanized "Litzmanstadt" for Lodz, the narrator remarks that Lodz was once known as the "polski Manchester," which makes Manchester, then, the English Lodz/Litzmanstadt. Translating the industrial city of Manchester to a Polish Holocaust-era equivalent, the narrator weaves together the Jewish spaces of Poland with the industrial spaces of England, recasting British history to include the ruined spaces of Europe. As we move, at the end of *The Emigrants*, from Manchester to Lodz, the "polski Manchester," we are left in Poland with the narrator, a Poland of historical photographs, a Poland of memory, in particular Jewish memory, a Poland in the imaginary space of a narrator who remains unexplained and unexplored, and a Poland in which the name of a place is forever in ruin, forever fractured: Lodz/Litzmanstadt, hovering, always, between its original Polish name and its translated, Germanized name, between the "polski Manchester," as it might have been known, and how it is known today, as the Lodz ghetto. We, the readers of this text, are at the end turned into émigrés, transported and dwelling, always, among languages, from Manchester to Lodz/Litzmanstadt, and back from Lodz to Manchester. In this way, Sebald suggests a new way of reading and writing German and Jewish memory, perhaps even a new way of being Jewish in England, Germany, and beyond.

Translating Europe in Alfred Kazin's America

In the works by Sebald, Federman, and Perec, narrative always contains the possibility of its undoing, its demise, its very impossibility. The meandering, associative prose of Sebald and Federman challenges the relationship between place and narrative text; that both writers are also self-translators only adds to the question of place in their texts. Sebald is the novelist as translator who moves seamlessly between his German "original" text and place of birth and his translated works into English, and also moves through spaces of Germany, eastern Europe, and, significantly, England. The act of walking or being conveyed through spaces, and the movement through the literary spaces, often are blurred in his work.

Similarly, the multidirectionality of Alfred Kazin bears a strong imprint in his literary works. The frontispiece to Kazin's 1951 autobiography, *Walker in the City*, is a reproduction of Alfred Stieglitz's 1907 photograph *The Steerage*, the paradigmatic image of Jewish immigration to the United States in the early decades of the twentieth century. Stieglitz shot this iconic photograph from the upper decks of the ship while looking down below at the Jews huddled in the steerage area. In his autobiography, *New York Jew* (1978), Kazin describes himself as

> another slave to Stieglitz's eye. I had become one from the moment I had seen his great photograph "The Steerage" and had imagined my mother as the woman who dominates the composition as she stands on the lower deck draped in an enormous towel, her back always to me. In some way Stieglitz's photographs of old New York possessed my soul, my unconscious past. . . . His was the New York my mother and father had stumbled along as young immigrants . . . my past is there without me.[65]

The woman in the Stieglitz photo whom Kazin describes as "dominating" the composition is draped in a large garment (more a shawl than a towel); the garment, draped over her head, the stripes at the side discernible although without fringes, serves as a visual trace, or tease (a woman would of course not be wearing a tallith), perhaps even a trompe l'oeil of the tallith that the photo evokes but never fully produces as "evidence."

Despite the iconic status of this photograph as the singular image of American Jewish immigration in the first decades of the twentieth century, discussion of the image in art historical scholarship has largely been limited to its formal composition and the photograph's iconography that established Stieglitz as the father of a "native" American modernism that was not simply an imitation of European aesthetics and which became the visual counterpart of the urban, democratic/populist modernism of American poets such as Walt Whitman and William Carlos Williams. Stieglitz, another complex German-Jewish American artist with a trajectory that moved back and forth across the Atlantic, went "walking" while on the ship *Kaiser Wilhelm II* from his first-class berth to the steerage cabin below. While the result was yet another iconic reenactment of European modernity's trope of the (American) German Jew looking at the *Ostjude*, or "eastern Jew" (inscribing him therefore into the textual tradition of other early-twentieth-century German Jews looking at the *Ostjude*, such as Döblin, Zweig, Wassermann, Roth, and others), Stieglitz himself did not address the content of the photo, stressing instead that the visual display of angles and the tension of visual oppositions compelled him to shoot it:

> There were men, women and children on the lower level of the steerage. . . . The scene fascinated me: A round straw hat; the funnel leaning left, the stairway leaning right; the white draw-bridge, its railings made of chain; white suspenders crossed on the back of a man below; circular iron machinery; a mast that cut into the sky, completing a triangle. I stood spellbound for a while. I saw shapes related to one another—a picture of shapes, and underlying it, a new vision that held me.[66]

Later he states even more definitively, exhibiting what can only be read as an expression of a German Jewish desire to repress his own Jewishness (masked by his scopophilic desire for the sight of the *Ostjude*) through an assertion of artistic formalism over content, that is, erasure of the Jews he had photographed and the very "Jewishness" of this photographic text: "You may call this a crowd of immigrants . . . to me it is a study in mathematical lines, in balance, in a pattern of light and shade."[67]

Yet while this photograph is usually read (and misread) as the authentic, definitive documentation of Jewish immigration to America, in truth the ship *Kaiser Wilhelm II* is not heading to Ellis Island, but in the opposite direction, back east over the Atlantic to Paris, filled with would-be immigrants returning to Europe after having been rejected by U.S. Immigration. Kazin, however, projects onto the photograph his own family history of immigration to New York, his own desire for the triumph of the new world over the old, a desire for the late nineteenth century and the departure from Europe which marked that era, and, metonymically then, his desire for the mother, given that he sees the woman draped in the shawl as his mother, "forever frozen on that lower deck"[68] and also with her back "forever turned" to him.

The departure of Stieglitz's ship not from Europe but from New York, bearing would-be immigrants refused entry into the United States, serves as my point of departure in exploring the textual traces of Europe in American Jewish writing and the complexity of reading and misreading the trope of an *Abschied von Europa* (departure from Europe). For if this photograph has been etched into the visual imaginary as emblematic of Jewish immigration to America, how can we retrace its visual impact to take into account a photograph of a ship that is itself a trompe l'oeil — not a ship bearing immigrants to the new world, but the very opposite? Kazin must have known that Stieglitz was traveling not from, but back to Europe, since Stieglitz made this clear in his statements about the photograph in 1932. Yet, the persistence to the present day of the reading of the image as one of immigration to America was circulating when Kazin wrote *Walker in the City* in the early 1950s. And if the Stieglitz photo, with its auratic evocation of Jewishness (through the visual tease of the tallith which is not one, white garments with stripes echoed in the lower left with the fabric hanging, bisected with the two lines) is, in fact, the anti-narrative of Jewish exodus from the pogroms of Europe, then how are we to read the Kazin text? How does Kazin translate the auratic Jewishness of the Stieglitz photo and the persistently ambiguous direction of the ship into narrative form — in other words, how does the immigrant son Kazin translate the pathology of the multiply displaced German Jewish photographer Alfred Stieglitz?

But most significantly, what Kazin's misreading of the Stieglitz photo (through its placement on the frontispiece to *Walker in the City*) attests to is Kazin's abiding desire for America and for its romanticized myths of immigration and nationhood, especially as these were filtered to him through poets such as Whitman and Williams. Kazin (1915–1998), one of the premier American men of letters in mid-century America, was representative of a key generation of American Jewish writing. Kazin's desire is the desire of the immigrant son for the English language, the desire not only to *go* native, but even more so to *be* native, all the while tempered with a hyperawareness of the Europe that lurks always just beyond that horizon, and which remains, as he describes his mother, "forever frozen." As the ship in Stieglitz's photo lingers in an ambiguous and indeterminate maritime course and equally indeterminate semiotic seas—read as traveling from east to west when in fact it was the opposite—so too does Europe, for Kazin, hover in an ambiguous relationship to America, the real source of his desire and longing. As he writes in the final chapter of *A Walker in the City*, evoking and explaining his desire for America:

> Anything American, old, glazed, touched with dusk at the end of the nineteenth century, immediately set my mind dancing. The present was mean, the eighteenth century too Anglo-Saxon, too far away. Between them, in the light of the steerage ships waiting to discharge my parents onto the final shore, was the world of dusk, of rust, of iron, of gaslight, where, I thought, I would find my way to that fork in the road where all American lives cross.[69]

The trace of Europe in the Stieglitz photograph, with its deceptive uncertainty of signification (is the ship going to or coming from Europe?), is an invitation to Kazin and others to read into it family history and even more, the history of American Jewry. Yet, significantly, Kazin counterposes the frontispiece of the iconic image of Jews with a line from Walt Whitman's poem "Crossing Brooklyn Ferry" in which the poet sings of a very different kind of crossing ("The glories strung like beads on my smallest sights and hearings—on the walk in the street, and the passage over the river"). If it is the mother who is "forever frozen" as the European immigrant never quite making it to the American shore, it is the son Alfred Kazin who becomes, like his poetic heroes Walt Whitman and William Blake, a poet/walker, in this case a "walker in the city" who walks, primarily around Brownsville, Brooklyn, with the trace of both Stieglitz's image and Whitman's text accompanying him.[70] (William

Carlos Williams, walking in Paterson, New Jersey, and Blake, as walker in London, are fellow-goers.)

The multidirectional movement of Jews between Europe and America, and the movement of his own walking through cities (Brooklyn and German cities) consumes Kazin in much of his autobiographical writing. Yet Kazin scholarship has bypassed the multidirectionality of his travels, claiming him as the "native son" he himself claimed as his birthright and with that, the Jewish writer who categorically resisted inclusion into the canon of American Jewish literature. As he walks, he reflects about Jews. In A *Walker in the City*, the rumination of the young Alfred Kazin is about Jewish life in the 1920s in Brooklyn and the question of an "America" that lies just beyond Brooklyn — with Brooklyn then figured as an extension of the Stieglitz steerage cabin just offshore: still in indeterminate space and not at all a part of America. Kazin, rather uncharacteristically for Jewish literary men of his generation, turns his attention obsessively to both Americanness and Jewishness, and equally obsessively ruminates about Europe.

Throughout Kazin's journals and autobiographical writing Jewishness erupts and Europe startles the page. In the final of his three memoirs, *New York Jew*, Kazin excavates the complex encounter between American Jewish and European intellectuals in the immediate postwar years and the Jewish refugees "filling" (in Kazin's words) the streets of New York. The most important of these refugees for Kazin was Hannah Arendt, whom Kazin first met at a dinner hosted by *Commentary* magazine in New York in 1947 in honor of Rabbi Leo Baeck. The famous walk with Arendt through the streets of Cologne is first introduced in Kazin's journals and later finds its way into *New York Jew*:

> UNSERE IST EINE OPTISCHE ZEIT proclaims the great banner in Cologne over the proud exhibition along the Rhine of sparkling bright, ultra-precise German telescopes, microscopes, and camera goods. Ours certainly is a "visual period," especially in a prosperous, resurrected Germany still full of ruins and ruined people exposing every period of its 20th century history. . . . Rebuilt Cologne is shiny, neon-lighted, looks as hurriedly and cheaply made as a housing project in Harlem.[71]

Kazin associates the provisional quality of rebuilt Cologne with, of all places, Harlem, with its cheaply made new housing projects, which signifies for Kazin as a site of literary modernism and not, one senses in this passage, as a sign of the entanglement between Jews and blacks in prewar America.

Walking with Arendt in the bombed-out streets of Cologne in 1952, Kazin reflects on the impact of Europe's destruction on the formation of an American—and in particular a Jewish American—sensibility. However, Kazin trained his eye not on the rehabilitation of German and European *Kultur* that would save a notoriously untempered American culture, but rather the haunting specter, in America, of the destruction of European Jewry, and the ways in which it shaped the emerging American Jewish intelligentsia in the wartime years and its aftermath. Kazin, unlike his peers at *Partisan Review*—all largely Jewish writers who were, in Kazin's word, "fugitives from orthodoxy and radicalism alike"[72]—is unique because he provides a sustained meditation on the very "Jewishness" of Jewish writing and Jewish writers in mid-century America. While very much in keeping with the patrician practitioners of New Criticism—Jewish critics such as Lionel Trilling, Philip Rahv, and Irving Howe whose struggle against being typecast as Jews took, in large part, the form of championing high culture (non-Jewish)—Kazin stands out because in the midst of this writing, one finds too the eruption of Europe and the question of Jewishness as concept in his writing.

What is singular about Kazin, compared to the other New York intellectuals or the *Partisan Review* group, is his obsessive return to the question of Jewishness in the context of a literary career devoted to everything but the Jewish. Kazin's literary encounter was with Anglo-American culture/literature, a classic feature of the Jewish literary intellectuals of that generation; he was one of the primary literary editors and critics of the mid-twentieth-century American literary scene (he published *The Portable Blake*; *On Native Grounds*; and numerous editions of American literature including Edith Wharton, Herman Melville, Ralph Waldo Emerson, Nathaniel Hawthorne, and Hart Crane). Reading into his journals and autobiographical writings, however, the other key figures that emerge are Arendt, Kafka, and Simone Weil. Kazin was first known as the critic who compiled *On Native Grounds*, the voluminous 1942 survey of American literature, proving first that there was a literature in the United States worthy of critical inquiry, and second, that a Jew was capable of doing this scholarly work on texts outside his tradition. Yet as Robert Towers points out in his review of *New York Jew* in the *New York Review of Books* in 1978, what is extraordinary is that Kazin did not mention a single Jewish writer (not even Henry Roth) or the massive influx of eastern European immigrants to America in *On Native Grounds*.[73]

Kazin's preoccupation with the genocide of the Jews in Europe can be detected in his journals as early as 1942. There he writes on September 9, 1942, "They are killing us off in Europe; they are killing us by the thousands from the Rhine to the Volga. The blood of the Jews is like the vapor in air that Faustus saw when the Devil claimed his due. But no one claims us but death; our due is, apparently, the 'sympathy' of a few men of goodwill."[74] In *New York Jew*, he suddenly, seemingly out of the blue, writes:

> It was now early 1944; the world was burning with war, and I was out of it, consumed with guilt. Everything was falling apart. I had a sudden horror of myself, and left Barrow Street, wandering in a trance from hotel to hotel, each more unreal than the last. I was as bad as any Nazi. The Jews burned every day in Europe were being consumed in a fire that I had helped to light. In my daily fantasies I saved bearded old Jews from attack in the subway, and was again a mensch, a son of the people.[75]

The first noteworthy literary act that set Kazin apart from his Jewish peers of the New York circle was a 1944 essay that appeared in the *New Republic*. The year before Kazin had come across an account on a small corner of a back page of the *New York Times*, of a Polish Jew, Shmuel Ziegelboim, who had committed suicide in London after his wife and child had been murdered by the Nazis. Ziegelboim wrote a letter to the president and prime minister of Poland, explaining his suicide as a way to call attention to the murder of 3,500,000 Polish Jews and 700,000 other Jews deported to Poland. The *New York Times* concluded the account by noting: "That was the letter. It suggests that possibly Shmuel Ziegelboim will have accomplished as much in dying as he did in living." Kazin got the *New Republic* to reprint Ziegelboim's suicide letter, adding additional commentary of his own. As Kazin notes in his journal, however, "this cry in a liberal weekly brings no handwringing or headshaking. Exactly three people—Lewis Mumford, Daniel Bell, Eugene Lyons—have responded. They praise my 'courage' in writing so directly about the 'Jewish tragedy.'"[76]

Kazin's profoundly American identity and his equally steadfast identity as a Jew emerges in the journals when he reflects on what it felt like to be an American in Europe right after the war. During the stay in Cologne where he takes the famous walk with Hannah Arendt, his wife has a traumatic response to being in Germany, prompting him to remark:

> No matter how casually [Hannah] tries to reassure her, we are in Germany, and we are Jews in Germany. I am endlessly curious about them—the language, their heavy civility, their terrible seriousness, the stories my colleagues at the university are always just about to tell me about the war or the pre-Hitler left. To Ann they are all murderers and dominate her dreams.[77]

Another passage in the journals elucidates what Kazin calls the "ineradicable strangeness" of Europe which is, for him, the strangeness of being a Jew in Germany right after the war:

> There are times in Europe, in the ineradicable strangeness of Europe, when I feel out in space rather than on land. I am swimming to the motion of planets I cannot see. Look: This is me: So let it be beyond praise or blame or disagreement. I am ending my apprenticeship, I am ending my apprenticeship, I am beginning to think. The German who sits next to me at lunch, whom I am prepared to fear and to flee, I can and shall be me with him. The Jews I incorporate in myself, I can and do leave as the occasion warrants, as and when some world truth larger than the Jews presents itself.[78]

Despite Delmore Schwartz's famous remark about Americans' preoccupation with Europe, Jewish American writing before and in the immediate aftermath of the war was more determined to elide and repress Europe and the trauma of the genocide against the Jews enacted on

European soil. A recent book by the American Jewish historian Hasia Diner attempts to undo and unmask the dominant narrative of American Jews' silence about the Holocaust and the claim that it was only in 1967, with a renewed sense of Jewish identity sparked by the Six-Day War, that American Jews began to turn their attention to the genocide against the Jews.[79] Diner presents ample evidence about the prevalence of discourse about the Holocaust in Jewish communal and public life and makes an important intervention in the national myth about Jewish repression of the Holocaust in the late 1940s and into the 1960s. However, the fact remains that the American Jewish literary world, with the exception of the publication of Saul Bellow's novel *The Victim* in 1947, veered away from literary representations of the genocide and the trauma in Europe. Yet despite the repression of the trauma in American Jewish literature in this period, Europe nonetheless circulates in American Jewish writing in the immediate postwar years as trace, as part of a landscape of textual ruin, and also as sign of a nostalgic encounter with modernity; not exactly what Delmore Schwartz meant when he called Europe the "biggest thing in America," but nonetheless in this ongoing circulation Europe remains a notable presence.

And for Kazin, it is Jewishness, as he is able to recall and remember it, that is carried in his writing as a sign of belatedness (*Nachträglichkeit*). Irving Howe notes something similar as he casts Kazin's Jewishness "as mainly a feeling of retrospect, mainly a recognition that no matter how you might try to shake off your past, it would still cling to your speech, gestures, skin and nose; it would still shape, with a thousand subtle movements, the way you did your work and raised your children. In the thirties, however, it was precisely the idea of discarding the past, breaking away from families, traditions, and memories which excited intellectuals."[80] In this way, Howe characterized Kazin and the other New York writers as existing in a state of intellectual belatedness: coming after the great debates and advances of modernism; after the end of true Jewish radical thought; at the end of Jewish immigrant experience. While it is clear that Kazin returns obsessively to the question of Jewishness and the puzzle of Europe, Irving Howe has claimed that

> the New York intellectuals were the first group of Jewish writers
> to come out of the immigrant milieu who did not define them-

selves through a relationship, nostalgic or hostile, to memories of Jewishness. They were the first generation of Jewish writers for whom the recall of an immigrant childhood does not seem to have been completely overwhelming . . . At the point in the thirties when the New York intellectuals began to form themselves into a loose cultural-political tendency, Jewishness as idea and sentiment played no significant role in their expectations — apart, to be sure, from a bitter awareness that no matter what their political or cultural desires, the sheer fact of their recent emergence had still to be regarded as an event within Jewish American life.[81]

This sense of belatedness is illustrated most sharply in a noted passage of *Walker in the City*, in which Kazin recalls the kitchen of his childhood apartment by "translating" the simultaneity of memory of the Brooklyn of his childhood with London right after the war:

> The last time I saw our kitchen this clearly was one afternoon in London at the end of the war, when I waited out the rain in the entrance to a music store. A radio was playing into the street, and standing there I heard a broadcast of the first Sabbath service from Belsen Concentration Camp. When the liberated Jewish prisoners recited the Hear o Israel, the Lord our God, the Lord is one, I felt myself carried back to the Friday evenings at home, when with the Sabbath at sundown a healing quietness would come over Brownsville.[82]

Julian Levinson notes that this passage is the only moment in *Walker in the City* that takes the reader out of New York, and significantly, to London, the site of the Ziegelboim suicide Kazin writes about.[83] Furthermore, as Julian Levinson argues, this definitive moment of hearing and then writing about the prisoners' recitation of the Shema is part of Kazin's preoccupation with the "perseverance" of Jews throughout time, so that, in Levinson's words, "writing the story of his life becomes for Kazin the symbolic equivalent of the prayer uttered by the survivors."[84] Levinson also notes, significantly, that this passage is the sole mention in *Walker in the City* of the Holocaust. In his reading of the passage, Levinson stresses

Kazin's burgeoning sense of Jewish identity, expressed through hearing the prisoners' recitation of the Shema, and his connecting Jewish history (i.e., the Holocaust) with his own history. Levinson concludes by stating: "Writing the story of his life became for Kazin the symbolic equivalent of the prayer uttered by the survivors."[85] Significantly, Levinson elides the fact that Kazin does not hear the prayers directly, but rather mediated through the radio broadcast he hears in the street as he waits outside, in the rain, outside a music store. The sound of the prisoners chanting the Shema does not make the young Kazin turn his mind to Bergen Belsen, where the prisoners are having Shabbat, but rather immediately back to Brooklyn, away from the trauma of Europe, and into the maternal sphere of the kitchen. Thus it is not so much the perseverance of Jewish history that is operative in Kazin's text, as Levinson argues, as it is a brokenness and rupture of experience that stretches from Bergen Belsen to London and then to Brooklyn.[86]

Kazin's work recalls an earlier American Jewish text: Henry Roth's 1934 novel *Call It Sleep*, which is without question the Ur-text for thinking about the eruption of Europe, through the layers of language, for twentieth-century Jewish writing and, in particular, for Alfred Kazin's body of work (Kazin wrote the preface to the rerelease of Roth's novel in 1991).[87] Roth's novel is organized around a series of eavesdropped conversations in Polish and Yiddish that the young protagonist, David Schearl, "translates" into the text of the novel; Europe then is inscribed as echo and trace on every page. If Europe is present as trace in Kazin's work, it is, always, mediated through the trace of Roth in Kazin's entire work.

Kazin was, first and foremost, an American writer for whom English was the sacred language—the sacred language of literature and, ultimately, the sacred language of Jewishness (like his peers in the New York circle, for whom the full embrace of the Anglo-American literary world was a way to escape the perceived provincialism of the Yiddish-inflected immigrant Jewish worlds into which they had been born). It is while sitting on the fire escape and reading, for the first time, soon after his bar mitzvah, illicitly, "in an agony of surprise, as if I could distinctly hear great seas breaking around me,"[88] the English translation of the siddur (Jewish prayer book) that Kazin first grasps the enormity of the biblical narratives that are being described: "The voice that spoke in that prayer book seemed to come out of my very bowels. There was something grand

and austere in it that confirmed everything I had felt in my bones about being a Jew: the fierce awareness of life to the depths, every day and in every hour: the commitment: the hunger."[89] Kazin confesses that he had never really looked at the English translation before, "had imagined from something even my parents had said, perplexed and amused as they were by my private orthodoxy, that it was not entirely proper to look at prayers in English translation."[90]

What is so striking about this passage is Kazin's description of a coming to Jewishness as sudden, as the "agony of surprise" of seeing the English and absorbing the ancient text into the Brownsville present, while perched precariously the day of his bar mitzvah on a fire escape no less, yet a sense of the eruption of the Jewish text as somehow consonant with the Anglo-American (i.e., the non-Jewish) literary world that Kazin adopted and over which he presided. Kazin was almost certainly reading the English translation of the Singer siddur, which was the leading English-language Jewish prayer book in the earlier part of the twentieth century.[91] However, the passages from the siddur in *Walker in the City* do not correspond entirely to the English translations of the Singer siddur; perhaps these prayers are mistransmissions or Kazin's embellishment, based on memory and not on the text, of the prayers, or they are mistranslations or—preferably, I argue—a rather Benjamin-like instance of the "more exalted" language than the "original" translation of the Singer siddur.

Furthermore, and more important, Kazin's rapturous entry into the English translation of the siddur, in his private fire-escape minyan of one, is matched by his creation of a pastiche, as he weaves together various sections of a number of prayers.[92] The pastiche he creates, in a new English that is reminiscent of the Singer translation but becomes its own text, conveys the author's euphoria in reading the English translation and discovering, in the beautiful English prose, similar to the King James version of the Bible, a more exalted world overlaying the shabbier, drab world of his Jewish immigrant family: "I had never realized that this, this *deepness*, lay under the gloomy obscurities of Shabbes in our little wooden synagogue on Chester Street; that my miserable melamed with a few dried peas sticking to his underlip and ready to slap my hands at every mistake had known *this*."[93] The "deepness" that he stutters toward ("this, this deepness") is the depth not only of a newfound wonder in Judaism, but simultaneously of the English in which he exults. Kazin recounts a kind of pornographic, guilty pleasure in the departure from the pious gestures of davening in Hebrew, and with a new ritualized and yet furtive reading on the fire escape—that place of danger and the provisional:

> Morning after morning now, the phylacteries forgotten, I sat on the fire escape with the Hebrew bible whose left pages in English I had looked into only to enlist the support of Deborah, fiery prophetess of Israel, and now glowed when I came to those lines in the Book of Ruth that seemed to speak for me to the Jews: Urge me not to leave thee, to return from following thee; for whither thou goest, will I go; and where thou lodgest, will I lodge; thy people shall be my people, and thy God my God.[94]

Kazin's exultation is also the exultation at discovering a new world of the "fathers," as he keeps repeating, in this passage:

> How many fathers I had . . . how many fathers! How, even as the elders smelling of snuff in our little wooden synagogue at evening service—how each of my fathers must have stood up alone, and each wrapped round and round in his prayer shawl, as at the moment of his death, addressed himself in the deepest prayer to God alone. We were a mighty people, a mighty people, and He our mighty father. I could feel in the surge of that prayer book the divine power of that Great One before Whom I had bound my left arm in the black thongs of my phylacteries and had strapped the little black box on my forehead, thus pledging my heart and my brain in devotion to Him. It was all One, I read now: from the Power of the All-Highest to the lowliest Jew in prayer, it was all One.[95]

Kazin continues in this vein, veering then to the *Avinu malkeinu* prayer chanted on Yom Kippur, with the many acts of transgression recorded and recited. It is at this point that he notes that the prayer book confirms what he has somehow already known about his Jewishness (again, that "the voice that spoke in that prayer book seemed to come out of my very bowels").[96] And yet alongside this rapturous response to reading the siddur in English on the fire escape, there is at the same time an admission of the sense of "abasement" and "supplication" against which Kazin struggles:

> As I read that prayer book on the fire escape, the English words, too, though so strangely fundamental that it moved me just to say them aloud, took on the same abasement before the monotonous God I had always known. There was a familiar dread in that prayer book, a despairing supplication, that reminded me of my mother's humility before the doctors in the public dispensary on Thatford Avenue and of my own fear of all teachers at school.[97]

And at this point in the autobiography Kazin returns from the ecstasy of the English translation of the prayer book to the reflection that guides the entire text of *Walker in the City*: the question of the relationship between Brownsville and the rest of the city (and the rest of the world). "Was being a Jew the same as living in Brownsville? Were they really Jews, those who lived beyond Brownsville?"[98] After the long reverie about the prayer book and the exultation about Jewishness, Kazin announces that if "you had sat too long on the fire escape, were getting dizzy and lonely in the sun with all your own thoughts locked up inside you — you had only to shake a leg, take up a book to read on the long subway ride, and getting off anywhere, walk it off."[99] And so the book about the walker in the city continues, out of Brownsville but always back to the heart of it, to the Jewish text that Kazin translates, over and over again. "Beyond Brownsville" means to move beyond Brooklyn, beyond New York, beyond the ocean separating America from Europe, with all its attendant ambiguities of signification as evoked in the Stieglitz photo, and to the creation of Jewish writing and Jewish text in which Europe flashes up and erupts in the text, ever present as echo and as trace.

Daniel Blaufuks and the Geometry of Memory

What I have attempted to do in the preceding pages is to create, through a reading of Kazin, a thick description of American Jewish encounters in Germany that resonated with the encounters between American Jews and the newly refigured Jewish spaces in Germany found in the works of Sebald and Federman. To thicken the description of American Jews and Germany is to thicken the thinking about the circulation of literary/visual/urban texts in what we now conceptualize as a transnational sphere.

Federman's mode of preterition—of "saying while not saying"—is reminiscent of another 1.5 generation child survivor novelist, Georges Perec, who famously begins his autobiographical W, or the Memory of Childhood with the claim, "I have no childhood memories." Federman, Perec, and Sebald all grapple with the difficulty and necessity of childhood memory and the literary figurations of forgetting and trauma.

Certainly, many critics have established that Sebald's entire oeuvre raises important questions about the relationship between trauma and narrative, and also between text/image and photography in post-Holocaust art and aesthetics. Yet it is in the work of the contemporary Portuguese German-Jewish visual artist Daniel Blaufuks that Sebald's poetics of photography, and the links between photography and poetry, become part of a constellation—what I call here a geometry of memory—whose points touch on, tangentially and interstitially, Perec, Kazin, and Sebald.

Daniel Blaufuks's 2015 exhibit All the Memory of the World, Part One (Toda a Memória do Mundo, parte um) at the Lisbon Contemporary Art Museum creates a series of precise yet diffuse and diasporic constellations between Perec and Sebald, as well as opening up the spatial relationship of text and image, both of which Blaufuks has described as enabling him to explore the "poetry of photography—its visual poetry, and the possibility of engaging with multiple potential paths. The possibility of taking Path A or Path B."[100] Geometry, which is concerned with similar questions of shape, size, the relative position of figures, and the properties of space, is a way to frame the many geometric patterns of Blaufuks's exhibit. (See figure 2.1.)

Blaufuks built an enormous installation that consists of photographs and found objects that work associatively, creating and amassing the geometry of the structures that are strewn throughout the texts of Sebald: asylum architecture, archives, the train station, and so on. Of course, Sebald was acutely aware of the discourse about the links between mathematics and melancholia, alluding to Dürer's engraving Melencolia I early in The Rings of Saturn, suggesting that the melancholic has, as its twin, the "typus geometrie"—a figure found throughout Sebald's work.

© Luis Pereira

Figure 2.1. Daniel Blaufuks, exhibition in museum (*Toda a Memória*). Courtesy of Daniel Blaufuks.

In other words, as has been suggested, mathematics is the ability to think in images, so that the melancholic is also, ultimately, the one with the larger panoramic view of the world.[101]

In an interview, Daniel Blaufuks states that he is not interested in the single photographic image, but rather "in the sequence or flux of images, in a kind of cinematic prose."[102] By thus simultaneously breaking and creating the frame of reference in the monumental sequence of photos that comprise the installation, Blaufuks's project also insists on the importance of the constellations he creates among images. As he writes in his essay in the museum catalog, he is interested in the "labyrinth of images and working with them as part of the chain of transmission between generations."[103] He goes on to say that "an image is a memory of something the photographer saw and that is about to be imprinted on the memory (long lasting or probably not) of the viewer. That is also one of the paradoxes of photography: we are actually seeing in our present something that someone saw in the past and eventually others will see in the future."[104] Daniel Blaufuks's entire project is to think about photography and text, image, and memory not as isolated events but as they circulate among viewers, across cultures, and across time and space.

The title of Blaufuks's exhibit in Lisbon, *Toda a Memória do Mundo, parte um*, forges an intertextual link between Blaufuks and Sebald through the interstices of a filmic text invoked toward the end of Sebald's novel *Austerlitz*. Austerlitz recalls the memory of having watched "a short black and white film about the *Bibliothèque Nationale*" and names it as Alain Resnais's 1956 film *Toute la mémoire du monde*.[105] Like Blaufuks, who is haunted by the image of the file room he first catches sight of in Sebald's novel, Austerlitz is similarly haunted by this film, which he "saw only once but which assumed ever more monstrous and fantastic dimensions in my imagination."[106] Resnais's film is an imaginative commentary on the obsessiveness of archiving information or, as Sebald puts it, "the library's nervous system . . . an immensely complex and constantly evolving creature which had to be fed with myriads of words, in order to bring forth myriads of words in its own turn."[107] Like Borges's stories "Library of Babel" and "The Book of Sand," the Paris library for Sebald and for Resnais holds all the possible images of the world's memory in its structure, confounding time (as Borges writes in "The Book of Sand," "none is the first line, none the last") and complicating the relationship between text and image. It is also a film that works with geometric patterns, suggesting that the massive archive fever that is the Bibliothèque Nationale is also part of a geometric system of images.

The archival impulse, or the archive fever at play in Resnais, in Sebald (and in Borges and Perec), and in Blaufuks can be traced back, archaeologically, to the work of H. G. Adler, the figure who haunts the end of Sebald's *Austerlitz*. Austerlitz describes reading Adler's 1955 monumental archival project, *Theresienstadt: The Face of a Coerced Community* (*Theresienstadt: Das Antlitz einer Zwangsgemeinschaft*):

> Reading this book, which line by line gave me an insight into matters I could never have imagined when I myself visited the fortified town, almost entirely ignorant as I was at that time, was a painstaking business because of my poor knowledge of German, and indeed, said Austerlitz, I might well say it was almost as difficult for me as deciphering an Egyptian or Babylonian text in hieroglyphic or cuneiform script. The long compounds, not listed in my dictionary, which were obviously being spawned the whole time by the pseudo-technical jargon governing everything in Theresienstadt had to be unraveled syllable by syllable.[108]

Weaving his own hieroglyphs of text/image, Sebald resurrects the archival script of Adler's text, inserting immediately after this passage the map of Theresienstadt, marked at the top "Sommer 1944," which is the frontispiece for Adler's book, but without the temporal marking found in the Adler text.

Although never mentioned by name in Blaufuks's own archival project, *Terezin* (2010), H. G. Adler is present as trace, deeply engraved into Blaufuks's unconscious, via Sebald, as Blaufuks, unconsciously, reads and recuperates Adler within a matrix of a layered series of texts that reflect on the meaning of the archival impulse and the circulation of German Jewish memory.[109] Reading Sebald's citations of Adler's work in *Austerlitz*, Daniel Blaufuks creates his multilayered and multimedia work *Terezin*, based on the photograph of the archive room from Theresienstadt found at the end of Sebald's novel. Daniel Blaufuks's *Terezin* is thus part of the intertextual matrix that links Sebald and Adler, an intertextuality that demands a reading—a "seeing," if you will—of all three texts as part of a matrix of the contiguous and the tangential. That Blaufuks never mentions Adler's name suggests the erasure or repression of the key figure for Sebald on the history and writing about Theresienstadt; perhaps Blaufuks is enacting a Bloom-like killing off of the literary (grand)father in his erasure/repression of Adler.

Blaufuks's text is an extended rumination on the image he finds in Sebald's book, which he only later discovers was a photograph in Dirk Reinartz's 1995 collection *Deathly Stills: Pictures of Former Concentration Camps* (Blaufuks later adds a note about this discovery on the final, copyright page of his book). Blaufuks begins his book with the map, although copied so that it is now nearly illegible, which serves as the frontispiece to Adler's *Theresienstadt* book, and which appears toward the end of *Austerlitz*. (See figure 2.2.)

Despite reprinting the map of Theresienstadt that Sebald takes from Adler, and the charts that follow it, Adler is still not mentioned. He is there, however, as trace. The circulation, or rather the migration of this map from Adler's *Theresienstadt* in 1955 to Sebald's *Austerlitz* in 2001 to Blaufuks's *Terezin* in 2010 marks the migration of memory through text, and marks as well a way of conceptualizing the movement of Jewish memory and its translation, from image to text to image, across a range of geographical locations (Theresienstadt/London/Norwich/Lisbon). Sebald's reading of Adler's book and his inclusion of the map are but a

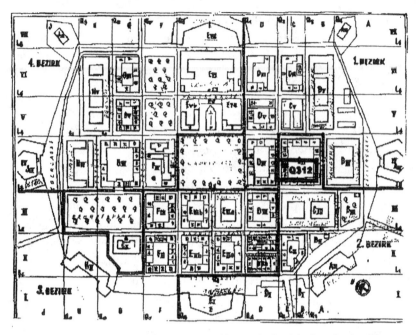

Figure 2.2. Daniel Blaufuks, map. Courtesy of Daniel Blaufuks from his book *Terezin*.

detour from his search for his origins. Rather than an intertextual reference that merely links Adler's book and Sebald's novel, the inclusion
of the map suggests perhaps something more analogous to the voices
of two women that Austerlitz hears on the "rather scratchy radio" when
he is in Penelope Peaceful's bookstore, where he hears the sound of the
word "Prague" through the radio's static as they describe their passage
as part of the *Kindertransport* to England on a ferry named *Prague*. Like
the "scratchy voice" on the radio that seems to emerge from Austerlitz's
unconscious, the presence of Adler's map in Sebald's book similarly suggests layers of textual and historical mediation; the map's appearance in
Blaufuks's book, without mention of its provenance but as the book's mo-
tivation, again suggests the touch or contact between authors that is airy,
impermanent, a spectral presence that hovers like the static of the radio.

Adler's book starts with the map, leading us into its spaces with text,
lists, observations, details, and information. Indeed, this map is the seed
that spreads, germinates, and creates Blaufuks's archival, monumental
collection about Theresienstadt, one that aims, as all maps do, for an ef-

fect of "total and exhaustive knowledge of bodies in space."[110] For Adler (and subsequently, Sebald and Blaufuks), the map is part of the archive that has the function of containing and creating knowledge about the past. In Blaufuks's book, this "archival impulse" is seen not only by his placement of the map as frontispiece (thus remapping, unconsciously, Adler), but even more so by the focus on the image of the file room (*Registraturkammer*) that he finds in *Austerlitz*, and which he returns to, obsessively.

Despite the prominence of the photograph in Blaufuks's memory (from reading the Sebald novel), he does not present the entire photo right away. Rather, he begins by breaking the photo, rupturing it, defamiliarizing the archival spaces so that the files look like patterns—like the pattern of the diary cover of "Ernst K." that Blaufuks finds and that becomes the frontispiece to his book and is interspersed throughout. This scattering of "text" and "image as text" is the key strategy in Blaufuks's book; indeed, if mixing text and image is one of Sebald's most noted textual methods, Blaufuks carries Sebald's signature text/image work farther. By breaking down the photo into an abstract composition (and, similarly, taking the diary's leaf pattern out of context and making it something merely decorative), Blaufuks breaks apart the strands of narrative and those of memory (Sebald, the diary of K.) into visual pieces that he then reassembles.

Blaufuks's text that is interspersed with the various manipulations of the photograph reads like a voice-over to a film. It is, in many regards, the anti-text to both Sebald and Adler: sparse in its use of language, filled with blank spaces on the page and multiple admissions of everything he does not and cannot know or see, and interspersed with images so that text and image become confused, and image eventually overpowers the text. And even more, the full repression of Adler signals Blaufuks's perhaps intentional failure as an archivist/historian. And indeed, the entire book can be read as a preamble to his reworked version of the Nazi-era propaganda film staged in Theresienstadt in which he enacts what Austerlitz does in the novel: slowing down the extant fourteen minutes of the film to sixty minutes and coloring the entire film red, in order to "find" Ernst K. in the footage. In this, Blaufuks becomes Austerlitz, making "real" what Sebald's fictive character does in the novel, which itself is a play on the propaganda film's own manipulation of the "real."

Blaufuks, in becoming Austerlitz, is unconsciously defined by the trace of Adler (in Sebald's work) that determines everything but that remains unacknowledged. Adler is, for Blaufuks's entire project, both the origin and the repressed.

The spectral presence of Sebald (and with that, Adler) is evident as well in the last image Blaufuks gives us of the file room, ostensibly taken by him in his visit there in 2007. This seemingly retouched, painterly photograph, which calls to mind the use of light in Flemish painting, is described by Blaufuks as he recounts his own pilgrimage, retracing Sebald's steps, to Theresienstadt in which he finally finds the room in the photograph in Sebald's novel:

> The furniture had been changed since the image was taken and there was a small desk. I cannot remember seeing the clock on the wall either. There is only a larger table in the middle of the room. With the clock or perhaps due to the fact that I was seeing it in colour for the first time, the urgency of the room seemed to have disappeared as well. It now appeared to me more like a working place for a company director than the bureaucratic room of the original photograph.

He notes too that the files in the cabinets had changed positions and are now perfectly aligned, although the door is still open in exactly the same position it is in the Sebald image. But he then writes:

> As I tried to go into the room I was unable: a modern glass door inside the open original doorway prevented anyone from passing through. I had to content myself with peering through the window from the courtyard to see the room. I noticed then that it was the same angle from which Sebald must have seen it as well, as this was the exact point of view of the photograph in the book.

Blaufuks, still operating under the belief that Sebald had taken the photograph, retraces the steps he thinks Sebald had taken; he follows Sebald who is following Adler's map, and encounters the glass door that "prevented anyone from passing through." It is at this point that he realizes that the photographer (still assumed to be Sebald) must have taken the photo from the window he peers through, but just as he cannot re-member seeing the clock on the wall, he also does not see that the glass preventing him from entering the room is analogous to the glass eye of the camera that took the original photograph.[111] Like Adler's archival project, with the map as its pointer, which attempts to offer a "true," com-prehensive account of the genocide, Blaufuks attempts to return to the "real" site of the photo in Sebald's book. Adler's archival impulse is ab-sorbed by Blaufuks via Sebald; reading in the other direction, the imprint of Blaufuks is now there on our readings of Adler. Reading Blaufuks read-ing Sebald reading Adler, or rather reading Adler back into Blaufuks, that is, reading tangentially, is a way to read Adler now and into the future.

In insisting on Adler as an Ur-text for Sebald and, by extension, Blau-fuks, we can—indeed, must—read Adler but also Sebald and Blaufuks "tangentially," as part of a "contiguous" Jewish literary history: reading him not simply as a major, although for decades forgotten, voice chroni-cling the experience of German-speaking Jewry in the Holocaust, but instead within a framework of German Jewish text since 1945 that chal-lenges the notion of the literary text as part of a seamless, continuous literary tradition. Rather, Adler must be read as participating in a German Jewish literary historiography in which figurative rubble dominates—the rubble of language, signification, epistemology, nationhood, and edifice in its broadest sense. This is a counter-narrative to the one espoused by postwar literary critics in which the German Jewish text struggles to assert an existence out of the ruins of history, standing as a textual triumph over genocide. I proposed to read Adler not to inscribe him into these causal, triumphalist structures that have defined and delimited German Jewish literary subjectivity, but instead to read tangentially, allowing for a more oblique or "airy touching" between Adler's works and a range of other literary and visual texts.

In an interview with Rémi Coignet in the catalog to the museum ex-hibit, Blaufuks notes that while Sebald uses writing "as a way to move towards photography," he moves "from photography towards writing." Greil Marcus has suggested that we have come to expect a certain "re-straint" from serious writers on the Holocaust—these writers (according to Marcus) do not explain the "abyss," but rather place us in relation to it.[112] What Blaufuks has done is to enter—literally—the abyss, that is, the photographic, concentrationary universe captured first by Reinartz, and then by Perec and Sebald. Blaufuks discovers only after he has completed the book project that the photo which prompts his own journey to Theresienstadt was not Sebald's but rather comes from a book of photographic stills by the German photographer Dirk Reinartz, *Deathly Stills: Pictures of Former Concentration Camps* (1995). He notes this in an endnote, on the very last page that contains the publication information: "As I was preparing this book in Göttingen, I suddenly found out in Steidl's library that the photograph in the book by W. G. Sebald was taken by the German photographer Dirk Reinartz. . . . My search for the image came abruptly to an end as my book was about to be printed in the same place as this was in 1995."[113]

And yet, of course, as the exhibit in the museum in Lisbon makes clear, the search is not over; instead, the constellations—indeed, the translations—between text and image are ever-present and ongoing. Blaufuks's *Terezin* book, framed by the photograph, has another nonphotographic framing device: the pages with the green leaf design from the found notebooks of Ernst K. that are placed in the center of the *Terezin* book. What is the relationship between the diary of Ernst K. and the Reinartz photograph found in Sebald's novel that prompts this entire journey to Theresienstadt? Like the photograph of the file room, the green patterned paper punctuates Blaufuks's entire book, reminding us of its status of found object (the diaries of Ernst K., the photograph in Sebald's book) and its remediation into Blaufuks's imaginary. The green patterned paper serves as the reminder as well, perhaps, of the role of figuration more generally in the creation of any kind of narrative or image of the Holocaust: itself an almost Jugendstil design that holds together the found writings of Ernst K., it breaks, like the ruptures Blaufuks creates as he consciously manipulates the file room photo, any sense of an organic unity to the Holocaust narratives that are at the very heart of Blaufuks's project.

In a photograph found in the Ernst K. section of the book we learn, several pages before we see the image, that "there were a few objects scattered among the pages of these diaries: one small photograph, a contact strip with three images, some annexed diary notes, scraps of paper with addresses, an unidentified lock of hair in transparent cellophane paper, a view from the mountains he had visited." Before this, describing some other photographs found in the diaries, Blaufuks says "for some reason I was reminded of the room in the image in the book by Sebald," and later in this section of the book he repeats this. The image of the mountains in the Ernst K. section of *Terezin* takes up both facing pages; it is the only instance, other than the Reinartz/Sebald picture of the file room, of a photograph taking up a full double page. And it bears an uncanny resemblance to the illustration in *Austerlitz* (also taking up facing pages) not of mountains in Switzerland, but rather an image Austerlitz recalls seeing in a large-print children's edition of the Bible that he had been given when he wanted to learn by heart the story of the Tower of Babel. What Austerlitz recalls, however, is the ensuing story of Moses:

> I particularly liked the episode where the children of Israel cross a terrible wilderness, many days' journey long and wide, with nothing in sight but sky and sand as far as the eye can see. I tried to picture the pillar of cloud going before the people on their wandering "to lead them the way," as the Bible puts it, and I immersed myself, forgetting all around me, in a full-page illustration showing the desert of Sinai looking just like the part of Wales where I grew up, with bare mountains crowding close together and a gray-hatched background, which I took sometimes as the sea and sometimes for the air above it.[114]

Transposing Austerlitz's recollection of being fully captivated by the story of the Exodus and the illustration that accompanies it, Blaufuks loses himself, similarly, in the illegibility of the images he finds in K's diary, in particular the sequence of the man and woman holding objects (at first Blaufuks says he thinks they are kites or paper planes, then conjectures that they are pieces of ice). And in this, like Sebald and his heteronym Austerlitz, Blaufuks too is on the shakiest of epistemological and even ontological ground: "Suddenly I realized the sea might not be a sea at all, but a wall. And the boats could be buildings or chimneys far away. Nobody seemed to notice the photographer, whoever he was. Is the woman Edith, the woman K. fell in love with? Is K. the man holding the ice with big bare hands and looking at the girl? Or is he the photographer?"

We cannot know the answers to these questions, of course, and it is here, in the epistemological uncertainty of the photograph, that Blaufuks shows his greatest affinity with Sebald. For like the scratchy voice on the radio through which Austerlitz gleans the sounds of the name "Prague" and with that, comes to a realization of his origins in Prague, so too does Blaufuks seem to embark, in a subtle way, on discovering the story of his grandparents.

Blaufuks's entire oeuvre engages debates about mediation, remediation, and the status of text/image in post-Holocaust art. The "airy" touching, the tangential, also draws together the work of Daniel Blaufuks, Sebald, and a contemporary American Jewish conceptual poet, Robert Fitterman, a "permutational poet" who is interested in the processes of textual reproduction and remediation (and whose work will be discussed in greater detail in the next chapter). Like Blaufuks, Fitterman is deeply engaged with the debates about the role of photography, and, like Blaufuks, he cites the Czech-born Jewish philosopher Vilém Flusser: "As inhabitants of the photographic universe we have become accustomed to photographs: They have grown familiar to us. We no longer take any notice of most photographs, concealed as they are by habit; in the same way, we ignore everything familiar in our environment and only notice what has changed."[115] Arguing that we need to break out of the endlessly repeating cycle of the "photographic universe," Flusser gives us a way to begin to approach the photographs in the works of W. G. Sebald and in the work of Daniel Blaufuks. Reading tangentially, then, is not only to read the literary text noncontiguously, but also to rupture the continuities of perception between memory and visual and written text.

CHAPTER 3

Untoward: Jewish Subjectivity at the Margins

All literature is scarry.

—HÉLÈNE CIXOUS, *Stigmata*

This chapter explores—with a nod to Kaja Silverman—Jewish subjectivity at the margins. Silverman's work opened up a way to conceptualize a range of male sexualities in order to explore the lines between the normative and the "marginal," establishing an anti-essentialist aspect to the discourse about sexuality and gender.[1] Similarly, the work of Sander Gilman, Daniel Boyarin, and Jonathan Boyarin, among others, has brought together the scholarship investigating the complexity of sexual identities with a sharper understanding of the ways in which Jewishness, and Jewish identity, can be understood in modernity.[2]

Drawing once again on Cixous's notion of the "stigmatext," I explore a diverse group of visual and literary texts that posit translation as foundational, since they enable an approach to the question of what constitutes Jewish and, at times, German Jewish textuality. Rather than reading these as discrete sets of texts brought together by a common linguistic, national, and spatial rubric, I instead put them together in order to push the very boundaries of the German and the Jewish.[3] The poets I consider in this chapter—Anne Blonstein, Alan Sondheim, Heimrad Bäcker, and Robert Fitterman—as well as conceptual artists such as Daniel Blaufuks—do precisely this. They all inhabit their own border zones among Jewish,

Holocaust, and German texts, as they challenge—sometimes overtly, sometimes obliquely—the now-weary debates about representation and Holocaust iconography. The work of these experimental, digital media, performance, and conceptual poets is intentionally non-expressive, embodying what Marjorie Perloff has lauded as "uncreative" and "unoriginal" writing.[4] Writing against the impulse to assign transparent meaning to the text, Sondheim, Fitterman, and Bäcker embody the poet as collector—or even, to use Fitterman's self-description, appropriator—of images and ideas that are in circulation.[5] Similarly, their works are not expressive of their experience or inner life, but are a compilation of "permutations," in which the poet rearranges and transposes existing texts, like "information designers."[6] They all write in the associative, "weighty and occupied," open-ended mode of the hyphen—the poetic space that Heather McHugh captures as the following: "the place of the poem is the place of our homelessness, our groundlessness. A poem is untoward."[7]

Translating Jewish Wryting/Jewish Writing

Like the work of the experimental poets who are the subject of this chapter, Daniel Blaufuks's work, as we have seen in the preceding chapter, is similarly concerned with the "found" object or, more precisely, what Derrick Price notes as the "occluded material history."[8] Blaufuks's "memento mori" book has thirty-one photographs of gravestones, with names but no other markers. He discovered these, or so he recounts, by chance in an envelope in a phone booth (itself now a nostalgic place of remembrance) near the Church of St. Sulpice in Paris. Blaufuks writes, "In the winter of 2006, for reasons which I do not care to explain, I walked into a telephone booth, near the Church of Saint-Sulpice in Paris. Inside, next to the telephone directory, I found a brown envelope, containing these photographs. The envelope had neither sender nor addressee."[9] The statement "for reasons I do not care to explain" is an elliptical nod to Georges Perec, whose collection of vignettes, *An Attempt at Exhausting a Place in Paris*, centers on the Place Saint-Sulpice. As Derrick Price notes,

> Given his discovery—his manuscript found in a bottle, as it were—he can lay claim to no special authority nor offer any sin-

gular insights in deciphering these anonymous pictures. Like us he can muse on the disjunction between the materiality of the images (what could be more solidly real than a gravestone?) and the realm of the imaginary in which they now exist. Like us, he is free to wonder about their provenance as photographs, or about the lives and history of the people who are represented only by stone-cut surnames.[10]

Taking his cue from Perec's lipogram novel written (and translated into English) without using the letter "e," *La Disparition* (*A Void*), Blaufuks, like the poets who follow, also works with the medium of erasure. In his video project, *An Absence*, Blaufuks erases the figure of Jean-Paul Belmondo from Jean-Luc Godard's canonical film *Breathless* (*À bout de souffle*), deleting every scene in which Belmondo appears.[11] Taking Godard's *À bout de souffle* and erasing, in the title sequence, both instances of the "e"—as homage to Perec—so that the title becomes *À bout d souffl*, Blaufuks thus enacts the very breathlessness, perhaps even suffocation, with the removal of the final "e" in *souffle*. Although the Godard film's English title is *Breathless*, the French expression "à bout de souffle" is better translated as "the last gasp," being at the very end of breath. It can also signify the smoke that lingers after a gunshot, and a "souffleur" is the one who mouths the words to an actor on stage from behind the curtain—a prompter.

The erasure of the letter "e" in Perec's novel suggests the vanishing, or disappearance, of Jews in the Holocaust; this is extended, in Blaufuks's video, to an insistence—there is no avoiding the void here—on the forever marred, displaced, ruptured, lacerated text/image of any classical canonical European work of art. Blaufuks reminds us not only of the spectral presence through absence of Jean-Paul Belmondo in this iconic film, but of the very presence of the memory of him. In the contemporary field of experimental erasure poetics, the poet Jen Bervin has, for instance, "erased" Shakespeare's sonnets (the volume is entitled *Nets*), explaining that she stripped "Shakespeare's sonnets bare to the 'nets' to make the space of the poems open, porous, possible—a divergent elsewhere. When we write poems, the history of poetry is with us, pre-inscribed in the white of the page; when we read or write poems, we do it with or against this palimpsest."[12] Similarly, the figure of Belmondo carries the cinematic memory of Bogart, after whom he fashions himself; by erasing Belmondo, Blaufuks also suggests the palimpsest of filmic images that we all carry with us. Blaufuks thus participates in the longer history of "erasures" in modernist art and poetics, from Dada to Rauschenberg's erasures of Willem de Kooning, all of which attest to the very modernist project of showing that the creation of art is simultaneous with its undoing.

Blaufuks's work challenges the very borderlines between presence and absence, between text and image, inviting us to contemplate the epistemological and representational void ("la disparition") of art in the aftermath of the Holocaust. Similarly, the experimental poet and digital code-worker Alan Sondheim has created a hybrid textual and visual universe that exists somewhere between English and codework, a term coined by Sondheim for this sort of digital media experimental writing, or [net.writing], filtering the English through the mesh of computer code languages to suggest a new process of encryption. Sondheim opens up the space between Jewish text and computer code language, creating an "intralingual" text that points to an ever-expanding notion of literary expression where the codework "infiltrates the surface" of the text, making it impossible to determine where code begins and poetry ends.[13]

The codework that animates Sondheim's poetry calls to mind the notion of minority writing coined by Deleuze and Guattari; as a writing "on the margins" that is done in a major language, Sondheim's codework (in the majority language of numbers and letters) positions itself on a number of borderlines. As Maria Damon has noted, it is "highly deterritorialized, not only from natural language, but, when corrosively and imperfectly integrated with it, from the language of computer programmers, who use it in their own hegemonic and hidden way."[14]

In a work from 2003, "After Auschwitz," Sondheim embeds Adorno's most famous (and misquoted) line about "poetry after Auschwitz" as one node among many in a matrix of digital codes.[15] Arguably the text that has shaped—and continues to shape—the discourse about German and Jewish memory after the Holocaust, Adorno's statement becomes the very fabric of the poem Sondheim creates. And yet, as "fabric," it is torn, fragmented, and ruptured, captured between the lines of codework and other internet debris as an eavesdropped conversation; as part of the acoustic memory of the postwar era, Adorno's heavily parsed and yet continually recited "poetry after Auschwitz" becomes, in Sondheim's text, simply broken. Comprised of hyphens and a host of other diacritical marks that disrupt any attempt at legibility, Sondheim's poem is broken beyond the tropes of unspeakability and incommensurability to which Adorno's statement is understood to refer. Sondheim breaks referentiality and meaning, creating in the polysemic flow of digital code and citation an asemic text that suggests, in the end, the dissolution of meaning after Auschwitz:

> After Auschwitz 0.109299 19k one might speculate that art may be the most powerful device to create some understanding, despite Adornos warning of No lyric poetry after Auschwitz... true /Reviews/reviews.html 35k death camps with the efficiency of a factory. No wonder Adorno said that to write lyric poetry after Auschwitz was itself 15k (She has read a later quote by him: I have no wish to soften the saying that to write lyric poetry after Auschwitz is barbaric . . . read a later quote by him: I have no wish to soften the saying that to write lyric poetry after Ausch-witz is barbaric true with the efficiency of a factory. No wonder Adorno said that to write lyric poetry after Auschwitz was itself barbaric. true Culler, Ch. 5. 09/19 No class. Translation as-signment due. Week 6 Lyric Poetry 10/01 Extrinsic criticism. Adorno essay on lyric after Auschwitz.[16]

Sondheim breaks the formative "statement" (in German, *das Wort*) about art after Auschwitz, nestling it with debris found on the internet, syllabi from classes in which Adorno's essay is read, and a series, significantly, of blank spaces that further break the text. The historical arc from Adorno's statement of 1955 to 2003, when Sondheim writes this poem and George Bush begins the Iraq War, is similarly suggested and also broken: historical continuity is as "historical" and "continuous" as the endless rumblings of Alan Sondheim's internet search that produces this poem. There is no end to this poem, as the codework signaling its end is also a part of the poem, looping back to earlier moments of the text:

> One more aside: it is quite possible that many of the people who are influenced by the ideas formulated by Theodor Adorno,

Erich Fromm Bush Judges = Bad true Zu George Bush, zu
George W. Bush, zu allen Bushs. Zu Theodor W. Adorno Zu
Fritz Ha JÃ¶rn Fritz@Joern.De â Â©Fritz JÃ¶rn MM ZurÃ¼ck
zur Äbersicht ZurÃ¼ck in joined the firm of Adorno Zeder in
1988, and quickly rose through support from Hispanics in South
Florida, many of whom already support Bushs re-election true
FIRST HISPANIC SUPREME COURT JUSTICE NAMED
Governor Jeb Bush announced the appointment of an attor-
ney and head of the appellate department at Adorno Zeder, PA
true pdf 40k Between them, Milgram and Adorno explain both
the Muslim and American responses to a It seems ironic that
bin Laden and Bush both behave in authoritarian ways. true
an.htm 38k Bush said he was well aware of that fact. Cantero
heads the appellate division of a Miami firm, Adorno Yoss and
was the only finalist who was not a judge. true Adorno and Bush
at ./looply.pl line 32 $ exit Script done on Fri Sep 12 15:36:48
2003 ___ [17]

Sondheim's "After Auschwitz" is exemplary of Heather McHugh's call
for a poetry that "is not exposition. . . . It is the place that suffers inscription. It bears the mark or scar of what was seen and what was grasped."[18]
Indeed, Sondheim's work bears the marks, or "inscriptions," of multiple
historical and cultural traumas and abrasions on the surface of his text.
Maria Damon has described Sondheim's codework as the "esoteric language of the underneath brought to the surface and forced to integrate,
bumpily and bumptiously, with natural language."[19] The abrasions and
textual lacerations that Sondheim creates from the hypostatized Adorno
text are, as Damon describes Sondheim's work as a whole, what Sondheim conceives as "wryting": "Wryting is wrything, an agonized, shimmy-
shimmy nod to 'writing's etymological kinship with 'writhing.' . . . To
carve, scratch, cut: wryting is laceration."[20] And yet, the words "writing"
and "writhing" are not linked etymologically, but certainly homophonically.[21]

Unlike Sondheim's "writing," which is, as Damon notes, an "agonized" series of textual lacerations,[22] Robert Fitterman's *Holocaust Museum* is a poem that consists solely of the captions, without the photographs, taken from the photo archives of the U.S. Holocaust Memorial

Museum (USHMM). In many regards, it is both anti-writing and also, in its lucid and seemingly straightforward reproduction of the captions, anti-"wryting": instead, Fitterman can be read, as Patrick Greaney has suggested, as a "permutational poet."[23] He does not lacerate language (digital, visual, or "natural"), but rather is interested in the processes of textual reproduction and remediation. Following each caption is the number, in parentheses, from the museum's archive. Fitterman organizes the book into seventeen chapters, listed in the table of contents: "Propaganda; family photographs; boycotts; burning of books; The Science of Race; Gypsies; deportation; concentration camps; uniforms; shoes; jewelry; hair; Zyklon B canisters; gas chambers; mass graves; American soldiers; Liberation."[24]

In a collection of his own essays entitled *Rob the Plagiarist*, Fitterman describes the "appropriator" as one who "sees all objects as equal, as equally up for grabs. The appropriator is interested in borrowing the material that is already available—not as a null set in retaliation to invention, but as a new way of participating in invention."[25] He goes on to elucidate his critique of the restrictions of seeing the poet as the "singular keeper and sharer of personal experiences," of the "poet as shaman," in order to "illuminate the hierarchical relationship that many readers of poetry express: that somehow original language expresses a deeper, truer experience." Earlier in the essay he states: "I am interested in the inclusion of subjectivity and personal experience; I just prefer if it isn't my own."[26] In the *Holocaust Museum* project, Fitterman borrows from the archive of stored images found in the USHMM (more precisely, in the online museum—the USHMM website), curating an "exhibit" that enters into the debates about mediation, remediation, and the status of text/image in post-Holocaust art.

Fitterman's project complicates Susan Sontag's claim that the caption is traditionally neutral and "informative," giving us "a date, a place, names" and that "while the image, like every image, is an invitation to look, the caption, more often than not, insists on the difficulty of doing just that."[27] The caption, for Sontag, helps to manage the shock of the visual. But the captions that comprise Fitterman's book work in an entirely different register of meaning than the one Sontag is describing. For one thing, the photographs, while not present in the text, are nonetheless present with us, the readers and viewers, as iconic images that circulate in media and are imprinted in our own memory bank of images. If, for Sontag, captions give us a sense, however false, of mastery over the shock of traumatic images,[28] Fitterman undoes the very possibility of mastery, giving us simply a pileup of text. Fitterman's project evokes the trace of the pictures that haunt us, reminding us that we have been haunted and, with the omnipresence of these captions, will continue to be haunted. Like Barthes's refusal to show us the Winter Garden photograph of his mother in *Camera Lucida*, claiming (in a passage inserted parenthetically) that it would merely be our "studium" but would not contain the "wound," Fitterman similarly disrupts the relationship between studium and punctum in *Holocaust Museum* in not showing us the photos from the museum.[29] A caption claims to be ancillary to the photograph (as narrative it is the studium, working against the punctum, for Barthes); in Fitterman's project, however, the entire relationship between studium and punctum is disrupted, deformed, set askew. For Barthes, "punctum" is

> the element that rises from the scene, shoots out of it like an arrow and pierces me . . . this wound, this prick, this mark made by a pointed instrument . . . the word suits me all the better because it also refers to the notion of punctuation, and because the photographs I am speaking of are in effect punctuated, sometimes even speckled with these sensitive points; precisely, these marks, these wounds are so many points . . . punctum is also: sting, speck, cut, little hole—and also a cast of the dice. A photograph's punctum is that accident which pricks me.[30]

Yet the question, in Fitterman's work, remains: do captions in *Holocaust Museum* contain the possibility of punctum—is a possible punctum created through the captions and manifested in the absence of the photographs themselves?[31]

In this, Fitterman's project is related to the work of recent erasure poets such as Uljana Wolf and Christian Hawkey, whose *Sonne from Ort* "erases" while simultaneously translating Rilke's translations of Elizabeth Barrett Browning's *Sonnets from the Portuguese*.[32] Erasure poetry reminds us, as Heather McHugh writes, that "all poetry is fragment: it is shaped by its breakages, at every turn. It is the very art of turnings, toward the white frame of the page, toward the unsung, toward the vacancy made visible, that wordlessness in which our words are couched."[33] Like Fitterman's project of giving us only the captions, erasure poems work by removing words from the page deliberately, with poetic "intention," forcing a confrontation of the reader with the traces that lie beneath the surface.

Fitterman's *Holocaust Museum*, as an instance not only of erasure but also of curatorial poetry, enables a rethinking of the role of the referent and representation in Holocaust art; by taking away or replacing the object and giving us instead only the caption, the absent photograph has led critics such as Charles Bernstein to want to anchor the project in the discourse about loss, absence, and the impossibility of representation in the aftermath of the Holocaust.[34] Fitterman does something more interesting here, however: rather than locating this as an elegiac project about loss and erasure, it is a highly generative project, one that is interested in transposing the "found object" of the caption and making it into a new (call it a) poetic text. The captions generate a memory of images that are unlikely to be the same as the actual images to which the captions refer; they call on our visual archive to supply these missing images. At the same time, they show it, and the whole procedure, as insufficient and in this insufficiency lies Adorno's "no poetry after Auschwitz." It is not, as Martin Glaz Serup claims, that the caption "now refers to a referent that is no longer there,"[35] but rather that the image—the referent, the Holocaust, the Disaster—is one more series of linguistic and visual displacements, always already there in its absence.

Fitterman's chapter "Propaganda" gets right to the heart of the debate he might be staging with Sontag. Since these propaganda photos are a conscious manipulation of image and fact, by giving us only the captions, Fitterman translates the images, relinquishing his ability to manipulate his readers. Instead, Fitterman strips the power from the original propaganda material, reducing the image/text to the emptiest and most meaningless of signifiers. The majority of captions in Fitterman's chapter begin with an anaphora—a rhetorical figure of repetition in which the first word or set of words in one sentence, clause, or phrase is repeated at or very near the beginning of successive lines—in the formulation "Propaganda slide entitled." By consciously placing the captions so that the anaphora dominates, the reader is confronted with the repetition of the phrase "propaganda slides" and the repetition of the withheld object (i.e., the image). This strategy of creating monotony and tedium of repetition produces a mesmerizing, intoxicating physical response to the enormity of the information (the visual proof and the historical fact) that is being withheld. What is absent in Fitterman's project is the Holocaust itself.

Fitterman's withholding, or possibly repressing, erasing, the information puts him, again, in the company of Vilém Flusser, Sebald, and Blaufuks, since the absent captions in his book of poems force a rethinking of the relationship between text and image, memory and time. Fitterman's project disrupts, in a productive way, the readings that many Sebald scholars have given of the translation of text/image. While this work has been important in shifting our focus from the print to the visual text, enabling readings that do not merely "read" the photographs as commentary or illustration of the literary text, more work needs to be done on the very materiality of the space in between text and image in Sebald's work. In fact, thinking with Blaufuks, let us imagine what it might mean to erase the text in Sebald's *Austerlitz* and instead let the images create the narrative (as Blaufuks has done in some projects). This would be a new way of thinking about the relationship between memory and material artifact, between text and image in Holocaust historiography.

Fitterman's project demands that we rescore the Holocaust in a new key; like Sondheim's poems that in their massiveness resist pointing to any referent and instead are a polysemic, lingual play with the endless signifiers of languages (both natural and digital), Fitterman's book of captions also forces a rethinking of the borders between original and translation, between creation and erasure, between the banal and defamiliarization, demanding that we think of the poetic text no longer as sacred or inviolable, but instead—to paraphrase Foucault—as part of the porous interplay among various nodes in a network.

One of the precursors for his project whom Fitterman acknowledges (in a series of epigraphs that also include Charles Reznikoff and the philosopher Vilém Flusser) is Heimrad Bäcker, whose *nachschrift* consists of quotations from a wide range of sources, including H. G. Adler's massive archival *Theresienstadt* volume, Raul Hilberg's *The Destruction of the European Jews, Mein Kampf*, and Albert Speer's memoir, as well as bits of letters, newspaper sources, and transcripts from the International Military Tribunal at Nuremberg. The Library of Congress designation for Bäcker's book is "Holocaust—Jewish (1939–1945)—poetry"; Fitterman's book is, however, listed as "Mass media—Philosophy," then "Photography," and finally "Conceptual Art." And yet, as I have tried to show, Fitterman's project is poetry in the largest sense of the word. Bäcker is more clearly classifiable: as a major figure in the German-language concrete poetry movement of the 1970s, his collage of the "found texts" of historical sources and documents in *transcript* is legible as part of a poetic project that addresses the fault lines between memory, narrative, and textuality more generally. A complicated figure in the postwar Austrian avant-garde, Bäcker, born in 1925, was a member of the Hitler Youth and joined the National Socialist Party at age eighteen. Yet as Patrick Greaney (Bäcker's translator) argues, Bäcker's documentary word-art projects are not to be understood as a form of atonement for youthful lapses into National Socialist ideology, but rather as an insistence on the always mediated and remediated nature of historical knowledge, including the blank spaces that fill each page of the book.[36] The book is a mix of concrete poetry, declaring allegiance to the power of the image/typeset/ blank spaces within the words, and also a piece of conceptual writing that prefigures contemporary work rethinking the status of the archive and the documentary image and text.

Bäcker's project, originally entitled *nachschrift* yet translated as *transcript* (and not, significantly, "postscript"), is nonetheless concerned with the after-writing or the writing *after* and, like Fitterman, with the act of appropriating as part of the process of invention. In Bäcker's work, it is impossible to determine the borders between the text, the after-text, the blank spaces, and the transcript. As Patrick Greaney has elaborated so elegantly, *transcript* is also not legible without the notes and bibliography that follow the text.[37] On the page separating the end of the "poem" and the start of the notes—perhaps the true "Nachschrift" of the project— Bäcker has written "Monumenta Germaniae Historica (q.v.)," and on the following page we read above the notes: "Every part of *transcript* is a quotation; anything that might seem invented or fantastic is a verifiable document. Slight changes and omissions (which allow the unaltered contents to stand out in sharper relief) are not explicitly indicated. The notations *from* or *based on* (for example, 'based on Hilberg') indicate that new textual patterns were configured from passages reproduced verbatim, sometimes to the point of a methodical gibberish that replicates a deadly gibberish."[38] The designation "Monumenta Germaniae Historica (q.v.)" is more than an ironic nod to the layers and complexity of the textual sources linking German nationalism and historiography; it renders his own *nachschrift* (the book as a whole and also the *Nachschrift* "Monumenta Germaniae Historica (q.v.)") as one more palimpsest layer in the already weighted vault of German history. The book is structured as a series of encryptions, but one in which the reader is only able to crack the code by referring to Bäcker's inclusion of the notes and bibliography. But even when one knows the "source" for the "poem"/text on any given page, the textual space (and the accompanying blank space of each page) suggests a sort of epistemological darkness and bewilderment. The inclusion, at the end of *transcript*, of the notes and bibliography is less an attempt to document the Holocaust than it is to point, indexically, to the impossibility of knowledge itself, telling us that we might know but reminding us of the always incomplete status of this knowledge. After all, Bäcker intentionally keeps the quotations and extracts brief and organizes them seemingly randomly. This is a book that arrests the reader on many levels: with its initial illegibility, with its mix of documentary and other sources, with its admission that there is indeed a "source" behind the texts that might "explain" or guide the reader, yet always with the suggestion of the fragmentary and the incomplete nature of this knowledge, which Bäcker suggestively alludes to by the overwhelming presence of the white spaces that fill each page. In this way, Bäcker's is erasure poetry on a grand scale: it does not just erase lines from one text to create a new one; it creates a collage, or assemblage of texts that can only exist on the page as partial truths.

The works of the digital codework poet Alan Sondheim and the conceptual poets Robert Fitterman and Heimrad Bäcker invite the reader/spectator to engage in a process of translation that entails simultaneously "knowing" and "not knowing" (or to see and not see), that is, to acknowledge the always fragmentary nature of knowledge and the limits of knowing *what* we are reading and seeing. The work of these poets also suggests that the digital circulation of texts (seen most clearly in the work of Sondheim) opens up a space for critical reflection and reassessment of the dispersed and forever textualized geographic spaces of Germans, Jews, and German Jewish culture in a post-Holocaust age. Conceptual poetry, as it seeks to create texts that disavow the very act of creation, dissolves the binaries of secrecy and knowledge, presence and absence (Fitterman's captions/the withheld images). The works by Sondheim, Fitterman, and

Bäcker open up the spaces between German, Jewish, and Holocaust text, enabling a rethinking of the status of textual knowledge: an epistemology of the hyphen.

Anne Blonstein's "Jewished English"

The British-born Jewish poet Anne Blonstein's 2008 book, *correspondence with nobody*, pushes this boundary even farther between German and Jewish text. Blonstein draws on the Jewish exegetical tradition of *notarikon* to translate (what she calls in one poem "jewished englished" translations) Paul Celan's translations of Shakespeare's sonnets. *Notarikon*, derived from the system of stenographic shorthand used by the *notarii* in recording the proceedings in the ancient Roman courts of justice, is a rabbinical hermeneutical system used to interpret the Hebrew Bible. It is a reverse acronym in which each letter of a word is "translated" into the initial letter of another word, thus expanding the original word into a phrase (that is, a five-letter word, say, becomes a five-word phrase: e.g., the word "Jew" could become "Jealous Evergreen Wrything").[39]

Blonstein's *notarikon* translation of Celan's Shakespeare translations thus asserts an originary exegetical basis to both the Shakespeare and Celan texts. In Blonstein's text, each letter of Celan's translation of Shakespeare's sonnets is expanded to a new full word; in addition, Blonstein's *notarikon* translation of Celan translating Shakespeare also includes parenthetical text, drawn from various sources Blonstein has been reading and inserted wherever Celan's German translation bears a comma. Each comma in Celan's translation is transformed and "translated" into additional parenthetical text, calling to mind Cixous's insistence on the "scarriness" of literature, the ways in which the "scar" "celebrates the wound and repeats the lesion"[40] so that the text is a laceration that aims "to flee the fatal nail, the sword, the knife, the axe which threatens to fix, to nail, to immobilize them in, by, death."[41] And as part of this process against being fixed or "nailed" Blonstein "translates" the comma; at the back of the book Blonstein lists the parenthetically inserted texts, a multilingual set of footnotes that dangle, however, without numbers, and which range from canonical figures such as Hannah Arendt, Simone Weil, Gertrude Stein, Gertrud Kolmar, and Ilse Aichinger to more obscure contemporary poets, artists, and writers. Citation has thus become incorporated text without the diacritical marks or traces of the quotation or the footnote; the parenthetical insertions absorb the shocks (the pause, the comma, the aporia, the place where language hovers into silence) of the movement from Shakespeare sonnet to Celan translation into German to Blonstein's *notarikoned* verse. The parenthetical is, therefore, as the sole "untranslated" text, the sign and mark that what we are reading *is* translation.[42] Added to this is the inscription at the start of each poem that shifts the anonymous address (a new form of "nobody-ness") of Shakespeare's sonnets to various deceased women artists, filmmakers, and other figures on the margins. The word "correspondences" of the title bears the trace, most immediately, of Baudelaire's poem "Correspondences" and then slides to the "nobody" which—for the English-language reader—evokes the "nobody" of Emily Dickinson ("I'm nobody. Who are you? Are you nobody too?") and, one translational layer removed from Dickinson, Paul Celan, as Dickinson translator and as crafter of the ever-present "Niemand" of the poem "Psalm" from the *Mohn und Gedächtnis* cycle.

Dickinson, Shakespeare, Baudelaire, Stein, Celan: with this series of translational slides and echoes, Blonstein blasts open the foundational English poetic form—the sonnet—and expands it, in her *notarikon* translation, as a form of midrashic commentary that bears the traces of poets and texts and literary figures that come much later. The sonnet is lovingly de- and reconstructed, via *notarikon*, taken apart and put back together again in a form that echoes, expands, and comments on both the original sonnet and the Celan translation.

As midrash on a literary form (of a particular national literary tradition, the English sonnet with its direct line of descent from the Petrarchan sonnet), the work of Anne Blonstein illustrates the dissolution between religious and secular text, and the breakdown between genre, national borders, and canonical poets (Shakespeare, Celan) as it exposes the foundational role of translation in enacting these textual dispersals. Blonstein's work also enacts Seidman's claim about Jewish text hovering in a perpetual state of translation—and in that piling up, accrual, of text, enabling a new taxonomy of the borders of Jewish text.

The eighteenth poem of Blonstein's cycle, the "translation" of Shakespeare's Sonnet CXV ("Those lines that I before have writ do lie"), begins with a nod to *gematria* (itself linked as exegetical practice to *notarikon*):

Shakespeare's sonnet is numbered in Roman numerals CXV (115) and Blonstein's *notarikon* "translation" is #18 in her cycle—significantly, the numerical value expressing *chai* (life) in *gematria*—she notes her poem #18 in Roman numerals and "translates" Shakespeare's Roman notation to the Arabic: XVIII/115. Below the translated numerical notations is the dedication, "in memoriam sheila blonstein (nee hyams) 10.ii. 1930–5. xii.1988," again using a hybridized notation merging Roman and Arabic numerals in the birth and death dates of her mother, thus joining her mother's birth and death dates—her *chai*—to the series of numerical substitutions that underlie the movement from Shakespeare's sonnet (CXV) to Celan's translation (115) to Blonstein's 18th *notarikon* of Celan's translation. The elegy for her mother, marked as the 18th poem of her cycle, the *chai* poem in a collection that revolves around commemoration (of Shakespeare, of the sonnet, of the other lost figures she remembers), contains as parenthetical inserts (where Celan had put a comma) only journal entries from her mother and one from her own journal. This is the only poem in the cycle that does not link to other poetic texts.

And yet the Shakespeare sonnet begins: "Those lines that I before have writ do lie," announcing itself as a poem that disavows the declaration of love found in each prior poem in the sonnet cycle.[43] And it also announces the moment of the poem—this poem—by virtue of all lines previously written being lies, as a newfound moment of text beginning, with the caesura of all that comes before. The final couplet—"Love is a babe: then might I not say so, / To give full growth to that which still doth grow"—is translated, the cadences of the Shakespeare text broken and more staccato, by Celan as: "Die Liebe ist ein Kind, das wächst. Ich ließ / sie reif sein, ganz,—ich durfte dies!" Here is Blonstein's *notarikon* translation of the last couplet of Shakespeare's sonnet:

> death is episemantic. life is everything but everything. inclu-
> sion seclusion transfusion.
> ends imprinted nominally. kindless in narrative dogmatism
> (Then there are those
> like my mother who are more resigned and give themselves
> over
> to medical technology rather like children running to their
> mothers

for bandages for a cut knee). daughterless and sisterless.
writing aunt epimerically configuring her spinstered terms.

invertiug certain hiddens. languaged in exceeding
    speech+script. self-inquiring
epitropes. roles expressed in fragments. subjectivity expressed
    in nonvision
(Most difficult of all now is to watch M.'s struggle
in the grip of the impossible). gratitude and not zugzwang
(Mummy died at 10 to 10) (Steven now talks
of a war—between our parents—finally being over).
ilking cloudy harmonies. dampening undertones ripple for
    temporized endings.
dust invalidates emotional snow.[44]

Blonstein's poem in memory of her mother, Sheila Blonstein, evokes from the sides and margins of poetry the elegiac impulse. It also bears the trace of the American Jewish poet Allen Ginsberg in his poem on his mother's death, "Kaddish." Much like the presence of the recently deceased mother, Naomi, in Ginsberg's "Kaddish" is invoked in voices both of the poet and the voice of the mother herself ("Get married Allen don't take drugs"), Blonstein similarly inserts text from her mother's journal as well as from her own journal at the time of her mother's illness and death, thus adding an additional midrashic layer to the "original" Shakespeare line of the sonnet: "Those lines that I before have writ doth lie." The "I" of Shakespeare's sonnet that confesses to having written lies, is translated from Celan's "ich" into Blonstein's *notarikon* translation as "interests conflict here." Immediately following Celan's "wie log ich," the comma in the German slides to Blonstein's insertion from her mother's journal: "(I don't think Anne quite realizes that I am really / still recuperating from my hysterectomy and can't do all I did / last year— she seems to think the more and more / I do the more I will be able to do)."[45]

Most interesting, it seems to me, in Blonstein's work is the status of this text as Jewish text that bears traces of hermeneutic practice, English poetic form (sonnet), and Shakespeare translations by Celan enacted at the moment of danger during the war. In this way, *correspondence with nobody*, and the "sonnet" elegy to her mother in particular, breaks apart taxonomies of writing and form. Blonstein's creation of what she terms a "jewished englished" is most striking in the *notarikon* of the third quatrain of the sonnet, where the Shakespeare text includes a self-citation ("Alas! Why, fearing of time's tyranny, / Might I not then say, 'now I love you best'") that suggests the inherent duplicitousness of declarations of love:

> now i enletters. lingering in english battles through. into
>   childless heterodoxy.
> dressed in contagious hues. we imagined elaborations.
>   jewished englished then
> zeugnissing this (:
>
> An accent overwritten by a voice).[46]

These lines form a central moment in Blonstein's elegy for her mother. First, the lexical law of Blonstein's *notarikon* is the absence of capital letters — more than the obvious nod to E. E. Cummings, although that of course is in there too, it is a "jewished englished" reenactment of Hebrew, with its orthographic democracy where no word is accorded a capital letter. "Now i enletters" — the "I" here not the poetic voice but a purely lexical "I" whose sole métier is that of language, letters, the lexical. The mother-daughter tension — the English battles, the childlessness of Anne Blonstein as a heterodoxy that merges with the mother's illness (the contagious hues), all of that is captured with the German noun *Zeugnis* morphed into an English gerund, *zeugnissing*, where the German *Zeugnis* (witness) becomes the "jewished englished" witnessing of the mother's slow dying. The "jetzt" of Celan's translation becomes in Blonstein's *notarikon* the multilingual neologistical line: "jewished englished then / zeugnissing this" that is then followed by the ambiguously demarcated parentheses with colon — either a web-based email smile peeking out to herald a digital layer to this translation palimpsest — or else the start of yet another parenthetically inserted piece of text from outside, from the margins of these translated texts. And it is here that Blonstein's text most piercingly evokes the dying of the mother:

. . . daughtering apart.
in collating hassles. managing in carefully heartbreaking.
    voices of resignation.
indigesting heavy roles (I had always hoped that once the
    children
were grown up I would have been able to travel
the whole world). discovering endless relativity. zuckerwerk—
    experiments in
twisting (I don't want to interfere with their lives
but I feel that a little more contact with them
might give my life a little more purpose). for uncertainty
embarrasses reasons certain hormonal triggers (I am frightened
being alone and long for someone to talk to
and confide in). so ought love curl here exposing
shouldhaves.[47]

Blonstein's "jewished englished" text is an English that is not fully English, an English that "zeugnisses" to the life force of translation, wordplay, neologism, German words, and words from the field of genetics (Blonstein held a Ph.D. in genetics) evoking the recombinant play of molecules and DNA. It is a "jewished englished" that is the Yiddish-inflected English ("Yiddish" often translated as "Jewish") and which suggests that both English and "the Jewish" are in simultaneous patterns of being *en passance* (they are continually being jewished, they are being englished). In this way, Blonstein's *notarikon* translation of Celan translating Shakespeare reconceptualizes German Jewish text and ruptures the diacritical mark of the hyphen linking and separating German and Jew, queering the boundaries of the German and the Jewish and pushing at the various iterations of the "trans-" (translation, transnation, and the transgression of disciplinary boundaries). Rather than establishing even more clearly demarcated zones of "German" or "Jewish," I propose instead that we consider German Jewish writing as inhabiting a new space of a trans- or a new imagined community that exists in a border zone of textual and historical memory, projection and fantasy, pathology and desire, and that will always exceed the geographic, linguistic, literary (genre), and ethnic/national markers in which these markers are enacted.

The Carnal Referent: Modified Jews, Indexicality, and Jewish Body Art

To think about the translated J/je/jew/juif/Jude—with its series of "klez-merical" slippages of the "J" between and among languages—is a way to approach the question of boundedness textually, at its most immediate visual level of orthography—that is, as multiple processes of translation that point to the ways in which the "J" is the "Jude" that is simultaneously the "Jew" and the "juif." The Jew has been, and can only be, "translated." It is into this disparate body of *Jewish* text which displays the "scarriness" that Cixous defines as constitutive of all writing, that I propose placing German Jewish writing: the canonical, marginal, trans-, provisional, and even imagined texts.

This next section turns from Cixous's declaration of the "scarriness" of literature to the more literally scarred body: the work of tattoo artists and performance artists who continue to open up new spaces for thinking about the shifting parameters of Jewishness today. Much of this work revolves around challenging, to various degrees, artistic representations of the Holocaust. In the culture at large, Auschwitz has taken on a certain iconic role. The icon always foregrounds the ontological status of the object it bears relation to—in the case of Holocaust art, Auschwitz is the end point, the ontological proof of the disaster of the genocide against the Jews. Thus, rather than focusing on the iconicization of Auschwitz, I instead turn to the icon's evil twin, the index, as a way to approach the question concerning the "thereness" of Auschwitz in a post-Holocaust imaginary. Peirce's law of the index states that "the index asserts nothing: it only says 'there'!" Since it only tells us that there is something "there" to look at, the index foregrounds the act of looking and deprivileges the object. Indeed, as it continues to signify in vastly different cultural contexts and situations, Auschwitz can be understood to be governed by the indexical, as a semiotic space heralded by the polysemic first letter, the aleph, or the A (of Auschwitz) which provides an open field. Mary Ann Doane has described the indexical as "perched precariously on the very edge of semiosis." Indeed, it is the position outside the margins and yet "on the very edge" of semiosis, of creating meaning, that is at issue here. Doane's observation enables us to move beyond much recent work on indexicality and photography, which has designated the index as part of a matrix of the trace or imprint; her approach initiates a way to open the interpretive field with which we might speak about Jewish space.[48]

While Doane, Gunning, Krauss, and others are interested in rethinking the status of the indexical in order to widen the frame of discourse on the role of photography, I turn to it as a textual strategy that suggests the forever contingent—a place of art that must by definition always be provisional. Thus, it is not the evidence of the real to which the indexical *might* point that interests me, but rather its potential in opening up interstitial spaces of meaning and signification. It is in the interstitial and precarious interpretive space of the indexical that I situate my reflections on Jewish memory, Jewish space, and the "aleph" that begins the textualizing of Auschwitz: Auschwitz—the aleph-schwitz, the first letter, an open letter, a glottal stop that is silenced, the point where language and signification begin.

To this end, I turn to the work of several Jewish performance artists who recast the central questions of the relationship between Jewish text, memory, and gender.[49] In what follows, I explore the work of the contemporary performance artist Marina Vainshtein, Shelley Jackson's tattoo project, and the Israeli artist Hagit Molgan, before turning to the phenomenon of Orthodox Jewish women's head-coverings to probe at the boundaries of what constitutes body modification, and (what I will be terming) the legibility of the Jewish female body in a diasporized world.

Kaja Silverman's *Male Subjectivity at the Margins* examines a "deviant" masculinity that asserts the lack of anything "natural" or "culturally innocent" about sexuality in general. In what might be an analogous notion of deviant Jewishness as Jewish subjectivity at the margins, I explore some instances of the Jewish body—the body as it translates memory, performs Jewishness, and, ultimately, diasporizes gender. Of course, all of these categories could be scrambled, since the acts of translation, performance, and the ontological state of diaspora are all, inevitably, intertwined and interdependent, drawing on tropes of spatial and discursive dislocation. Silverman critiques what she terms the "present dominant fiction [dominant ideological order] as above all else the representational system through which the subject is accommodated to the Name-of-the-Father. Its most central signifier of unity is the (paternal) family, and its primary signifier of privilege the phallus. 'Male' and 'Female' constitute our dominant fiction's most fundamental binary opposition."[50] In shifting the optic here from male to Jewish subjectivity—a move that might be more seamless than not, with masculinity the default inscription of identity for Jewishness—I will attempt to explore what a Jewish subjectivity at the margins might be: that is, Jewish subjectivity outside the dominant fiction of Jewish unitary subjectivity.

The following set of disparate texts all bear a resemblance to Hélène Cixous's notion of the stigmatext as being "stitched together, sharing the trace of a wound." Similarly, these various visual and performance art texts share the trace of the wound, both individually and even more so as I bring them together as a strategy to disharmonize and disrupt the seemingly apparent links between memory, gender, and Jewishness. Moving from a discussion of Jewish body art (tattoos) to Orthodox women's head-coverings, I claim these disparate phenomena—tattoos, the violation of Jewish law's prohibition against marking the body, and wigs, adherence to the Orthodox command to cover the hair—as instances of body modification that probe the contours defining Jewish law and the body and, with that, the lines constituting the margins of Jewish subjectivity. Both tattoos and head-covering create Jewish bodies as sites that demand to be read, as places of legibility—in particular, Jewish legibility. Furthermore, the diasporic quality to all of the projects discussed below do not illustrate only the literal sense of art enacted outside the borders of Israel. They are a diasporic poetics that embodies dislocation, dispossession, and discontinuity.

Jewish tattoo artists, paradoxically, assert a legible Jewishness by turning to practices that violate Jewish law. They are the very embodiment of Cixous's stigmatexts that are "stitched together sewn and resewn . . . [and] share the trace of a wound. They were caused by a blow, they are the transfiguration of a spilling of blood, be it real or translated into a hemorrhage of the soul."[51] And yet the work of one of the principal Jewish tattoo performance artists, Marina Vainshtein, poses a challenge to the open-ended, diasporic scarriness that defines Cixous's understanding of the stigmatext. Jewish body art, or body modification, as well as the contemporary movement of "Jews and tattoos," posits itself as a provocative reclaiming of Jewish identity through the violation of the Jewish prohibition against tattooing the body. Reversing the mark of difference through the self-conscious and ironic reference to the tattoos Jews were forced to bear in the camps, Vainshtein and other Jewish body artists attempt to recast Jewish difference and the significations of the Jewish body and thus create a new Jewish subjectivity. Vainshtein has tattooed Holocaust imagery throughout the canvas of her body, seeming not to miss a single iconic image or trope from Holocaust accounts. Dora Appel sketches in detail how Vainshtein has created a full body narrative of the Holocaust, which moves across her body to encompass the totality of the Holocaust narrative:

> On her upper back, the central image represents a train transport carrying Jewish prisoners in striped uniforms toward waiting ovens. Smoke billows above the train cars while a swastika, represented in negative space, wafts through the ashes that are spewed forth by a crematorium chimney. Across her shoulders, Hebrew letters carry the message, "Earth hide not my blood," from the Book of Job's passage. Atop the train car, figures, some blindfolded, hold each other or reach their arms hopelessly upward, one clutching a flag marked with a Star of David. Other figures are pressed together inside the cattle car, one shaven-headed person staring forlornly through the bars. Ribbons of barbed wire float upward from broken fence posts. Below the train and the brick-lined ovens, a tattoo represents the notorious inscription on a number of concentration camp gates: Arbeit macht frei, while the results of that absurdly false promise are presented as tombstones, engraved with Hebrew text, and a column of skeletons. A can of Zyklon B, screaming faces of prisoners being gassed are tattooed in her right breast (also pierced).[52]

Vainshtein creates Jewish visibility by inscribing the iconic Holocaust narrative—ghetto to ashes—on her body. She thus holds a position as "secondary witness" to a trauma that she did not personally experience, but that she, as a member of her generation, experiences as postmemory; the postmemory is then reinscribed, literally, on her body.

Vainshtein's body art proclaims itself as Jewish art that enacts the signification of the Holocaust. Yet how are we to read the iconography of Vainshtein's body? Or, to twist W. J. T. Mitchell's question: "what do *tattoos* want?" How can we complicate—smear, render illegible, de-ink—

the totalizing and dangerously legible Jewish master narrative (ghetto to ashes) with the referent inked and intact on Vainshtein's body?

By re-creating a master narrative—both bodily and visual—about Auschwitz on the body, Vainshtein is operating in a different interpretive framework from performance and body art from the 1970s, notably the work of Vito Acconci. The feminist body artists Carolee Schneemann and Hannah Wilke created "self-exposures" that "insistently pose the subject as intersubjective (contingent on the other—the spectator) rather than complete within itself (the Cartesian subject who is centered and fully self-knowing in his cognition)."[53] Vainshtein's body art, however, insists on a narrative of completion and on a sense of unitary subjectivity of the tattooed body artist. Rejecting the biblical prohibition against writing on the body, she aligns herself with other tattooed Jews in order to explore new meanings of Jewish visibility and the range of body art in a distinctly Jewish context. These Jewish body artists proclaim that the act of inscribing their bodies with a visibly Jewish iconography is an act of Jewish observance that makes them "feel" more integrated and "whole" as Jews.[54]

Yet even in displaying the memory of the Holocaust on her body as postmemory, Vainshtein constructs—in contrast to other artists such as Art Spiegelman, whose reflections on postmemory insist always on the inherent rupture between history and memory—a totalizing Jewish master narrative (ghetto to ashes). Vainshtein's performance, in which the referent (Auschwitz) is inked on the body, neither disrupts nor transgresses, but rather creates unitary subjectivity, in which the body is synonymous with the canvas displaying a similarly unitary narrative of the Holocaust. Furthermore, Vainshtein's tattooed body suggests that an untattooed, uninscribed body is not a site of discourse, does not, in Judith Butler's term, "matter." Yet bodies do matter, as not only Butler has made clear, since they are always already sites that are contoured and constituted discursively, made material through discourse. Vainshtein's tattoos suggest that only the tattooed body is a discursive field; however, bodies are always "marked," always discursive. Thus Vainshtein's body is (was) already readable, as a site of discourse that also demanded to be read, even before the tattoo.

Vainshtein's writing on the body denaturalizes the idea of legibility by literalizing it.[55] The tattooed body also denaturalizes the idea of transparency, the notion that we can read and know a person, that there is not only legibility but a firm epistemological ground on which we do this "reading." The act of becoming a public Jew by presenting the Jewish body as a Jewish text, filled with Jewish narrative, to be read, demands a reinscription of the category of Jew as a unified subject. In contrast to contemporary art practices that disrupt the notion of referentiality in art, Jewish tattoo art such as Vainshtein's fully tattooed body reifies the referent. As Dora Appel observes, "Although extreme, or precisely because of its extremity, Vainshtein's tattooed body, while establishing a unique late twentieth-century form of Jewish identity, ironically reproduces central aspects of traditional Jewish identity: the Jew as outsider, the Jew as Other, the body of the Jew as deformed, the Jew as excessive and inassimilable . . . where there is no cultural specificity to distinguish the newly conscious Jew, the Holocaust tattoo itself becomes the mark of difference."[56]

Vainshtein transposes memory (as postmemory) onto her body, imprinting "an experience of pain never actually felt on the feeling body, to physically inscribe herself into a history for which she was born too late."[57] Vainshtein's body art is not only a representation of the Shoah. It also performs, by writing it on the body, the postmemories of the trauma and pain of the event itself. Vainshtein's performance consists of displaying her body, and its inscribed Jewish and Holocaust narrative, in public spaces, creating spectators and readers from encounters in daily life. She produces and reproduces a familiar Holocaust narrative, whose images are part of the repository of kitsch and the banal. But going beyond this, Vainshtein's tattooed body is itself a witness to the belatedness of trauma as it lives on into this generation. Vainshtein's tattooed body raises questions about both its artistic and political gesture, and also of Jewish body art more generally. Its intention is transgressive and performative, but does Vainshtein's visual performance actually help to rethink the relationship between gender and Jewishness, or does it instead reify categories of difference? How do word and text function in this body art? Does the visual reassertion of Jewishness reinscribe the category of Jew as a unified subject? Is the text of Vainshtein's body "translatable" as a mediation between aesthetic forms (that is, between text and image) and between German and American cultures? Does it rethink the status of Jewish text, creating from the material body a more diasporic notion of text that takes into consideration the way in which texts traverse spatial, historical, and personal memory?

Finally, Vainshtein's body art raises the question of whether Jewish tattoo and body arts force a rethinking of the forever vexed question of Jewish art—and, even more significantly, the question of whether this is a truly transgressive art. Certainly, as an out lesbian with visible markers of punk (twenty-five piercings and a red Mohawk), Vainshtein positions herself within the larger sphere of body modification and lesbian punk performance, consciously linking the historically outsider status of the Jew with other socially marginalized groups associated with tattoos. In addition, Vainshtein and other body artists seem to embody the medicalized discourse of the Jewish body and the construction of the racial and physical otherness and difference of the Jew. In the performance piece *Jewess Tattooess* (in which the work is the act of being tattooed) by the British Jewish performance artist Marisa Carnesky, the burlesque, the gothic, and the tradition of the tattooed lady are all at work. Like Vainshtein and Carnesky, the Jewish body artists in the film *Tattoo Jew* see themselves as consciously rejecting the biblical prohibition against writing on the body in order to explore new meanings of Jewish visibility and the range of body art in a distinctly Jewish context. These young body artists proclaim that the act of inscribing their bodies with a visibly Jewish iconography is an act of Jewish observance: these tattoos often consist of Hebrew words (such as Yahweh, *shekhinah*), passages from the Hebrew Bible, and Kabbalistic words and names. A number of websites have appeared recently that help instruct the tattoo artist in the proper translation and transliteration of Hebrew words. These websites are not necessarily aimed at prospective Jewish tattoo customers; they are more likely an outgrowth of a Madonna-inspired frenzy for all things Kabbalah and for Jewish words written on the body. Yet young tattooed Jews ("modified Jews") claim that to violate the biblical prohibition, and to consciously reenact "branding" as a Jew, which has functioned historically to mark the Jew as Other (not only in the Holocaust but before as well), is to create a more fortified and, paradoxically, less marginalized and less ruptured sense of their Jewish identity. As Joshua Burgin, one of the creators of the film *Tattoo Jew*, writes, "For me to take the star of David as a Jewish symbol of identity and mark myself permanently with it, makes me feel more Jewish than I ever felt before." Ezines and other websites devoted to Jews and body modification echo Burgin's claim that the tattoo, a violation of Jewish law, ironically makes them feel more integrated and "whole" as Jews.

Yet this narrative of wholeness and unitary subjectivity works against the transgressive and performative potential of this kind of art. Burgin's claim to "feeling more Jewish than ever before" with the Star of David tattooed on his body undoes the radical potential of tattoo in this context. Jewish tattoo art and Jewish body modification more generally have the potential to suggest the mutability and indeterminacy of Jewish culture, especially as it intersects with pop, hip-hop, and alternative cultures more generally. This new Jewish body art is committed to exploring new ways of "being" Jewish that take as a given the diasporic underpinnings of Jewish culture, questioning and even queering Jewishness, creating in new and unexpected ways a Jewish subjectivity that can only be at or even outside the margins. Michael Kimmelman's review in the *New York Times* of the 1995 Drawing Center of New York's exhibit *Pierced Hearts and True Love* (examining a century of drawings for tattoos) observed that "the images are banal. And in any case, they're simulacra: drawings are beside the point, which is that tattoos are about the body. This is why people called tattoo 'collectors' actually wear their tattoo collection. Tattoos must be worn to be tattoos, after all, and everything involved with that hard fact—the pain, the scarification, the exhibitionism, the permanence of tattooing—is what makes the phenomenon intriguing."[58] Yet the question still remains: how transgressive is tattooing as art, and in particular, how transgressive are tattoos within the context of Jewish law, beyond their obvious stance as violating not only the prohibition against graven images but against writing on the body? Can banality in art be transgressive? Starting with the prominence of rhinoplasty as a defining mark of postwar American Jewish culture, Jewish body modification has a long and complex history.

Joshua Burgin's assertion that the Star of David inked on his body makes him not only *feel* more Jewish, but also *makes* him more Jewish raises a question. What is the nature of the signifier in the production of cultural identity? Is the inked Star of David on Burgin's body analogous to the Israeli passport that currently serves as the one true marker of Jewish authenticity under Jewish law, since it signifies epistemological certainty of who is a Jew under the law of return? Do tattoos of Jewish iconography hold the promise of a sort of eternal return, an endless possibility of proliferation of Jewish signifiers that can be reproduced over and over again? Burgin would claim that it is the memory that the symbol—the star—carries with it, the traces of the past that link the sight of the Star of David to historical memories of Jewish trauma. Rather than creating a transgressive intervention in the production of Jewish memory and culture, Burgin's conception of his own tattoo depends on a traditional, static notion of the referent in art, thus forbidding the Star of David tattooed on his body to bear the function, in any way, of a transgressive artistic act that can exceed the margins of his (Jewish) body.

What is striking in the Burgin project is the adherence to seeing the inked image as part of a linear, unitary narrative of self. In contrast to this, I propose that we read tattoos in the way in which we read texts: to recognize, as Mark Taylor suggests, that "a tattoo is never a sign that can be read with certainty."[59] Rather, figurative ornamentation on the body is part of an ongoing play with identity and difference. Taylor argues against the notion of tattoos as merely an expression of the primitive, insisting on their function to inscribe social and political codes and structures onto the body, thus becoming marks of civilization.

Claiming the art of tattoo drawing as a "submerged" art form, the catalog to the Drawing Center's *Pierced Hearts and True Love* exhibit chronicles the history of tattoos from their earliest appearance on the mummified body of an Egyptian woman (2200 B.C.E.) and moves from there to include tattoos from Nubia in the fourth century B.C.E., to biblical prohibitions that stifled it for centuries, until its rediscovery in the South Pacific by colonialist seafarers and its reimportation into Europe, primarily in the domain of marginal social groups and the arena of the circus, carnival, and the underworld. As a cultural and social practice, tattooing has been understood to reinforce the boundaries of socially marginalized groups, while at the same time it has the potential to undermine these social regulations and serve as a transgressive trans-act.[60] The status of the tattoo—the shifting meanings of its social function on the body, its proclamation of signification (writing on the body as an act of asserting identity), and its challenge to any transparent relationship between text and image—plays out, often, as paradox. All of this has implications for the larger questions about the meaning of Jewishness and the circulation of the Jewish body in contemporary culture.

There are, of course, artistic antecedents to the modern primitive and body art movements. Scarification, branding, and cutting have been part of performance art for decades. In addition to the work of the body performance artist Fakir Musafar, the so-called father of the "modern primitive movement," who gained notoriety in the 1980s and 1990s for his vivid body modifications, contemporary body modification artists cite artists such as Manzoni, a Fluxus artist who signed human bodies with his signature, thus turning the body into a canvas that bears his "art" through his signature. Vito Acconci in the late 1960s inscribed his own skin with a bottle cap, and in another project, "Trademarks," he bit his own skin in as many places as he could reach. In a performance piece entitled "Crucifixion," he burned off the hair on his chest. The function of tattoos as straddling both word and image is evident in the provocative portrait by Catherine Opie, *Self-Portrait/Cutting 1993*, a chronogenic color print showing the back of a woman with a tattoo on the right shoulder. In the middle of her upper back is a cutting that is done like a child's drawing, with two stick figures, and on the left of these figures a house and clouds. Above the artist's head is what seems to be a curtain, suggesting that the cutting, the photographing of it, and the spectacle and the witnessing of the act are all theater, staged, a performance of the body. The spectator next to me at the Whitney Museum said, in response to the installation entitled *Skin*: "That's disgusting."

The implied indexicality of the spectator's spontaneous expression of disgust, "*that's* disgusting," suggests that the image indeed refers to something beyond the artwork. And of course it is disgusting, in the everyday sense of the term and even as it echoes Kant's condemnation of art that is not "in accordance with nature" in creating aesthetic pleasure. But is it truly disgusting? What constitutes disgust in art? What constitutes beauty, the work of art, aesthetic pleasure and desire? Where is the line between art and the transgressive?[61] These performance artists, and body art more generally, raise precisely the questions that have occupied the field of aesthetics since Kant, and which have resurfaced in the 1990s in Anglo-American literary, feminist, and cultural theory that returned to investigating "beauty," with theoretical work on the topic ranging from Elaine Scarry's "On Beauty and Being Just" to Arthur Danto's collection of essays, *The Abuse of Beauty*. At the same time, extended inquiry into the nature of disgust has resurfaced alongside the reflections on beauty.

While it is understandable that Catherine Opie's cutting or the body modifications of Fakir Musafar would arouse Kant's sense of disgust, what is it about the tattooed body of Marina Vainshtein that evokes a similar response? Is it the excess of signification on the body, in the case of Vainshtein, or the "body in pain" in Opie's work that turns the body, quite literally, into what Cixous termed the *stigmatext*?

Shelley Jackson's *Skin: A Mortal Work of Art* is a radically different body art project that highlights precisely the limitations of Vainshtein's Auschwitz-tattooed body and its reliance on iconicity. In 2003 Jackson issued the following on the website announcing the project:

> Writer Shelley Jackson invites participants in a new work entitled "Skin." Each participant must agree to have one word of the story tattooed upon his or her body. The text will be published nowhere else, and the author will not permit it to be summarized, quoted, described, set to music, or adapted for film, theater, television or any other medium. The full text will be known only to participants, who may, but need not choose to establish communication with one another. In the event that insufficient participants come forward to complete the first and only edition of the story, the incomplete version will be considered definitive. If no participants come forward, this call itself is the work.
>
> Prospective participants should contact the author (shelley@ drizzle.com) and explain their interest in the work. If they are accepted they must sign a contract and a waiver releasing the author from any responsibility for health problems, body image disorders, job-loss, or relationship difficulties that may result from the tattooing process. On receipt of the waiver, the author will reply with a registered letter specifying the word (or word plus punctuation mark) assigned to participant. Participants must accept the word they are given, but they may choose the site of their tattoo, with the exception of words naming specific body parts, which may be anywhere but the body part named. Tattoos must be in black ink and a classic book font. Words in fanciful fonts will be expunged from the work.
>
> When the work has been completed, participants must send a signed and dated close-up of the tattoo to the author, for veri-

fication only, and a portrait in which the tattoo is not visible, for possible publication. Participants will receive in return a signed and dated certificate confirming their participation in the work and verifying the authenticity of their word. Author retains copyright, though she contracts not to devalue the original work with subsequent editions, transcripts, or synopses. However, correspondence and other documentation pertaining to the work (with the exception of photographs of the words themselves) will be considered for publication.

From this time on, participants will be known as "words." They are not understood as carriers or agents of the texts they bear, but as its embodiments. As a result, injuries to the printed texts, such as dermabrasion, laser surgery, tattoo cover work or the loss of body parts, will not be considered to alter the work. Only the death of words effaces them from the text. As words die the story will change; when the last word dies the story will also have died. The author will make every effort to attend the funerals of her words.[62]

Jackson's manifesto for the creation of her stigmatext makes clear that the tattooed person "becomes" and "is" a "word," a single mark on a single body that forms part of the whole text that exists in its dispersal and dissemination. Substituting "word" for "person" in the last paragraph, Jackson insists that the person bearing the one word from her text is not a "carrier" or "agent" but rather an embodiment of the text; significantly, if the tattoo becomes erased or lost (through dermabrasion or dismemberment), the stigmatext as a whole is not "altered," but when the person ("word") dies, they are finally effaced from the whole. The eventual death of all "words" will mark the death of the story.[63]

Skin: A Mortal Work of Art thus enacts textual memory on the body; the text is embodied, literally, and also, significantly, dispersed, displaced, alive and living in multiple locations at once, a stigmatext spread across continents that forms, nonetheless, a unitary text. Jackson's skin-text embodies precisely what Cixous might mean when she asserts that "all literature is scarry," since "it celebrates the wound and repeats the lesion."[64] It also, significantly, insists on the fundamentally indexical nature of the

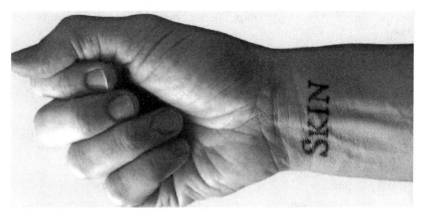

Figure 3.1. Shelley Jackson, "skin." From *Skin: A Mortal Work of Art*, courtesy of Shelley Jackson.

object, since it makes the object into language and tells us to look at it. (See figure 3.1.)

With the inked word "skin," for instance, Jackson recasts Magritte's "ceci n'est pas une pipe": the inked word, pointed to in the photograph, is everything Magritte's pipe is not. The word "skin" is inseparable from the signified and does not, as in Magritte's famed project, point to the rupture between the real and the representation. In Jackson's project, the inked word "skin" labels the "matter" of the canvas onto which it is inked. As a text-body that "matters," as Butler would have it, *Skin: A Mortal Work of Art* repeats the lesion, the wound of language, existing as pure citationality; in this, it also suggests the borders and margins of Talmudic text in its existence as both center (Jackson's 2,095-word short story) and dispersal, as both text and midrash (multiple bodies; multiple readings). It is, like Anne Blonstein's *correspondence with nobody*, another paradigmatic diasporic text, hovering above and beyond any conceivable nation-state or border, and constantly in flux as the "words" travel, move, alter, age, and eventually die. One participant in the project says her tattoo— "words"—is at the "center" of who she is. Significantly, she placed the word ("words") on the crown of her head, which was shaved to create a window/frame for the inked word. Until now, she says, "I existed and interacted outside of the word itself. Now I am a word. Who is going to read, consume, and interpret me? Who is in my sentence? Am I part of an independent clause or a dependent clause? Is someone my adjective? Who verbs me? Would I like the other words in my sentence? Will I ever meet them?"[65] The ironic expression of a longing for the other, the longing for completion and for coherence, lexical stability and legibility, is a fundamental part of the tension (and the beauty and brilliance) of Jackson's project. (See figure 3.2.)

Jackson's *Skin: A Mortal Work of Art*, like many of the "word-art" projects by other conceptual artists, enacts writing "severed from its role as mere visual description and is experienced instead as both a verbal and visual phenomenon."[66] It is writing as art and art as writing, demanding a new relationship between the work and the viewer, dispersing and fracturing the whole of the text and creating ever-changing communities of readers and viewers. It disrupts the relationship of reader to printed text in ways that are analogous to cyberpoetry and other new media. As Maria Damon suggests more generally about "post-literary" cyberpoetics and e-poetry: "It's a taste of outer space, that diaspora-to-be . . . 'natural' home to the queer, distorted and dissonant, the parasites (in the creative sense of the word) of the planet; the misfits, the whackos."[67] Jackson's *Skin*, its own variation of a site-specific art installation, casts the word and text into the outer space of perpetually moving bodies.

In an analogous mode, the Canadian Jewish performance and cyber-poet Adeena Karasick has conceptualized word as body, creating performance pieces in which language is brought onto the page and the stage as effluvia, as body fluids, as organic matter that flows and oozes and stutters. Karasick's texts create a sonic dissonance between memory and the body, between literary theory and nonsense verse, that is dysemic in sound and meaning. In *Genrecide*, for instance, Karasick invokes the necessity of narrative — one need only think of Coleridge's Ancient Mariner, as he is forced to wander the earth retelling his story. Similarly, in *Genrecide* and other books (such as *Dysemia Sleaze*) language itself is forced to wander, nomadically, in exile, creating meaning through traces, ellipsis, marking, echoes. As Karasick herself stated about the project of *Genrecide*: "Its only mishkan (temporary, portable tabernacle) in the desert are occasional ideogologems, memes, brief respites for it to cling to, as it wanders in errance, travels travailles in agony and extasis, nomadic monadic . . ."[68]

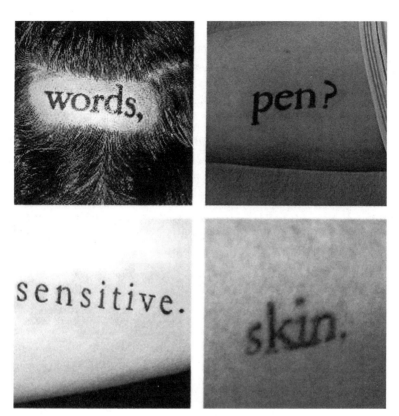

Figure 3.2. Shelley Jackson, collage. From *Skin: A Mortal Work of Art*, courtesy of Shelley Jackson.

The performance artist Adeena Karasick and Jewish body artists such as Vainshtein and Carnesky ask us to rethink categories of Jewish art, Jewish text, and difference. In doing so, they also invite consideration of Arthur Danto's ideas of the end of art. Danto acknowledges his debt to Hegel and, in fact, the debt that conceptual art in general has to Hegel "for knowing philosophically what art is."[69] Danto's formulation of post-historical art—that we are at the end of the era in which we can map a linear art history of art movement begetting art movement—draws on Hegel's conception of the end of History and the notion of absolute knowledge, in which knowledge and its object are one. Danto goes on to assert that art in our time is similar to Hegel's formulation of knowledge, "for the object in which the artwork consists is so irradiated by theoretical consciousness that the division between object and subject is all but overcome, and it little matters whether art is philosophy in action or philosophy is art in thought."[70] For Hegel, art was transported to the world of ideas; Danto sees art as increasingly dependent on theory for its existence, "so that theory is not something external to a world it seeks to understand . . . all there is at the end is theory, art having finally become vaporized in a dazzle of pure thought about itself, and remaining, as it were, solely as the object of its own theoretical consciousness."[71]

Does contemporary Jewish body art subsist in this vaporized form of pure thought, as art that is inseparable from its conception? In one sense, Danto prefigures Dan Miron's quest for a post-historical Jewish literary historiography grounded in the tangential and the contiguous. Unlike Danto, however, Miron attempts a new sort of literary historiography, one that challenges the continuous model of literary history. Danto's point is a different one: that "there can now be no historically mandated form of art, everything else falling outside the pale."[72]

Despite Clement Greenberg's pronouncement that "all deeply original art is initially perceived as ugly," it is hard to take this as a pronouncement on the future decidability of the beauty or even interest in body art and tattooing. In fact, as Kimmelman points out, the art itself is, at best, banal. Emerging from the culture of seamen and criminals, the tattoo has always had a particularly strong relationship to its own indexicality: a tattoo of an anchor, for instance, indicated a particular seaport. Suffused throughout is an erotic pull that defines the tattooed male body as participating in a social structure that is homosocial, closed, masculinist, militaristic, and nationalistic. Does the advent of Jewish body art alter the earlier paradigm of a nationalistic, militaristic masculinity of the tattoo? Does the tattooed Jewish body automatically carry the trace of the Holocaust? There is the new phenomenon of third-generation Israelis having their grandparents' KZ numbers tattooed on their arms, thus linking their bodies to the memory of their grandparents' bodies, creating of their body the simulacrum that is at the same time both sameness and difference.

It is into this nexus of philosophical musings about the object and subject of art that I place this inquiry into Jewish body modification, in order to open up a new set of questions about post-Holocaust art, beauty, translation, and the transgressive. If, as Hegel enjoins us, art invites us not to create more art but to reflect philosophically on the nature of art itself, what can we say about Jewish body art? Is there a link between Andy Warhol's Brillo Box as "art" and Vainshtein's tattooed body? Danto has remarked recently that "it is still true that works of art constitute a restricted set of objects. What has changed is that these cannot easily be identified as such, since anything one can think of might be a work of art, and what accounts for this status cannot be a matter of simple recognition."[73] Danto's reflections on art take us far from the original reflection in aesthetics that often accompanies discussion linking tattoos and art — namely, Kant's celebrated reflections on ornamentation, which decorate current critical work on the tattoo.

In the introductory lectures on aesthetics, Hegel observes that art consists of the attempt to impress oneself on the external world. To illustrate his point, Hegel uses the example of a child throwing stones into the river and then admiring the circles that trace themselves on the water "as an effect in which he attains the sight of something that is his own doing." This notion of art Hegel then extends to the human body and alterations done to it, which Hegel identifies as the "cause" of all ornamentation and decoration, "though it may be as barbarous, as tasteless, as utterly disfiguring or even destructive as crushing Chinese ladies' feet or slitting the ears and lips." As is true also of Kant, the examples Hegel draws on are from non-Western, so-called primitive cultures that have not attained "spiritual education," in contrast to the "enlightened" European who possesses a "universal need for expression in art" that would consist of the art object (outside the self or possibly even the self) in which he recognizes his own self. Kant's reflections on Maori tattoos and Hegel's examples of body modification practices such as Chinese foot-binding and African body-piercing are folded into modernity's project of turning the lens back on itself by casting an Other as counterpoint.

Body art (including but not limited to tattoos) and body modification can therefore be understood when placed within the context of late 1960s conceptual art, in which there no longer has to be an object, an artifact. One could make art without being an artist, and be an artist without making art. So where does that cast these body artists? If for Kant and Hegel art was intended to arouse feeling, in particular pleasurable feeling, what are we to make of this body art that is, as Michael Kimmelman admitted, banal and ugly? Can these body artists' aim of merging art and religious identity offer a way to reconcile the debates in art circles about beauty and politics? Does this new body art suggest or demand new ways of seeing the relationship between art and religion? Does the perceived transgressiveness of this art consist in its rejection of idealist notions of the function of the artwork, or is there another way in which it is transgressive?

Conceptual art replaced the art object with the idea of art. Our question here is where to place body art, tattooing, and other forms within this framework. What is the status of the sign in body art? Of word and image? Body art, as it came into being in the 1960s on the heels of conceptual and pop art, has been explained as a radical instance of conceptual art. As conceptual art is grounded on the dematerialization of art, so too body art, taking this a step further, makes the body, quite literally, "matter." For conceptual art the project was to radicalize abstraction to get at the immaterial idea that lies behind the material object that had once been the site of "Art." Mark Taylor has suggested that the reason why tattoos are so popular now is that "tattooing represents the effort to mark the body at the very moment it is disappearing." Jackson's *Skin* project and the Jewish body artists simultaneously reinscribe the body with text and with signification—materialization—of their status precisely as bodies.

A similar but more sustained reflection on gender transgression and the body in Jewish art can be seen in the work of the Israeli artist Hagit Molgan.[74] The artist focuses on the practice of *niddah*, the ritual laws of purity, in particular menstruation, which decree that a married couple is forbidden to have sexual relations while the woman is menstruating and for seven "clean" days after. Molgan's art opens up the social and theological implications for Jewish women of the laws of *niddah*. In one installation, Molgan creates canvases that are patchworks of the *bedikah* cloth that is used to determine if the woman's menstrual period has come to an end. The canvas, an enormous surface with roughly 50 to 60 *bedikah* cloths taped to the surface, displays the cloths with spots of blood on each one. The "unclean" cloths are displayed, row upon row, shocking the viewer who, for that brief moment, is transported both into the role of the woman and into the role of the (male) rabbi whose job is to inspect the cloths to determine her state of "purity." The image of what looks like serialized cloths on the canvas defamiliarizes, for the museumgoer, the already unfamiliar cloths, since the practice of *niddah* is confined to ultra-Orthodox Jewish observance and is not something that the visitor to the art museum would most likely have encountered. The *bedikah* cloth installation, a feminist critique of the purity laws, exposes the sign of the body at its most private, interior, and intimate, making the body, quite literally, "art"; with this, too, it exposes practices from the Orthodox world to which secular and less observant Jews have no access. Molgan creates a different form of the stigmatext: by marking, scarring the canvas with the sign of the "impurity" of the female body, she scars as well the perception of orthodoxy from the outside, translating biblical custom into a conceptual art frame that has artistic antecendents such as Judy Chicago, Karen Finley, and Eleanor Antin.

In another part of the exhibit entitled *Kosher, Kosher,* there is an equally large canvas with the *bedikah* cloths arranged as in the first piece, and stamps — U (for Union of Orthodox rabbis), K (kosher), D for Dairy, and so on — with which the visitor is invited to stamp the cloth. This sort of interactive installation places the question of the gendered Jewish body as one that is resolutely, and quite literally, in the eye of the beholder. It is up to us, the viewers, to determine what passes as "kosher." Molgan's attempt to address head-on the relationship between Jewish law and gender inequality is startling, given Molgan's own position in the Orthodox community. The questions of ritual purity and the female Jewish body, which might seem anachronistic to modern, nonobservant Jews in the United States and Europe, nonetheless link her project to work done by visual, conceptual, and performance artists (most of whom are Jewish) such as Eve Ensler, Karen Finley, Eleanor Antin, Carolee Schneemann, and Judy Chicago. In this, the memory of art that seeks to displace the borders between gender and the body continues to live in the work of this Israeli artist.

Molgan's art projects raise the question: is there an aesthetics of Jewish body art beyond its status as transgression of the biblical prohibition, and if so, how does Jewish body modification create Jewish legibility? The primal scene of Jewish legibility and the modified body is circumcision, where the mark on the infant's body becomes a site of erasure and absence that defines Jewish male identity. Significantly, Jewish male ritual clothing (*tallitot; kipot;* hats among the ultra-Orthodox; *peyes*) creates the iconic visual image of "the Jew": the male Jewish body that is marked by clothing and hair (beard, *peyes*). These are the iconic images of the Jew in the media that "modify" the body of the male Jew, making it forever legible as a Jewish body.

But what about women and the visual imprints and legibility of their Jewishness? In a sense, one can say that the female Jewish body is marked by what is not there. In the postwar period, rhinoplasty became the most common form of Jewish body modification; it was largely used by Jewish girls and women who were trying to pass as American and appear less Jewish or "ethnic." The Jewish nose job, immortalized in American Jewish fiction from Philip Roth to Herman Wouk, became the marker of a cultural moment in American Jewry in the postwar period. It was a sign of the burgeoning assimilation and attempt to "pass" in WASP American culture. The key text for this phenomenon was Philip Roth's 1959 novel *Goodbye, Columbus,* in which Brenda Patimkin's rhinoplasty not only modeled the desire of American Jews (in particular, women) for assimilation into the dominant WASP culture by modifying Jewish difference, but also served to highlight the class difference among Jews (in this case, between Brenda and the novel's protagonist, Neil Klugman).[75] The nose job, however, always bears the mark or trace of the Jewish nose left behind. Although in an entirely different social and historical register than Jewish tattoo body art, the nose job nonetheless is an act of body modification that exists as a similar interplay of memory and the gendered body. Thus the nose that is "done" is as much a marker of the Jewish as the "undone" Jewish nose that hovers as its spectral absence. The nose job is a bad copy, a translation of the non-Jewish body onto the Jewish body, which reveals the fact that there is no stable original (non-Jewish nose). Furthermore, rhinoplasty reveals that materialization of all kinds — Jewishness, gender, sexuality — as legible in the body is a repeated process of stylization which through its repetition reveals its own failure and instability. This is what Judith Butler identifies as the performative way in which "matter" is made, how bodies matter. As with tattoos, where the binarism between material and discourse breaks down, the nose job simultaneously places the Jewish woman not only as "modified," but, more significantly, as having been in need of modification. In both the act of tattooing and of the nose job, discourse is being inscribed onto, and is modifying, matter (the body). The Jewish woman with a modified nose reveals herself, through the modification, as much as a Jewish woman (with a nose job) as the woman without the nose job. The nose job itself becomes the marker, through the absence of the original nose, of the Jew.

Finally, I want to consider briefly a form of Orthodox Jewish practice that is not usually conceptualized within the framework of body modification: the practice among married Orthodox Jewish women of wearing a wig as a sign of modesty. Thinking of wigs as a form of body modification demands not only a rethinking of the gendered Jewish body as it has moved through history and memory, but even more significantly, the line separating the real and the simulacrum. The wig, like the indexical sign, asserts that something (in this case, adherence to a religious community and its belief system) is there to be looked at, but at the same time it cannot be seen. A scarf tied around the head satisfies the command for modesty. A wig does more than this, creating a new aesthetic category by taking the biblical command to cover the hair in public. Whether the wig consists of real or artificial hair is not, however, a matter of simple preference, style, or aesthetics. The wig modifies the body by covering the real hair with a simulacrum of the real (often in fact it is real hair, but not the hair of the actual woman wearing the wig). It is intended to impose modesty by concealing the hair; yet, paradoxically, at the same time that it conceals the hair it also asserts itself as excess and as ornamentation.[76]

The Orthodox woman's wig marks the wearer as Jewish; in its stylized presence, it alters the silhouette and creates, through artifice, a visible, recognizably Orthodox Jewish woman. The practice of allowing a small amount of the original hair to be visible at the temples (a *tefach*, or a hand's breadth), with a headband then attached to the wig hair, illuminates the artifice that is at the very center of this religious practice. Another sort of line between the real and the simulacrum, the *tefach* is as potentially transgressive as the outrageous tattoo art on the bodies of lesbian punk performance artists. Although socially sanctioned, it consciously plays with the borders between self and artifice, between sensuality, modesty and concealment, between the real and the simulacrum, between the Jewish body as natural and the Jewish body as the site of text, midrash, construction.

It is precisely this play with borders that joins together a reading of the Orthodox woman's wig and the conceptual poetry—to return to the start of this chapter—of Alan Sondheim, Daniel Blaufuks, Robert Fitterman, Heimrad Bäcker, and Anne Blonstein. All these works concern themselves with the performance of Jewishness and all insist on the fundamentally "scarry," stitched-together text, in which the Ur-text is not only no longer legible, but has transformed into its own textual material.

CHAPTER 4

Translating Place, Placing Translation

This final chapter is a case study of a place outside the margins, Czernowitz, and a poet outside the margins, Rose Ausländer. Today, Czernowitz's currency as the embodiment of a vanished world, as an elegiac place of memory, is largely due not to the work of Rose Ausländer but rather to the critical reception of its best-known poet, Paul Celan. Looking closely at Rose Ausländer and Czernowitz, this final chapter considers what it might mean to translate place and to rethink the status of a Czernowitz poet who is *not* Paul Celan, for it is unquestionable that Czernowitz has become metonymic for the poetry of its best-known native son. The poetry of Rose Ausländer is, with a few exceptions, the radical opposite of Celan's anti-representational poetry that is, as critics such as John Felstiner and Charles Bernstein have observed, inextricable from the "hermeneutic necessity" of translation.[1] Indeed, it is axiomatic that to read Celan is to grapple always with the limits of language, representation, and the possibility of dwelling on the border zones of translation. Yet this is also the case with his *Landsmann* Ausländer, a self-translator who translated her own works back and forth between English and German, and also a translator of mid-century Yiddish and American poetry.

There has been a great deal of scholarly attention given to Paul Celan; his stature as one of the foremost European poets of the postwar generation is uncontested. Rose Ausländer, on the other hand, has had a different critical trajectory. Yet both poets have been read largely through the prism of their Holocaust experience, with attention also given to the significant role that translation plays: Celan translated Pessoa, Shakespeare, Mandelstam, Dickinson, and Valéry, among others, and his own poetry demands an engagement with the principles of translation, since it is replete with neologisms and at times impenetrable images.[2] Ausländer, in contrast, wrote deceptively simple texts; indeed, as I will argue later in this chapter, her poems are popular in part because of their accessibility and, much of the time, their banality. As a self-translator, it must be added, she is unparalleled.

The Translated Jew thus gives its final pages not to Paul Celan—that favored poet of readers who do not seek a transcendent or spiritual voice of Holocaust "experience"—but rather to Rose Ausländer, a poet who is harder to categorize. She is both canonical and outside the margins of a poetic community that has embraced, indeed—to use Charles Bernstein's word—"venerated" Celan.[3] Bernstein makes the important point that this veneration has created the "crippling exceptionalism" that "has made his work a symbol of his fate rather than an active matrix for an ongoing poetic practice."[4] What Bernstein addresses is the way in which Celan has been approached by Anglo-American poetry critics and poets; what he leaves out is the fact that there has been much serious scholarly work on Celan in the field of German Jewish studies that grapples with the legacy of Celan as the quintessential Holocaust poet but also with his famously impenetrable poetic practice.

Bernstein, however, opens up the suggestion of a reading that is what Miron would advocate as "tangential," in his plea to place Celan in a conversation with poets who are not from Czernowitz nor German-speaking Jews of east-central Europe. Reading Celan as an American serialist poet (à la Jack Spicer) for whom "poems in a book were linked open-endedly, each poem another pass rather than a finalized articulation,"[5] Bernstein does indeed rescue Celan from the strictures of a Holocaust poetry, even though serialism can be read as a post-Holocaust refusal of signification.

The task of the translator and the reader of Jewish text, post-Benjamin, is to grapple with its status as Jewish text, proclaiming its fundamental diasporic quality and insisting that the relationship between language and place, or language and national origin, no longer coheres. Indeed, Bernstein adds his playful homophonic translation of Celan's "Todtnauberg" poem to the lineup of noted Celan translators (Pierre Joris, Michael Hamburger, and John Felstiner) as part of this project of breaking language, sound, and place apart. The first line of Celan's poem "Arnica, Augentrost, der" he translates as "Arnica, hold-in-trust, tear."

Homophonic translation tears language from meaning while challenging the project of locating an originating text and differentiating it from its translation. What might it mean to translate the place, Czernowitz, homophonically? (Share novice? Chair know wits? Cherry no whisk?) For the task of "translating Czernowitz" participates, inescapably, in the project of writing and thinking elegiacally: in one sense, all literary translation (with the possible exception of the homophonic) is elegiac in that the struggle between copy and original contains within it the search (and the lament) for the irretrievable original. In the post-Holocaust aesthetics of postmemory, the "original" consists of reproductions or circulations of images that ultimately confound notions of origin and copy. Furthermore, translatability in the larger sense depends on a notion of legibility, a reading of texts that either forges from the illegible and indeterminate a more rooted and legible "copy" or grapples with the illegibility of both copy and original.

While Ausländer wrote extensively about Czernowitz and the Bukovina in a series of poems and fragments, Celan did so only in the *Meridian* speech (1960), the Bremen Prize speech (1958), and, most obliquely, in a poem entitled "A Rogues' and Gonifs' Ditty Sung at Paris Emprès Pontoise by Paul Celan from Czernowitz near Sadagora" ("Eine Gauner- und Ganovenweise gesungen zu Paris Emprès Pontoise von Paul Celan von Czernowitz bei Sadagora"). Echoing in his title a poem by Francois Villon in which he describes his Paris birthplace as being near (*emprès*) Pontoise, Celan reverses the usual phrase in which Sadagora is described as being near Czernowitz: "Czernowitz near Sadagora."[6] In reversing the usual order of both places in the title of the poem, Celan suggests a displacement of the city of his birth to the place of Hasidic culture and legend, Sadagora, an even more Jewishly sacred site.[7] Otherwise, Celan distanced himself from the poetry produced in Czernowitz in the interwar years, poetry that was largely antimodernist and derivative, of which Ausländer's neo-romantic first volume of poems, *Der Regenbogen* (The Rainbow), was a prime example. Unlike Ausländer, Celan elided the place of his childhood, Czernowitz and the Bukovina, while writing, as many have argued, incessantly about and around Auschwitz, however elliptically.

Translating Czernowitz

"Czernowitz really exists, and not simply as a topos of a literary world."[8] This proclamation by the historian Karl Schlögel serves as both the point of departure and the point of contention for what follows: Schlögel's challenge is to probe the contours of the relationship between real and imaginary literary and geographical spaces, and between text and memory. The first part of this chapter will address the rhetorical and textual re-creations of Czernowitz as "place" on contemporary maps of Jewish mourning and, specifically, in the work of the Czernowitz-born poet Rose Ausländer. Like the work of Daniel Blaufuks, Robert Fitterman, Alan Sondheim, Raymond Federman, and W. G. Sebald, examined in previous chapters, Rose Ausländer's enormous corpus of poetry suggests a new way of engaging with post-Holocaust art and aesthetics, since it raises large and abiding questions for a critical Holocaust discourse about representation, figuration, Holocaust aesthetics, and German Jewish sites of memory.

Czernowitz poses an interesting problem for contemporary literary and cultural theory that seeks to map the fault lines between literary text, cultural and historical memory, and geographical and textual sites of memory. This legendary Jewish city, once a part of the Habsburg Empire and now in Ukraine, is present as a textual site of memory, embodying the absence of Jewish culture in east-central Europe. Yet at the same time it is, paradoxically, off the map of the new wave of Jewish tourism in eastern Europe. Marked in Paul Celan's *Meridian* speech by a "nervous" finger on a map of a place that no longer exists, Czernowitz is a paradigmatic "non-place" that carries the trace and the echo of a largely literary and textual past.[9] It is both a heavily remembered place and, at the same time, a forgotten place on and outside the margins of an already marginalized east-central Europe.

Rather than inscribe the city of Czernowitz into its historical and geographical "real," as Schlögel urges, I stress how the reiteration of the name of Czernowitz figures in contemporary German Jewish discourse about loss and mourning, particularly in Ausländer's poetry. Indeed, Czernowitz has come to stand in for an elegiac place of remembrance, and not a current city in the now bleak (and no longer Jewish) landscape of east-central Europe.[10] Thinking in Jewish, and thinking and reading tangentially, I turn to Italo Calvino's *Invisible Cities*, a pivotal text about the interplay between city spaces and poetic spaces, to explore the contours of Czernowitz as city, text, place, and non-place. Czernowitz is a "non-place" that embodies what Calvino calls the "redundant" because it repeats itself and, in the repetition, creates the echo of memory so that "the city can begin to exist."[11]

My point of departure is a provocation: namely, that Czernowitz has emerged in popular and literary discourse about vanished Jewish life in the former Habsburg lands as an invisible city. Like Calvino's exploration of the imaginary and constantly reimagined spaces of Venice, Czernowitz comes into being within a textual matrix that has shaped and constructed its meaning in the years since 1945 and after 1989. Like the cities in Calvino's text, it too exists in the imaginary, as a repetition of signs. Yet Czernowitz did, of course, truly exist—as the capital of the Bukovina and the city revered as both the "Paris of the east" and "little Vienna," the city in the Bukovina with the largest Jewish population before the war, and the renowned site of the first and most significant congress on Yiddish in 1908.[12] And it still exists; one can, with whatever difficulty, go there, even if the *there* is now part of Ukraine and not Romania or the former Habsburg Empire.

Axiomatic as the Atlantis of eastern European Jewish experience, Czernowitz has become, as Winfried Menninghaus declares, an "idealized cipher for the absence that lies at the heart of the fervor of memorialization of past Jewish life."[13] Indeed, Yasmin Yildiz's challenge of the veneration of the "multilingual" and her turn to the notion of the "postmonolingual" is particularly productive for thinking about Czernowitz, the exemplary site of German Jewish polylingualism in the prewar period. Menninghaus critiques the renewed nostalgia for Czernowitz that celebrates the city and the region as a multilingual, multicultural land of "books and thinkers," as both Celan and Ausländer famously characterized it. Arguing that Czernowitz thus serves as a German fantasy of an imagined Habsburg past, Menninghaus calls attention to the ways in which nostalgia for the golden age of Czernowitz demands at the same time repression of the memory of the antisemitism in the Bukovina that flourished, and continues to spread today.[14]

The repetition of Czernowitz within contemporary discourse about the absence of Jewishness in east-central Europe does more than simply recall another, more glorious historical era. The panegyric to Czernowitz is part of the project of commemoration in the post-Holocaust landscape of Europe, in which Czernowitz has been revived as a center of humanism and, more significantly, German *Kultur*. Parallel to this reconstruction of Czernowitz as a site of German *Kultur* and *Bildung*, the more diffuse spaces of the camps are reviled as its very negation. Czernowitz serves then as a cipher within contemporary German Jewish discourse, not only for a literary trope that returns again and again but more significantly for the absence underlying the zeal to commemorate past Jewish life.

Literary studies that seek to remap the fault lines between historical and cultural memory of the Holocaust must do more than simply (re)inscribe Czernowitz onto the tombstone of vanished Jewish culture and Jewish cities—Czernowitz, Vilna, Kovno, Kyiv, Lodz. Instead, contemporary approaches to urban space—by thinkers such as Italo Calvino, Edward Soja, and Marc Augé—can help us reshape our understanding of the spaces of east-central Europe—past and present. Soja's analyses of Los Angeles, Augé's conception of the non-places of supermodernity, and Calvino's evocation of the invisible city facilitate a critical move away from merely elegiac and nostalgic re-creations of Jewish cities that no longer exist as Jewish cities, to new ways of imagining these "lost cities" of east-central Europe as places suffused with memory, history, narrative; as places that demand an ongoing reflection about Jewish presence and absence in east-central Europe today. Within the contemporary rhetoric of mourning, a metonymic slide creates the litany of disaster stretching from Vilna, Kovno, Lodz, and Czernowitz to Auschwitz; the re-created and reimagined spaces of east-central Europe create a tabula rasa of "authentic" Jewish experience, distilled through the putative lens of "history" to provide a landing pad for the tourist—in the case of Czernowitz, a virtual and largely literary tourist—eager to consume these spaces.[15]

It is imperative that we move beyond the critique that east-central Europe today has been commodified and even "Disneyfied."[16] Instead, the task is to think about the interrelationship of text (urban space *and* literary text), ruin (literary ruin *and* architectural ruin), and memory. Czernowitz is more than merely a literary topos or an elegiac site of remembrance. Not only is it erased from the map of Jewish tourism in eastern Europe (in contrast to Prague, Warsaw, and Krakow), but even more significantly, the ossification of its fabled literary past dominates the contemporary narrative about the city, so that it is not thought of as part of the ongoing encounter with the Holocaust.

Reading Rose Ausländer beyond the Biographical: Czernowitz and the Elegiac

Rose Ausländer's biography has become inseparable from the readings of her poems; in turn, the poems have become testaments to the poet's biography. This tautological stranglehold of the biographical is often the fate of women writers and also Holocaust survivors who write. Rose Ausländer was born Rosalie Scherzer in 1901 in Czernowitz and immigrated in 1921 to New York, where she later married Ignaz Ausländer. In 1931 she returned to Czernowitz, where she survived the war in the ghetto. In 1946 she returned to New York, and stayed there until her return to Germany in 1965. For the last decades of her life she lived in the Nelly Sachs House in Düsseldorf, where she died in 1988. Yet despite the many years in New York and later in Düsseldorf, Ausländer was very much shaped by the Jewish culture of late Habsburg Czernowitz. Ausländer is part of a generation of Habsburg Jews writing in German (Ruth Klüger, Hans Mayer, and H. G. Adler) who were shaped by the belief in German *Bildung* and retained a strong affinity for the German language and culture while in exile, even while acknowledging the trauma of the rupture from the language and culture to which they still held fast.

Significantly, the popular and critical reception of Ausländer has placed more emphasis on her associations with Celan than Celan scholarship places on his ties to Ausländer. They knew each other in Czernowitz before the war through a mutual friend and mentor, Alfred Margul-Sperber, and Celan attended the reading in Czernowitz on the occasion of the publication of Ausländer's first volume of poems, *Der Regenbogen*, in 1939. There is documentation in the critical literature on Rose Ausländer that one of the poems in that volume was the source of the celebrated first line, "Black milk of morning," in Celan's most famous poem, "Death Fugue."[17] Yet despite the many years Ausländer spent in New York, the critical reception of her work has tied her to a largely postwar imagining of Czernowitz. This association of Ausländer primarily with Czernowitz anchors her to her fellow Czernowitz poet Celan, despite the fact that the poets to whom she cites the greatest debt are the American poets she met and corresponded with in New York after the war: Marianne Moore, Wallace Stevens, and E.E. Cummings.[18]

Ausländer scholarship has largely approached the theme of rupture and loss in her poems solely in biographical terms, focusing on the profound alienation, poverty, and loneliness experienced by the poet during her years in New York, her longing for *Heimat* (homeland), and for her native language. At the end of the poem "Age" ("Alter"), from 1980, for example, she expresses, with characteristic sparseness, the affinity between poetry and loss:

> I look for my dead friend
>
> in dreams
>
> Writing
>
> hurts[19]

The act of seeking the dead friend in the unconscious world of dreams is enacted in the eternal present, in a time that the poet, at the start of the poem, describes as "these hard days" in which "the anemones shine in vain."[20] The anemone is the flower that is perhaps most textually saturated with loss and the elegiac, since it derives from the Greek myth in which Aphrodite sprinkled Adonis's blood with nectar, causing the short-lived anemone to grow. This joining of the elegiac impulse to remember the dead friend with the recognition of the pain of writing stretches from Virgil through Milton, Spenser, Shakespeare, Shelley, and Tennyson to Derrida's collection of writings for friends who have died, in which every essay begins with a reflection on the sheer difficulty of writing about, or for, the dead friend.[21] Similarly, Ausländer's poem "Age" links poetry and loss by suggesting the futility of writing, the purposelessness of rendering mourning, grief, and melancholy into text, as the poetic "I" seeks the dead friend again and again in a timeless unconscious. Like many of Ausländer's most evocative poems, this one challenges the viability of writing and the acts of mourning and creating text. The poet's assertion that "Writing / hurts" could, in fact, serve as a coda for her entire oeuvre, a coda that is met, at the same time, with a nearly constant, perhaps even obsessive, need to confront the pain that ensues from the attempts at, and often the failures of, mourning and grief. The recognition of the intimate link between loss and the pain of writing constitutes the rupture of writing.

This link between writing and loss is also present in Ausländer's textual re-creations of Czernowitz and the Bukovina. The dominant critical response to the elegiac mode of Ausländer's Czernowitz poems insists on it as a place of historical and geographic loss, and even more so as a place associated with the Holocaust and mourning. Instead of this, I want to propose a thought experiment of turning to the French anthropologist Marc Augé in order to conceptualize Czernowitz as "non-place," situating this former Habsburg Jewish city as a textualized space that exists apart from the historical, anthropological narratives that have created its status as an "idealized cipher." Augé locates as the "real non-places of supermodernity" those marked by the "invasion of space by text," spaces such as the supermarket, the highway, and the airport lounge, in which words and texts dominate—"No smoking"; "You are now entering the Beaujolais region"—as their "instructions for use."[22] Augé defines these "non-places" situated in "supermodernity" as spaces that are neither "anthropological" (e.g., places of identity and social relations) nor historically situated, but instead places of solitude, "lieux de memoires," where the traveler exists outside of relations and identity.[23] While the Jewish spaces of east-central Europe are not the objects of Augé's analysis of the non-place, his attempt to think about place as distinct from its historical or anthropological layers is a new way to conceptualize the discourses about Czernowitz. For Augé the non-place comes into existence through the interplay between place and text; similarly Czernowitz, as a cipher for debates about Jewishness in eastern Europe, takes on the status of a non-place.

The relationship between text and place that marks Augé's linking of supermodernity and the non-place is central to the project of "translating Czernowitz." Variously approached in terms of language, style and aesthetics, conceptual art and performance, or cultural contact and politics, the many projects of "translation" that are included here both enable and complicate notions of language, culture, and text. First, to "translate Czernowitz" is to locate Czernowitz as textualized space—not to conceptualize it solely as a geographical or historical place, but as the non-place identified by Augé. Second, to "translate Czernowitz" is to be concerned with the act of moving between interior poetic spaces and geographical spaces of dispersion, with the tension between poetic utterance and assertion and negation of place, and the relationship between sound and echo. In other words, the task is to "translate" paradigms of diasporic thought into a poetics of diaspora, seeing in the interplay between the once-Jewish city of Czernowitz and the vanished traces of this Jewishness not a nostalgic or elegiac recuperation of loss, but rather the forever provisional, indeterminate nature of Jewish text that exists as part of a system of translation that carries the echoes, dispersed, of previous texts.

Czernowitz exists as text, as a system of signs that has signified in various ways in different historical periods; as a system of signs, it invites the project of translation on multiple levels. On the most obvious and "literal" level, to speak of "translating Czernowitz" thus refers not only to the multiple languages that were part of the Bukovina, but also to the translation of texts by its major poets, most notably Paul Celan, Rose Ausländer, Dan Pagis, Aharon Appelfeld, Elieser Starnberg, Alfred Margul-Sperber, Alfred Gong, Alfred Kittner, and Itsik Manger. Significant too is the fact that many of these poets were also noted translators, and translation and self-translation played formative roles in their own poetic work. Celan, although legendary for his own untranslatability, translated, among others, Giuseppe Ungaretti, Shakespeare, Emily Dickinson, Robert Frost, Marianne Moore, Osip Mandelstam, and Fernando Pessoa.

Rose Ausländer not only translated the work of the Yiddish poet Itsik Manger, her fellow Czernowitzer who went to New York, she also translated her own poems. Many of the English poems she wrote in New York in the 1940s she translated into German, and her German poems she translated into English. The drafts of her poems that are available in the Ausländer *Nachlass* make clear, in fact, how difficult it is to determine if a given poem was written first in English and then translated into German, or the other way around.

These questions about textuality, translation, self-translation, repetition, and legibility are especially salient in the work of Ausländer. On the surface, her poems seem eminently accessible and citable, often reducible — and this in part accounts for her popularity — to epigram-like statements that would seem to capture the "experience" of Jews in east-central Europe before and during the war, thus contrasting starkly with the tantalizing obscurity of Celan. Yet present in these poems is also a stuttering, a repetition, an echo of her own previous poems. Furthermore, since she translated many of her poems back and forth between German and English, the question of "original" language arises; the repetitions, translations, and retranslations of her own poems call to mind Walter Benjamin's reflections on the unstable relationship between original and translation, and perhaps even more, his proclamation in the *Arcades Project* that "the text is the thunder that continues to roll."[24] Translation is a form of poetic *repetition*—"the thunder that continues to roll"—re-creating in the various languages iterations of the once original and thus evoking the absence and loss of that first text. Similarly, the different modes of repetition in Ausländer's poetry lead to the fundamental paradox that defines her oeuvre: the poet reflects, over and over again— she wrote more than 2,600 poems—on the central dilemma regarding silence, language, and writing after Auschwitz. She creates new iterations and translations of the poet's role, generating an echo of her poems and translations and creating the "more exalted language" Benjamin identified as the mark of the translated text.[25]

Ausländer's poem "Jerusalem," written first in English in 1953 and later translated by the poet into German, serves as a good example of Benjamin's notion of this "more exalted language." It is also indicative of the way Ausländer worked, since there are at least five extant versions of the poem. Here is the first, the "original":

I have never been in Jerusalem
When I hang my blue-white scarf toward east,
Jerusalem comes to me
with the Temple and Solomon's Song

I am 5,000 years young
In the arena I was introduced to lions
embraced by one
Rats were my companions
in the ghetto

※

At the moment another style prevails

*

My scarf is a swing
when I close my eyes toward east:
On the hill
Jerusalem
5,000 years young
in orange aroma
swings to me

Of the same age

We are

having a game in the air[26]

A German inflection creeps into the first line of the poem with the use of the preposition "in." Standard English would read "I have never been *to* Jerusalem." This faint grammatical slip does more than simply reveal a poet not fully at home in the English language: the unusual use of the preposition wounds the English, creating an abrasion on the body of the text and thus marking it as not natural or whole. It is a text subject to rupture, to a "breaking in" of language. Neither a translation nor a text in the poet's mother tongue, this version of the "Jerusalem" poem occupies a liminal space between original text and translated text, signaling Ausländer's status as a poet who crosses borders — literally and figuratively — and does not, perhaps cannot, occupy any sort of unified or coherent national or linguistic subject position.

In this early version of the poem there is a Jewish poetic subject who has not been to (or in) Jerusalem, which is presented not only as a place but as the very location of Jewishness and Jewish identity. The repetition of the poem — through the multiple drafts, versions, and translations — is what calls the place, Jerusalem, into being and what binds the poet to that place. Jerusalem and "the east," spaces of the imaginary for the poet, emerge through the many iterations of the text. Jerusalem, imagined when the poetic subject closes her eyes "toward east," becomes the imaginary space that lies east of the eastern *Heimat* of the Bukovina. Czernowitz, alluded to only in the English version with the line "Rats were my companions / in the ghetto," is present in the poem as the site of the other "east." Drawing on the persistent trope of longing for the east found in Jewish poetry from the twelfth-century poet Judah Halevi to the Bukovina-born Israeli poet Dan Pagis, Ausländer links the longed-for east of the Bukovina to the east of Jerusalem.[27] In this way she creates metonymic substitutions of east-central Europe for "mizrach"—the east toward which Jews in the diaspora face in prayer, and the direction of all longing for Zion, captured emblematically in Halevi's "My heart is in the East." Ausländer's Jerusalem, a place of refracted easternness, is not an unproblematic or unreflective place; rather, it functions here as the non-place, conjured through text, in which the poet can only express a fragile, provisional, and always uncertain Jewish identity.

The second version of the English poem (in the *Nachlass*) contains changes that are important for the subsequent publication of the poem in German.[28] While the original English version continues after the first line that declares, "I have never been in Jerusalem": "When I hang my blue / white scarf toward east, / Jerusalem comes to me," the third line in the second German version becomes "Jerusalem *swings* to me."[29] The verb "swings" is more elusive than "comes," suggesting that Jerusalem is also in the air, ethereal, not fixed or static. A dialogic relationship thus emerges between the lyrical I and the land of Israel.[30] The reciprocity between the autobiographical and the poetic becomes even more marked in the German version of the poem, in which the declarative first line from the English version ("I have never been in Jerusalem") is omitted. Instead, the German version begins with the English version's second line, since in the intervening years between writing the poem in English and translating it into German Ausländer did in fact make a trip to Israel.

The displacement of Jewish longing from Czernowitz to Jerusalem and the displacement enacted through translation in the "Jerusalem" poems suggest contradictory meanings of each place. At the same time that Jerusalem is the axiomatic place of Jewish identity and longing, it remains in Ausländer's work elusive, a place of the imaginary that "swings," that is conjured through closing the eyes and through aroma. Similarly, the multiple meanings of Czernowitz for Ausländer need closer scrutiny. The poem "Jerusalem," in its many drafts and versions, serves as a reminder of the ways in which translation and repetition point to the ever-provisional status of language in Ausländer's work, where the poetic landscape is characterized by translation and by the echo of both what the poet hears and sees and what she cannot grasp or experience: "I have never been in Jerusalem." Jerusalem is the cipher for the Czernowitz that is both a source of nostalgic longing and a site of absence and emptiness.

A closer examination of Ausländer's Czernowitz and Bukovina poems shows how she participates in an elegiac re-creation of Czernowitz and the Bukovina more generally, while at the same time undercutting this nostalgia. In the poem "Czernowitz before the Second World War," for instance, Czernowitz is evoked as a

> Peaceful Hill-City
> surrounded by beech forests . . .
>
> . . . Four languages
> in accord with each other
> spoiled the air
>
> Until the bombs fell
> the city breathed
> happily [31]

In the poem "Bukowina III," the Bukovina is invoked with the first line, "Green Mother / Bukowina / butterflies in your hair," and the poem also contains the lines

> Four languages
> Four-language songs
>
> People
> who understand each other[32]

At least seven of the poems contain the refrain "four languages" and the image of a harmonious mix of languages and people. Another poem, "Bukowina II," opens with the invocation "landscape / that invented me" and goes on to describe the Bukovina as "water-armed" and "forest-haired."[33] Ausländer thus inverts the images to suggest that it is the "green mother Bukowina" that produced and invented her. While expressing the received idea of Czernowitz as a center of multicultural humanism, she also conceptualizes it in a specular relationship to herself: she comes into the world in Czernowitz, and Czernowitz continually comes into her. This specularity is expressed as well in a famous prose fragment from 1971, "Everything can be a Theme" ("Alles kann Motiv sein") written in response to the question "Why do I write?" Ausländer responds: "Perhaps because I came into the world in Czernowitz, and because the world in Czernowitz came into me. That special landscape. The special people. Fairy tales and myths were in the air, one inhaled them. Czernowitz, with its four languages, was a city of muses that housed many artists, poets, and lovers of art, literature, and philosophy."[34]

The nostalgic undercurrent in this often-cited fragment about Czernowitz is undercut in several of her poems from the 1970s, written after her return to Germany. In a poem from her 1974 volume *Without a Visa* that begins "I too was born in Arcadia," Ausländer creates a palimpsest of the classical trope "et in Arcadia ego" from Virgil's *Eclogues*, the first line of Schiller's poem "Resignation," and Goethe's inscription on the frontispiece to his *Italian Journey*. However, despite Ausländer's conscious use of this line to signal the insertion of her poetic voice into a longer trajectory of elegiac writing, she departs from the tradition of pastoral poetry or even memento mori art by inscribing the "Motherwords" she finds blooming in this Arcadia into another landscape, one decidedly less Arcadian, a bleak landscape populated by the nameless and "nothingness":

> I too lost
> my name
> among the nameless
>
> I too
> asked Nothingness
> about Being [35]

The repetition of the word "too" signals Ausländer's participation in the world of poets and also signals that the memory invoked is not just her own historical memory, but intertextual memory, through Virgil, Goethe, Schiller. The voice of resignation, heavy with the voices of poets past, at the beginning of the poem is also a voice of postmemory, joining personal loss to earlier texts so that elegies to earlier lost Arcadias are also elegies to Czernowitz and the Bukovina.[36]

Read in this way, Ausländer's elegy "I too" ("Auch ich") situates the poet as self-consciously and self-reflexively engaged in the process of remembering and, in part, in the process of re-membering her own texts. For instance, in the second stanza we hear "Also to me / bloomed fragrant Motherwords / I too grew up / among fantasy-filled legends."[37] The neologism of "Motherword" (*Mutterwort*), which appears in other poems in Ausländer's work (most notably in another formulation as "Mutterland / Wort"), signals the placement of this poem in the larger oeuvre. The reminder of the "fantasy-filled legends" is the cultural landscape and Jewish legacy of east-central Europe and the Bukovina in particular, a metonymic reference to the *Wunderrabbiner* and other Hasidic sages and storytellers of Sadagora.

In the poem "The Inheritance," from the 1975 volume *Other Signs*, however, the Bukovina is evoked as a memory in this "Austrian-less time," where the act of thinking about "das Buchenland" produces only the fragmented and anti-nostalgic stanza "uprooted Word / birds vanished without a trace."[38] Yet the "Buchenland" remains a place that the poet can summon from memory and call into text, however broken the metaphors she uses; to think about the "Buchenland" is to show as well a different notion of "inheritance," that is, the poetic legacy of another German Jewish poet, Heinrich Heine, and the first lines of his poem "Nightthoughts" ("Nachtgedanken"): "Thinking of Germany in the night / I lie awake and sleep takes flight" ("Denk ich an Deutschland in der Nacht / dann bin ich um den Schlaf gebracht").[39] The sudden, singular use of the German "Buchenland" instead of her more customary use of "Bukowina" at the beginning of the poem ("I think about the Buchenland") marks an abrupt change from the other Bukovina poems, in which she calls the region the "Bukowina," adding a note of nostalgia as she attempts to realign the place with its former position as part of the Habsburg Empire. Even more significantly, to move from Heine's "Thinking of Germany" ("Denk ich an Deutschland") to "Thinking of the Bukowina" ("Denke ich ans Buchenland") is to move from Heine's nineteenth-century "Deutschland" to the resonance, post-1945, of Buchenwald. In other words, "das Buchenland" carries, inevitably, the trace of Buchenwald in the aftermath of the Holocaust. This is, perhaps, the linguistic "inheritance" of Rose Ausländer. In "The Inheritance," the possibility of text as ruin emerges for the first time in the series of poems; here text is "uprooted word," and metaphor and image have "vanished without a trace," replacing the poetic invocation ("O green Mother Bukowina!") and nostalgic rewriting of history found in the earlier poems.

Although scholarship on Rose Ausländer has tended to cast her unequivocally as a Holocaust poet whose origin in Czernowitz is "proof" of her legible Jewishness, "The Inheritance" suggests that even within the apparently seamless construction of Jewishness in her poems, there exists an indeterminacy of Jewish history and Jewish identity vis-à-vis the Bukovina. In other words, if—for contemporary German Jewish discourse—Czernowitz is an idealized cipher for the absence underlying the fervor of memorialization of past Jewish life, these moments evoking the brokenness and fragmentation of place and text in Ausländer's poems demand a new reading—indeed, a new translation—of the interrelationship of text, city, and ruin. As "The Inheritance" suggests the indeterminacy of place and of reading, it challenges the legibility of Jewishness in the former spaces of east-central Europe.

Both Rose Ausländer's poetry and the place of her birth, Czernowitz, need to be "translated" beyond the paradigms that have created the critical impasses Menninghaus so acutely identifies; that is, the challenge of her poetry is similar to the challenge of "reading" and "translating" Czernowitz, in that both demand that we move past easy critiques of Disneyfications and the quaint recapturing of vanquished Jewish life to a fuller consideration of the relationships of memory, loss, space, and text. The critical task in reading a poet such as Ausländer is to read allusively when the text does not automatically yield allusion, when it is still rooted in mimetic notions of the referent and of representability. In many of Ausländer's poems the allusive, the unspoken and the not-quite-spoken, the elliptical, hover, as seen in the lines from the poem "Age," in which the difficulty of writing is proclaimed at the end of a poem that paradoxically enacts writing.

The poet's assertion that "writing / hurts" (*Das Schreiben / tut weh*) could in fact serve as a coda for the entire oeuvre, a coda that is met, at the same time, with a nearly constant, perhaps even obsessive, need to not confront this pain that ensues from the attempts at, and often the failures of, mourning and grief. The recognition of the intimate link between loss and the pain of writing constitutes the failure of writing.

It is precisely this persistent rupture and loss that have been examined and rehearsed by Ausländer scholarship in largely biographical terms: first citing the fact of her departure from Czernowitz in 1921 and immigration to the United States, and then her return to Czernowitz in the 1930s, where she survived the war, and her subsequent return to America after the war. To be sure, these ruptures, marked by historical and personal experience, take shape in the poems, to the extent that many of the poems articulate the profound alienation, poverty, and loneliness experienced by the poet in the years in New York and the desire for *Heimat* and for the mother tongue. Yet it is vital that we extend the notion of rupture beyond the historical and biographical facts of her life, to think about how this functions poetically within the texts and as part of the larger cultural production seen in art more generally.

The biographically based scholarship on Ausländer always mentions that she was Jewish, with a focus on what is often characterized as a Jewish fate: ghetto, persecution, emigration, refugee, war, survival. Yet more significant, it seems to me, is to contemplate how her texts, and not solely her life's history, all evoke and grapple with trauma, loss, translation — that is, how they participate in a tradition of Jewish writing. Ausländer is a paradigmatic example of the difficulties of locating what constitutes Jewish writing after Auschwitz. Like Sebald and even Celan, the question remains of how to place Ausländer into a trajectory of German Jewish writing. How "Jewish" is her work? What is the encounter of her work with a religious, sacred, and literary tradition? Ausländer was also paradigmatic for many late Habsburg writers steeped in German *Bildung* and ambivalent about the lines dividing secular and religious Jewish cultures. As we have seen in some of the poems above, she writes as a consciously Jewish poet, although much of the time this assertion of Jewishness is presented as indeterminate, provisional, and forever shifting. In this, Ausländer, like her *Landsmann* Paul Celan, is an exemplar of the "translated Jew" for whom Jewishness is always provisional and Jewish text must always be read as a node in the ongoing network of the proliferation of text. We can thus not only read Ausländer as a post-Holocaust poet who laments the loss of her *Heimat*, but also see her texts as forming a contiguous network of the displaced landscape of German Jewish text after 1945.

In part, this is done through her participation in a community of poets who write about angels.[40] In his book on angels in the work of Kafka, Benjamin, and Scholem, Robert Alter noted that all three writers inhabited a "no man's land" between Judaism and secularism. In an analogous fashion, Ausländer's poems are filled with references to Jewish rituals and to Shabbat, yet at the same time there is a profound ambivalence concerning the observance of Judaism. This is nowhere more pronounced than in the poem she wrote about angels, "Jacob Wrestles with Angels." Jacob wrestling with the angel in Genesis is often read as the universal struggle with belief in God. Yet in Ausländer's poem, the wrestling is part of her larger poetological project of wrestling with the viability of poetry after Auschwitz. Her conscious mixing of two Jacob narratives (the wrestling and the ladder) is an insistence on the indeterminacy of the textual and of Jewish identity; that she makes the angel into a plural, yet without the definite article, also suggests the indeterminacy, almost abstraction, of her use of angels.

Rose Ausländer's poem "Janus Angel" ("Janusengel") begins with a citation of Benjamin's Angel of History.[41] The opening lines begin: "Engel der Geschichte / Rose and Sword / in Feathers."[42] The motif of the rose, a self-reflexive poetic gesture found throughout Ausländer's work, appears four times in the poem "Janus Angel." However, in this poem the self-reflexive use of "Rose" is not an assertion of oneness between the poetic subject and the voice in the poem, but, rather, an expression of ambivalence: the ancient Roman god Janus was the god of beginnings and of transitions, doors, time, gates, passages, and endings. The two faces of Janus enabled him—like Benjamin's Angel of History—to look simultaneously into the future and back into the past. Janus's two-faced existence expresses the fundamental split in Rose Ausländer as a German-speaking Jew, the "Jewish gypsy" who speaks German ("jüdische Zigeunerin / deutschsprachig")[43] and the poet whose lyrical I "does not speak about roses" but rather about mourning, persecution, "the yellow star" in the "time of the gallows": that is, who speaks instead about her survival and the darkness.[44]

In the poem "I vouch" ("Ich stehe ein") from 1976, Ausländer weaves together biblical motifs with a pointed poetological message. In the first line: "With my People / I went into the desert / I did not pray / to the God of snakes and the / Sandgod,"[45] the neologism "Sandgod" (*Sandgott*) links the motif of sand with writing, evoking Celan's "Sandkunst" and the metaphor-world in which sand suggests the difficulty, indeed impossibility, of writing.[46] In the work of Ausländer's contemporaries Paul Celan and Edmond Jabès, sand emerges as the medium through which words and language attempt to form, only to become dissolved, erased, traceless in the process. Ausländer's poem ends without punctuation, without an end, as the poetic I wanders through the "Sand desert" (*Sandwüste*) or, possibly, the Celan-like "Sand Art" (*Sandkunst*), "from word to word," itself a near echo of the Hebrew "l'dor v'dor" (from generation to generation).[47] This last stanza links the sand in the desert, in which Rose Ausländer has wandered "for many hundreds of years," with the biblical topos of the "word." For Rose Ausländer, the assertion of the primacy of language (of inhabiting her "Mutterland / Wort") is at the same time an assertion of the poetic and of the Jewish. The two are not separable in her *Sandkunst*.

Rose Ausländer's Translations of Itsik Manger: Getting Lost in the Yiddish

The Yiddish Czernowitz-born poet Itsik Manger, in exile in London, wrote to Rose Ausländer in English in 1947: "My dear Roisele, I am very glad that you got rid of our 'beloved' country."[48] Placing the word "beloved" in quotation marks, Manger adds a note of irony that undercuts any possible nostalgia for their *Heimat*; even more significantly, he conceptualizes this *Heimat* as a place the writer can, through exile, "get rid of." Yet while Manger's critical assessment of their homeland serves as counterpoint to the nostalgic, sentimental re-creations of Czernowitz and the Bukovina that were to come later, scholarship on Ausländer has tended to forge a more univocal relationship between the poet and her place of birth. In fact, her poetry has become central to the nostalgic impulse identified by Menninghaus among others, in which German critics create a Jewish fairyland from the ruins of the now-absent Jewish culture in Czernowitz.

This unusually sarcastic and ironic formulation serves as a leitmotif for the correspondence of Ausländer and Manger (the actual correspondence in the form of letters, as well as the affinity between the two poets). In the letter to Ausländer, Manger presents a provocatively critical portrait of the Bukovina that demonstrates how important but also how complex the relationships among *Heimat*, language, memory, and text are.

Manger's wry formulation in his letter to Ausländer ("I am very glad that you got rid of our 'beloved' country") invites a critical reassessment of the Bukovina as a place of idealized multiculturalism. The poetic and personal encounter of Rose Ausländer with her *Landsmann* Itsik Manger is linked to both poets' relationship to their place of birth. While Manger writes caustically about the "beloved country," Ausländer praises the Bukovina in a number of poems.[49] Ausländer writes about the "dead Fatherland" in the "Mutterland" poem, and about her survival in the "Mutterland / Wort," thereby linking place and language. In any case, the role of translation is central — not only her translation of Manger's ballads into English and German, but rather the constant moving back and forth between English and German in her own poems. Between the lines of the correspondence between Manger and Ausländer lies the question of the Jewish absence in eastern Europe and its trace in Yiddish text.

After Manger first contacted Ausländer in 1947, a relationship between the two poets developed whose importance for Jewish culture in Czernowitz cannot be underscored enough. Of course, the significance of Yiddish culture for Czernowitz is legendary. Czernowitz is still synonymous with the Yiddish conference, convened there by Nathan Birnbaum in 1908. In his speech at the start of the conference, the Yiddish writer I. L. Peretz proclaimed the importance of Czernowitz as the location of this first Yiddish conference, and the importance of translation in integrating Yiddish into a larger cultural trajectory: "And in this language we want to amass our cultural treasures, create our culture, rouse our spirits and souls, and unite culturally with all countries and all times."[50] Peretz believed that the central meaning of Yiddish was to promote the relationship between language and the autonomy of the Jewish people: "We no longer want to be fragmented, and to render to every Moloch nation-state its tribute: There is one people — Jews, and its language is — Yiddish."[51] Furthermore, Peretz elaborated his hope that in order for Yiddish to be part of "world languages," Yiddish had to be part of the world. In order to achieve this end, Peretz believed that as much literature as possible must be translated into Yiddish—and the Bible, in particular, must be translated into Yiddish. And not only translated, but these texts must also be transliterated: "We no longer want to be crude, unrefined parvenus or upstart newly-rich. Culture includes tradition! And we don't want to introduce our culture to the peoples of the world through mechanical translations that deaden the living word."[52]

Like Ausländer, Manger was only seven years old when the Czerno-witz conference took place, yet the so-called Prince of the Jewish Ballad accomplished many of the things that Peretz had demanded of Yiddish culture in his speech. Manger, who immigrated in 1939 to London via Paris, and whose immigration to the United States in 1951 coincided with Rose Ausländer's second New York period, was an influential fig-ure for Yiddish modernist poetry. According to Alfred Kittner, he lived impoverished and like a "vagabond" in Brooklyn and in other places. The repeated description of Manger as a "vagabond" in the recollec-tions of him by Kittner and Edith Silbermann also helps to explain Man-ger's formulation in the 1947 letter: "I am very glad that you got rid of our 'beloved' country," in that Manger expresses an identification with Ausländer's exile and poverty in New York. The style of the English is unusual and stilted yet also symptomatic of Manger's disrupted and dis-placed relationship to Czernowitz. He and "Roisele," as he calls her, did not leave the homeland, they got rid of it, he writes. This reversal of the usual formulation of exile reveals a bitterness toward the homeland that is rarely seen in Ausländer's own poetry. It also reveals—through the awkward English syntax—that Manger's mother tongue was Yiddish. Other letters also reveal this ("I would like you should write to me about yourself and what you know about my sister").

Manger's sarcastic tone contrasts with the nostalgic, melancholic tone of much of Ausländer's verse, such as the poem "The Inheritance" ("Das Erbe"), in which the Bukovina is a memory enacted in the "Austrian-less time" (österreichlose Zeit), or "Bukowina II," in which the poet evokes the Bukovina, famously, as "a landscape that invented her."[53] Despite the nearly constant nostalgic evocation of the Bukovina, Ausländer's poetry contains a critical voice that incorporates prewar longing and nostalgia with post-Holocaust trauma, seen perhaps most markedly in the poem

"Motherland" ("Mutterland," 1978), perhaps one of her best known, that ends with the lines: "My fatherland is dead / they buried it / in fire.[54]

Yet Manger's experience of exile was substantially different from that of Rose Ausländer. Whereas Ausländer returned to Czernowitz in 1931 from her first stay in New York, and survived the war there until returning to New York in 1946, Manger left Czernowitz in 1939 and never returned. While Manger, who primarily wrote ballads, is often considered emblematic of a pre-modernist Yiddish culture, his poetry, especially from the time of his exile in New York, emerged through an intensive interaction with American modernist poets such as Eliot, Pound, Williams, and E. E. Cummings. At the same time, however, Manger participates in an older narrative poetic tradition, drawing explicitly on biblical and mythical elements from Jewish text. For example, in a well-known poem, "For years I wallowed about in the world" ("Ikh hob zikh yorn gevalgert"), Manger consciously asserts an identity as a poet in exile, a wanderer in the diaspora:

> For years I wallowed about in the world,
> now I am going home to wallow there,
> With a pair of shoes and the shirt on my back,
> And the stick in my hand that goes with me everywhere.[55]

This poem, written in 1958—shortly before his immigration to Israel—draws on the work of the twelfth-century Hebrew poet Judah Ha'levi, whose poems (from *Songs of Zion*) sing of the landscape of the Holy Land. Manger takes Ha'levi's unequivocal love for Jerusalem ("I would bow down, my face on the stones, I would love your stones") and transforms it into images that are far more broken than unitary: "I'll not kiss your dust as that great poet did, / Though my heart, like his, is filled with song and grief. / How can I kiss your dust? I *am* your dust / And how, I ask you, can I kiss myself?"[56] The plaintive lament for the impossibility of oneness with the land (here, Jerusalem) in Manger's poem contrasts with the poems of Ausländer, in whose work the lost *Heimat* is always the Bukovina. Itsik Manger instead inserts an originary "Holy Land" for the *Heimat* that stands in opposition to exile.

Yet despite the difference between both poets' conception of *Heimat* and exile, Ausländer translated three of Manger's poems into German, and one into English: "The Ballad of the Necklace of Stars," "The Ballad of the White Bread," and "Do Not Follow after Me, My Brother" ("Die Ballade vom Kränzlein Sterne," "Die Ballade vom weißen Brot," and "Folg mir nicht nach, mein Bruder"). "The Ballad of the White Bread" was translated into German not only by Ausländer but also by Alfred Margul-Sperber and Hubert Witt. Ausländer eliminated the eighth stanza in her translation of the poem into English: "the children smile at the glow of the white bread / and die an easy death" ("shmaykhln baym shayn funem veysn broyt / di kinder un shtarbn a gringen toyt"). Comparing Ausländer's translation of this stanza with Margul-Sperber's, Ausländer pushes the metaphorical sense of the "white bread": in Ausländer's translation, the bread is not only an illusion, as it is also in Margul-Sperber's poem, but rather is more abstract; rather than being a presence, in Ausländer's translation it is only there as trace.[57]

Ausländer's translation contains traces of her encounter with American modernism; in particular, the first lines of her translation echo Marianne Moore, with whom she also had an extended poetic correspondence. Manger's poem begins "shtehn mames in tserisine shaln / oyf tunkele ovntike shvelln."[58] Ausländer's version begins: "Mothers standing in gloomy doors / wrapped in tatters. The evening roars." The line "the evening roars" does not correspond at all to the Yiddish ("oyf tunkele ovntike shvelln"); a more precise translation would be "Mothers stand in torn shawls / in dark twilit doorways." Furthermore, the word "roars" is in an entirely different semantic and acoustic register than the verb in Manger's poem. The rhyme scheme and choice of words ("door" instead of "threshold" as the translation for the Yiddish word "shveln" and its rhyme "roar") is reminiscent of two poems that Ausländer dedicated to Marianne Moore, in which the word "door" ("the door / evermore") and its acoustic echoes are a wordplay on the name of the revered poet Marianne Moore.

Itsig Manger's poem "Ikh bin der veg keyn maarav" ("I Am the Path to the West") and Ausländer's German translation of it entitled "Folg mir nicht nach, mein Bruder" ("Do Not Follow Me, My Brother") recall a number of Ausländer's poems, with the trope of wandering and exile linking the two poets not only through their shared *Heimat* and exile, but also linking them textually:

I am the path to the West
  the blond sunset
the brown shepherd birds
  the tired evening sounds

Do not follow after me, my dear friend,
  My going is a passing
Do not bind your young belief
  to my blue lament

Ikh bin der veg keyn maarav,
der blonder zunfargang
das broyne pastun-feygl
der mider ovnt-klang.

gey mir nisht nakh, mayn khaver—
mayn geyn iz a fargeyn;
heng nicht dayn jingn gloybn
oyf mayn bloy geveyn.

Ich bin der Weg ins Leere,
das blonde Sonnensinken,
die braune Hirtenflöte,
Das müde Abendwinken.

Folg mir nicht nach, mein Bruder—
mein Gehen ist Vergehen!
Es wird dein junger Glaube
An meinem Weh verwehen![59]

In the first stanza of Manger's poem, the Yiddish term *maarav* (from the Hebrew *ma'ariv*), meaning "the West," is translated by Ausländer into the more abstract, placeless "emptiness" (*Leere*). The emptiness that Ausländer replaces with "the West" suffuses her translation of this poem; even more, however, it marks the entire body of Ausländer's poetry. To be sure,

Manger's use of the Hebrew *maarav* is difficult to translate into German. However, Ausländer's translation of it as "emptiness" erases Manger's deliberate intertextual reference to Judah Ha'levi's well-known poem about exile: "My heart is in the east, but [as for me] I am at the very end / edge of the west" ("libi b'mizrach v'ani b'sof maarav"). Ha'levi's poem, one of the most emblematic poems about exile, expulsion, and longing for a forever unattainable home, is echoed not only in Manger's poetry but in the work of other Hebrew-language poets from the Bukovina such as Dan Pagis, Aharon Appelfeld, and Yehuda Amichai. Manger's poem, "I am the road to the West" ("Ikh bin der veg keyn maarav"), imagines a poetic subject who is not at home in "mizrach," that is, in the East, but rather in exile, en route to the West. That Rose Ausländer translated this poem into German is not an accident: as Ausländer translates Manger, she is at the same time participating in the poet's injunction to not follow him to the West. In translating Manger who admonishes us, in the second stanza, "Do not follow me, my dear friend, / my going is a passing" ("gey mir nisht nakh, mayn khaver — mayn geyn iz a fargeyn"), Ausländer goes with her friend ("khaver"), a going that is simultaneously a writing with and a translation that is a getting lost ("vergehen"). Ausländer moves with Manger on the path into the emptiness ("das Leere") that is simultaneously, through her translation, the West but also an emptiness that is a way into the lyrical and textual.

Reading Rose Ausländer reading Marianne Moore reading Nelly Sachs reading Ingeborg Bachmann reading Paul Celan reading . . .

The poetic correspondences between Ausländer and Manger are multivalent, based in their shared place of birth, shared experience of immigration, and also their shared translation back and forth between German and Yiddish. More precarious as "correspondence" are the other significant literary relationships the poet had with the American modernist poets E. E. Cummings, Wallace Stevens, and Marianne Moore. In particular, her friendship and literary correspondence with Marianne Moore are important; yet while Moore figures prominently in critical works about Ausländer, Ausländer is virtually unknown and absent in the scholarship on Moore.

At first glance, Rose Ausländer and Marianne Moore are the unlikeliest of correspondents or friends, yet in the years of Ausländer's second New York sojourn, there was an intensive exchange of poems and letters between the two poets. Beginning in 1956, when they met at a writer's conference at Wagner College, Ausländer felt a strong affinity with Marianne Moore. Moore was already a poet of great note by the time they met in 1956: she had won the Pulitzer, the Bollingen, the National Book Award, and the Gold Medal of the National Insittute of Arts and Letters, to name just a few; Ausländer, on the other hand, was an impoverished Jew in exile from Czernowitz, who worked a day job in the office of a shipping company. During the 1950s, Ausländer's poetic style became increasingly laconic and minimalist, whereas Moore's poems were elliptical and elaborately wrought, almost baroque, filled with countless citations from other texts. If Marianne Moore had a clear place within American letters, Rose Ausländer was not only an outsider—she was the proverbial exile who lived with suitcases packed.

In "a note on the notes" that Moore included in front of the footnotes to the *Complete Poems*, she wrote the following:

> Some readers suggest that quotation marks are disruptive of pleasant progress; others, that notes to what should be complete are a pedantry or evidence of an insufficiently realized task. But since in anything I have written, there have been lines in which the chief interest is borrowed, and I have not yet been able to outgrow this hybrid method of composition, acknowledgments seem only honest.[60]

The hybrid nature of Moore's poetry is analogous to Ausländer's constant moving between English and German, her ongoing translations of her own poems. In an unpublished fragment, "The Poet in Two Worlds," Ausländer describes three possibilities for non-native speakers of English who were not born in the United States: "There is a third category of poets and writers who lead a double life; while they remain deeply rooted in their original language, they have also absorbed the new language, English, its idiomatic flavor, rhythms, images, word-magic to the extent of identifying themselves with this language-world."[61] It was, primarily, the

poetry of Marianne Moore that Ausländer absorbed. In a poem entitled
"Marianne Moore," published in 1978, she addresses both Moore and
Wallace Stevens:

One hour may change the world
(it happened many times before)
backward forward inward
or toward
Marianne's minute humor
Wallace's metaphysical magic.[62]

In another poem, "Miracle," the poet writes:

I am an ear
and must record
the dreams I hear:
A rainbow word
a genuine smile?
the wonder of star
Wallace Stevens
Marianne Moore
And so forth.[63]

In a postcard to Ausländer from July 20, 1956, Moore writes that "Rose
Ausländer . . . has a gift for verbal invention, a propensity to reverie that is
synonymous with reverence, poetic sensibility and depth."[64] In a Christmas letter from 1958 Moore writes, "A rare scene. You send me, Rose—
reverence, worship with the hand of the infant Christ on the head of
the king in his raiment of violet, white, and gold. And your wishes—for
health, inspiration and joy I wish you every blessing, Rose. One of my
rewards for going to Wagner college. May 1959 bless you and you have
many a joy. Marianne Moore."[65] A few years later (June 3, 1962), Moore
writes, in response to Ausländer's invitation to attend one of her readings:
"I know your poems have joy and reverence in them . . . and I love German, that soulful tongue."[66]

In 1956 Ausländer sent Marianne Moore three poems dedicated to
Moore: "Der Urbaum," "Overmore," and "The Door." Moore responded

with a letter that cites from all three, making a collage in the middle of the poem with the following lines drawn from the three poems:

Der Urbaum in mir in jeder Kreatur
Overmore
Overmoon
and then
The door
Not the thing of wood[67]

Moore wrote in her letter: "Unique work that is inward private very personal beauty . . . I am to have the poems; I think you mean that. I treasure them. The German words—so enticing and the English their real counterpart?"[68] Yet despite the compliments bestowed on her friend, Moore urged Ausländer, repeatedly, to return to writing in German. The English that Ausländer gravitated to showed that she was, as she herself noted, living a bifurcated life in two languages. The poem "Overmore" begins

Light wrapped in rays.
Baskets praise.
Pears plums grapes praise.[69]

The poem is written in a number of poetic registers; Ausländer also translated the poem into German, yet as is often the case with Ausländer's translations of her own poems into and out of English, the English poem is a distinctly different poem than the German one. Moore was herself a translator (of La Fontaine's *Fables* and, with Elizabeth Mayer, Adalbert Stifter's novella *Bergkristall*). Ausländer's translations of poems to Marianne Moore exist in a sort of gray zone, an in-between space between languages in which it is impossible to determine which is the original and which the copy—these poems hover between translation and original, between present and past, between language and silence, remembering and forgetting. This instability of language and the movement between original and copy creates the sense of a disfigured language that is reminiscent of Moore's poetic project of citation from multiple languages and sources so that the referential meaning of any given word is impossible to locate. This is seen most explicitly in Ausländer's poem "The Door," one of the poems dedicated to Moore.

Another difficulty in considering these two poets together is Moore's stature as the foremost American woman modernist poet of mid-century America who was decidedly American: not only her fabled love of baseball and her antiauthoritarian claims against poetry ("I, too, dislike it"), but the absence of European culture, especially in contrast to Eliot and Pound. For instance, the citations in her work, in contrast to the multilingual references found throughout the work of Eliot, are exclusively American; even more, they consist of conversations, letters, or texts from marginally known authors. In her poem "To a Snail," Moore elaborates on the poetic principle of "compression," lauding the snail's "contractibility" and "compression," "the principle that is hid."[70] Indeed, it is the veiled that marks Moore's work, including the many unattributed citations throughout her poems. In this, Moore is the quintessentially "unmarked" poet, asserting an American poetic identity through the process of concealment; this is in stark contrast to the always-marked Czernowitz poet Ausländer who lived between languages, between places.

Rose Ausländer's turn to writing in English, and her correspondence and friendship with Marianne Moore, show the pivotal role that living and, for a time, writing in English played for the poet.[71] Her work as self-translator led her to identify with other writers who lived a "double life," living abroad but writing in their native tongue. As she elaborates in the essay "The Poet in Two Worlds":

> While they remain deeply rooted in their original language, they have also absorbed the new language, English, its ideomatic [sic] flavor, rhythms, imagery, word-magic to the extent of identifying themselves with this language-world. As a natural result, this poet is moved to express his poetic experiences also in English.[72]

A bit later in the essay, she recounts how

> suddenly and unexpectedly, about ten years ago, I had the irresistible urge to write an English poem, and did so. With shorter or longer intervals, I have been writing English poetry ever since, and during my "English periods" I am—with a few exceptions—

unable to write in German, and vice versa. I have become, in this respect, a "split personality," shifting from one language plane to the other.[73]

Despite this unambiguous articulation of what it means to write in two languages and to live in exile in a language different from one's mother tongue, Rose Ausländer does not explain *why* it is she began to write in English. It is significant that during the periods in which she wrote in English she was unable to write in German. And yet she does not write about her self-translations, leaving scholars and readers of her work uncertain about how she navigated through the many poems she wrote and their constant movement back and forth between English and German. Here, it is clear that Ausländer operated in a different poetic and philosophical register than Raymond Federman, for instance, for whom the creative act of writing "always proceeds in the dark" and the act of translating, "also a creative act, is performed in the light."[74]

Reading Nelly Sachs Reading Paul Celan Reading Rose Ausländer

To read Moore and Celan and Ausländer, tangentially, it is imperative to also bring in the voice of Nelly Sachs, the German-language poet who emigrated to Sweden in 1940 and who received the Nobel Prize for Literature in 1966. Sachs's reverential and soaring incantations to trauma, memory, and the poetic invite, as a counter-force, Marianne Moore's arch statement of poetic disavowal, of complete nonbelief: "Poetry: I, too, dislike it."[75] Marianne Moore's autocratic, self-ironic pronouncement about poetry (which she wrote and then rewrote countless times) seems worlds apart not only from the poetry of Ausländer but also from the oeuvre of Nelly Sachs, a poet consumed not with Moore's sardonic voice but rather with the voices of "the people Israel" for whom, she claimed, she spoke. Yet Moore, in the many revisions she made over five decades to her poem about poetry, compressing and condensing it to three lines in the final version, in 1967, does in the end give her readers a reprieve from the sardonic: "Poetry: I too dislike it. / Reading it, however, with a perfect contempt for it, one discovers in it, after all, a place for the genuine."[76]

Sachs's place in the canon of Holocaust poetry, and particularly in the body of work written in German, is uncontested. She occupies, along with Celan—often referred to as her "poetic brother" or *Dichterbruder*—and Rose Ausländer, a key position. And yet, the pathos in so many of her poems—bordering, in the words of Aris Fioretos, on a kind of "Holocaust kitsch"—is also reminiscent of the work of Ausländer.[77] Sachs is generally read as the poet of reconciliation, of forgiveness, the poet who, when given the Peace Prize of the German Booksellers' Association in 1965, was lauded by the West German president Heinrich Lübke for giving a "German voice to the Jewish dead," thus serving an official function as poetic suture to the rupture between German and Jew.[78] Sachs participated in this role willingly, and her oeuvre has only served to confirm the prevalent view of Sachs that Fioretos wryly notes: "in the beginning was the Shoah."[79]

The paradigmatic example of a poetic exchange about Jewishness and the poetic is the dialogue and correspondence between Paul Celan and Nelly Sachs. And it is in this correspondence that the differences between the two are most apparent: Sachs was a believer, Celan a skeptic. In fact, the existence of the correspondence with Sachs elevates her, in a similar way that the even briefer exchange and encounter between Celan and Rose Ausländer has served to elevate Ausländer.

Reading Nelly Sachs, then, tangentially, as part of a contiguous Jewish literary history, is to read her not simply as a poet who laments "Oh the Chimneys" ("O die Schornsteine," that is, as the Holocaust poet par excellence) or the poet who stated that "it is entirely unimportant that it was me who wrote all this, it is the voice of the Jewish people speaking and that is all."[80] Rather, to read Nelly Sachs tangentially is to read away from her status as representative German Jewish/Holocaust poet, and instead to attempt to place her in the ever-shifting landscape of German Jewish text after 1945.[81]

To read Sachs tangentially means, then, to read Paul Celan reading Ingeborg Bachmann reading Nelly Sachs. There is a large body of poems inspired by Sachs and dedicated to her by a number of (largely but not exclusively Jewish) postwar German-speaking poets: Paul Celan, Ingeborg Bachmann, Rose Ausländer, Johannes Bobrowski, Hans Magnus Enzensberger, and Hilde Domin. The German word for such poetry is, aptly, *Nachdichtung*, with the German preposition *nach* meaning both "after" and "towards." Thus the *Nachdichtungen* to Nelly Sachs is a *writ-*

ing after, a writing that suggests the link between writing and death and which carries the trace of the poet to whom the poem is dedicated, but also a writing that suggests the poetic text can bear the reader (and the writer) into the future.

The correspondences—epistolary, affective, poetic—between Sachs and Celan have been documented and interpreted, with the affinities and the points of divergence between the two poets parsed at length. Paul Celan, with whom Sachs corresponded for nearly sixteen years, was critical of Sachs's official position as the Jewish woman writer "per se." In a letter written in verse to his wife in 1965, Celan writes that the German literary establishment has used Sachs as a poet of "forgiveness," as a "Jew per se."[82] For Celan, this status meant that Sachs was not only misread but instrumentalized by the German public (however much she willingly took on this role). The other key poetic exchange about the role of Jewishness and text is found in the first poems Celan read by Sachs, "Chorus of Stones" and "Chorus of the Orphans," from the thirteen-poem cycle from *In the Houses of Death* (*In den Wohnungen des Todes*, 1948). Celan's own poem "Whichever stone you lift you lay bare" (from *Schwelle zu Schwelle*, 1955) is taken from a line of Sachs's poem "Chorus of Stones": "We stones, . . . whoever lifts us / lifts millions of memories."[83] As Vivian Liska has noted, for Celan "every act of speaking that does not aporetically take itself back, that does not mark its own impossibility and presumptuously claims to actually revive the dead by speaking in their name, implies for Celan a denial of the destruction."[84]

The readings of Celan and Sachs have served to schematize both poets, creating a trajectory of German Jewish writing in which Sachs has been read as the conventional poet who believes in the transcendent possibility of art, and who held to a belief in God and to Jewish identity, and her *Dichterbruder* Celan has been the embodiment of the poet who ruptured language, thought, and belief with (perhaps paradoxically) exquisite beauty. Sachs's poems are filled with references to Jewish text, Jewish traditions, Jewish history, and work within a poetic idiom that is still able to assert an identity as Jewish poet in a way that Celan usually (although not always) resists. This dichotomous reading of Sachs and Celan creates a narrative of continuity that is simultaneously discontinuous, as it suggests a move from an illusory wholeness to an exquisitely crafted rupture of German Jewish writing. The poem that famously highlights this contrast is Celan's "Zürich zum Storchen," in which he chronicles their meeting in Zurich in May 1960 (the Day of the Ascension) as Sachs was en route to receive the Droste Prize of the city of Meersburg: "Our talk was of Too Much, of / Too Little. Of Thou / and Yet-Thou, of / clouding through brightness, of / Jewishness, of your God."[85] And later in the poem, "Our talk was of your God, I spoke / against him . . ."[86]

Rather than highlighting and reifying these nonetheless foundational differences between the two poets, I suggest instead that we place Nelly Sachs in the ongoing debates about the status of German Jewish text (or about Jewish text in Germany) in order to consider the ways in which Sachs's work forms part of the complex repatternings of Jewish text and the trace of Jewish history in Germany. For in doing this, rather than schematizing the difference between the poets—in particular their relationship to both language and silence—we could begin to read Sachs, as Jewish poet, against the grain of her postwar German reception (as the "Jew per se"), enabling new readings of her work that open up the borders between her and other German Jewish poets. The affinities between the two poets are present in the letters. In a letter from 1958, Celan writes to Sachs to reassure her "with what words, with what silence?—that you must not believe that words like yours can remain unheard."[87] It is in fact the interplay between language and silence that marks the correspondences between the two poets, that point in which, as Celan also notes in a letter to Sachs in July 1960, her darkness is his darkness too: "You are feeling better—I know. I know it, because I can feel that the evil that has been haunting you—that haunts me also—is gone again, has shrunk back into the nothingness where it belongs; because I feel and know that it can never come again, that it has dissolved into a little heap of nothing."[88]

It is this shared point of touching—the tangential and contiguous between Sachs and Celan, and not the counterpoint—that indicates how we should read Sachs and Celan; it also suggests a way of reading Rose Ausländer with Sachs and Celan. In the final two lines of "Chorus of Things Left Behind," Sachs calls for the abandoned "things" earlier in the poem (the jug in the rubble, the half-burned candle, the shoes) to be "read" like "reversed writing in the mirror": "So read us like a reversed writing in / the mirror, / first the dead thing and then the / dust of man."[89]

Calling to mind the "reversed" (*verkehrt* can also mean "wrong") nature of Hebrew script, Sachs inscribes the abandoned objects into a new form of Jewish textuality that can emerge from the rubble of history. At the same time, the image of the "reversed script" suggests the rabbinic exegetical technique of *akbash*, in which the letters of the Hebrew alphabet are reversed (so that the first letter is the last, etc.), forming a code. It is the very materiality—the "things" earlier described in the poem—of the sign, of language, that is the trace of what has been destroyed. As Vivian Liska observes about Sachs's use of the metaphors of reading and writing in this poem:

> The objects left behind now want to be *read* as signs and translated into a new reality. The revival cannot take place through direct invocation, but only by way of the detour of reading the traces that lead in a slow, groping journey backward to the past.[90]

It is in this plea to be "read like a reversed writing in the mirror" that Sachs affirms the necessity of the backward trail of Jewish text.

Finally, let me offer two tangential readings of Sachs that help move us toward a contiguous reading of the poet that places her in a poetic world of greater indeterminacy than the usual readings her poems invite. First, Celan's inscription to Sachs of the offprint of his Emily Dickinson translations contains a quatrain from Dickinson: "who dwelled in Possibility / a fairer house than prose. / More numerous of windows / Superior of doors."[91] That Celan and Dickinson both dwell in the subjunctive of possibility, in a poetics of contingency and undecidability, bleeds into the work of Nelly Sachs and, by extension, Ausländer. And finally, there is Ingeborg Bachmann's reading of Sachs in her poem "You Words," dedicated to "Nelly Sachs, friend and poet, in reverence," in which she begins with the incantation, "You words, arise, follow me!" and then moves to, "The word / will only drag / other words behind it, / the sentence a sentence." Bachmann "reads" Sachs as achieving a kind of poetic indeterminacy—a dwelling in possibility—that echoes Paul Celan's relationship to language:

Into the highest ear
whisper, I say, nothing,

don't collapse into death,
let be, and follow me, not mild
nor bitter,
nor comforting,
without consolation
without significance,
and thus without symbols —

Most of all not this: the image
cobwebbed with dust, the empty rumble
of syllables, dying words.

Not a syllable,
you words![92]

The Banality of Grief: Ausländer, Warhol, and Serialist Poetics

Rose Ausländer has had an iconic status as both Holocaust and exile poet,
but, at the same time, her enormous body of work poses a problem for
the literary scholar in that many of her poems are deceptively simple and
often quite banal expressions of loss and hope. The critic must resurrect
questions of valuation that have long since been buried to read into the
banality of countless lines of poetry an indeterminacy of meaning. The
banality of Ausländer's poetry expresses the banality of grief: the echoes
and repetitions, and the centrality of translation within the oeuvre, provide points of entry to rethink the relationship between poetry and banality amid the shifting configurations of the meaning of Czernowitz. In
reflecting on the role of banality and the interplay between banality and
sublimity in the ongoing circulation of grief and mourning that marks
our (forever still) post-Holocaust age, I hope to add an additional layer
to thinking about trauma, art, mourning, and banality in all its guises.

Ausländer's evocation of the link between poetry and loss in the poem
"Age" is a reminder of the fundamental ways in which her work participates in the theoretical and critical discourse about mourning and
poetic text circulating in literary and Holocaust studies. The task for

readers of Ausländer's poetry is to read into the simplicity of countless lines of poetry an indeterminacy of meaning. These poems are simple, and also remarkably banal. The task, therefore, in reading Ausländer is to make the banal as phenomenon interesting, to see it as yet another symptom of trauma, such as the repetition found throughout her verse: in other words, Rose Ausländer's poems *express* the banality of grief.

This suggests that tropes and figurations of loss and grieving have, by their repetition, themselves become banal. The trope of unspeakability hovers between the assertion of the unrepresentability and incommensurability of the Holocaust on the one hand, and on the other the insistence on new ways of configuring the possibility of representation. Ausländer's poems—more than 2,600 of them—are expressive of a pathos and a banality that unlike Andy Warhol's self-proclaimed descent into the banal ("there is nothing there") are entirely unselfreflexive and "unintentionally" banal.

The starting point for these reflections on the "banality of grief" is Hannah Arendt's *Eichmann in Jerusalem: A Report on the Banality of Evil*.[93] While the phrase "the banality of evil" has migrated from the specificity it bears in Arendt's text to serve as a tautological equation between evil and the mundane, Arendt offers us the chance to push the aesthetic challenges posed by debates within Holocaust studies and German Jewish studies about authenticity, representation, and unspeakability. Significantly, Arendt characterizes the banality of evil as "word-and-thought-defying," as rooted in a stupidity so extraordinary that it is simply banal.[94] It is precisely the absence of thought and deliberation, the absence of "artfulness," that for Arendt links evil with banality. But what might it mean to link banality with grieving, with mourning, and with loss?[95] Can we probe the contours of banality and art to navigate the endless circulation in critical Holocaust discourse about representation, figuration, Holocaust aesthetics, and German Jewish sites of memory? My aim is to find a way to take in Ausländer's banal yet tremendously popular "Holocaust" poems, and to think about the relationship between figuration and abstraction, between memory and "fact."

In making the link between Ausländer's poetry of banality and the serialism of Andy Warhol, the first question that arises is whether banality can be recuperated as part of the process of working-through—as part of the repetition that must take place in order to move past trauma. These repetitions of loss can be seen as the "banality of grief" (and the grief of banality), the tropes of repetition and circulation, the echoes of grief and mourning that mark remembrance of the Shoah in Germany today (and that circulate between the United States and Germany), and the echo of earlier texts on grieving and banality.

The master statesman on boredom and banality is Warhol: as he wrote, "if I'm going to sit and watch the same thing I saw the night before, I don't want it to be essentially the same—I want it to be exactly the same. Because the more you look at the same exact thing, the more the meaning goes away, and the better and emptier you feel."[96] It is precisely this struggle with meaning and the desire to evacuate the artwork from any sense of redemption (through emotion) that can help make the poetry of Rose Ausländer more compelling.

Germany itself never produced major figures of pop art. However, Warhol exerted a strong influence in Germany and on the debates that stretched from the United States to Germany by figures such as Clement Greenberg, Arendt, Adorno, Enzensberger, and Marcuse on kitsch, the culture industry, consumerism, ideology, and the avant-garde; these debates straddled American and European/German culture.[97] Andreas Huyssen has characterized American pop of the 1960s as a "colorful death mask" of a classical avant-garde shattered by Hitler and Stalin, thus locating pop, and its reception in Germany, as part of both the student movement and the critique of bourgeois art sparked by Adorno and Marcuse and championed by Enzensberger and others.[98]

In contrast to poems that position themselves as spaces of closure, coherence, and legibility, in which the event of the Holocaust is conveyed on the experiential level, post-Holocaust poetic text that does the opposite is my focus here: elegiac texts that create what has been termed an "aesthetics of uncertainty," a sustained reflection on the indeterminacy of meaning and the uncertainty of the relationship between banality and art.[99] Elegy, of course, is a literary form that exceeds any strict taxonomy; there are a wide variety of texts (literary, visual, sound) that are elegiac meditations on loss and absence. There is elegiac awareness of the loss, through slippage, of the boundaries between the banal and the sublime.

Paradoxically, Rose Ausländer's positive reception is tied to the fundamental banality of her work. Her poems forbid a reading process that aims to establish a chain of signification of the allusive (and elusive). Hers is a body of poetry that despite its repetition and echo of its own lament about the impossibilities of speaking the unspeakable, forbids an "aesthetics of uncertainty," attempting instead—reiteratively, finally impossibly—to create textual spaces of epistemological certainty. Indeed, the critical task in reading a poet such as Ausländer is to read allusively when the text does not suggest allusion, when—in contrast to the belligerent transparency of pop art—it is rooted in mimetic notions of the referent and of representability. While the presence of repetition and poetic echo in Ausländer's work can be tied to a traumatic reenactment in text, in which the trauma is returned to, textually, over and over again, it buries its own potential allusive pull in a poetics of banality.

The repetition that forms the basis for Andy Warhol's series of photographic silkscreens, which were well received in West Germany in the late 1960s, consists of reproductions of reproductions, of echoes of echoes, displacing any notion of the original, dismantling not only the existence of high vs. low art or art as sacralizing object, but even the possibility of it. Pop proclaims that there is nothing outside the text (the canvas, the silkscreen, etc.), insisting, as Roland Barthes says, instead on "the banal conformity of representation to the thing represented."[100] For Barthes, the very banality of pop art lies in its rediscovery of the "Double," or the once-mythic theme of the "Doppelgänger": "in the productions of Pop Art, the Double is harmless—has lost all maleficent or moral power, neither threatens nor haunts: The Double is Copy, not a Shadow: *beside*, not *behind*: a flat, insignificant, hence irreligious Double."[101]

Pop art's creation of layers of reproduction, where the "real" is untraceable to any original, marks its affinity with the ideas of postmemory circulating in Holocaust studies. Postmemory takes as a given that the nature of memory itself is mediated, never transparent, an "imprint," as Liss terms it, of its prior representations. This notion of postmemory insists on the impossibility of a transparent relationship to the past and to language, announcing itself instead as mediated between the various layers and levels of memory—experiential *and* textual. Postmemory, as I am using the term, is memory that cannot be traced back to the Ur-text of experience, but rather unfolds as part of an ongoing process of intertextuality and translation and a constant interrogation of the nature of the "original."

Pop art provides the earlier textual layer to post-Holocaust art that foregrounds its own impossibility as art object and challenges the representation of history and memory. Like Eco's observations about the relationship between the "real" and the fake in the wax museum, and the spectator's desire for the reproduction of art that can substitute, exceed, and challenge our desire for the "original," "post-Holocaust" texts (literary and visual) take up Eco's challenge to the notion of the "original" in art. Holocaust remembrance in these texts is a postmemory that "after Auschwitz" cannot be traced back to an originary moment of the Holocaust itself, but rather circulates endlessly as representation, as melancholy, as elegiac repetition. Challenging the viability and possibility of history, knowledge, and subjectivity, these texts are marked by meta-reflection about the Holocaust, memory, and the limits of art. Most significantly, in their attempt to problematize the limits of representing the Holocaust, they become elegies to the once-supposed viability of Holocaust representation.

In 1963, in response to the first appearance of the da Vinci *Mona Lisa* at the Metropolitan Museum, Andy Warhol did a series of paintings entitled, variously, *Mona Lisa, Thirty Are Better Than One*, and then later, in 1978–80, another series including *Four Mona Lisas, Four White on White Mona Lisas, 63 White Mona Lisas*, and *Double Mona Lisa*.[102] Warhol's response to this cultural, social event — *Mona Lisa* at the Met — is a response not to the painting as painting, that is, art as art, but to the event of the painting (the most famous, most reproduced, and most mocked painting), to the event of "Art," and to the event of the *Mona Lisa* being shown for the first time in New York. By proclaiming that "thirty are better than one" and reproducing what is already a reproduction, Warhol breaks and manipulates modernity's adherence to notions of the original and the authentic. Yet at the same time, to declare the presence of banality in this way is to utilize a shock effect — reductio ad absurdum — that is ultimately tied to modernist notions of the bounds of transgression in art as much as to what art can and cannot do. Benjamin Buchloh argues that Warhol's technique of the photographic silkscreen enabled him to break pictorial and representational boundaries by extracting the image and foregrounding its reproducibility, while at the same time remaining firmly within the boundaries of the pictorial framework.[103] The tension that Buchloh identifies between breaking and preserving pictorial space is what constitutes the possibly elegiac nature of these images, creating their link to a post-Holocaust aesthetics that can be traced to the early 1960s developments in pop art.

Warhol's break with the aesthetic strategy of "appropriation and simulation" insists on the connection between art and banality. The tension between appropriation and simulation is also found in much contemporary art that grapples with questions of representation and the "original" after the Holocaust, notably in the controversial *Mirroring Evil* exhibit at the Jewish Museum that exposed once again the fault lines between kitsch and art. Lisa Saltzman's observations in the catalog to *Mirroring Evil* bring this into focus:

> In the wake of Pop, art no longer cloaks its continuous aura of originality and creation. Any claims to beauty, to sublimity, give way to a posture of studied sophistication and ironic detachment. Any possibility of parody is lost to its semblance as pastiche. Art after Pop is predicated on the postmodern convention, if not conviction, that each act of visual representation is but one more act of representation, repetition, or reproduction of a set of culturally available and assimilable signs. It feeds relentlessly, unabashedly, and conspicuously upon the virtual archive of images that constitutes its present.[104]

Saltzman's précis links postmodern aesthetics and post-Holocaust art, challenging the relationship between referent and simulacrum in contemporary art. Warhol's work contains traces of the referential (referents to iconographic themes or to real things in the world) as well as an insistence on image as simulacrum—images that represent other images in a seemingly endless chain of signification.[105] The *Mona Lisa* series suggests the elegiac notion of the loss of true art, but a more suggestive link between pop and post-Holocaust art is Warhol's *Marilyn Monroe* silkscreens. Like the *Mona Lisa* series, these photographed silkscreens take the object—here, a photo of Marilyn Monroe—and reproduce it again and again, creating an elegiac visual text that mourns not only Marilyn Monroe, whose death in 1962 sparked Warhol's works, but also the photographic event of her fame. In thus creating an elegiac text that references a popular iconic figure, Warhol prefigures the preoccupation with reproducibility—the trace of the photograph—that has come to play so central a role in Holocaust art and aesthetics in the past few decades.

Post-Holocaust art must, in this sense, be seen as post-pop, in that pop art, even when described by Peter Bürger as neo–avant-garde, constitutes a definitive break with mimetic ideas of representation. Pop makes conscious play with the idea of the original, an assertion that echoes Benjamin's but moves it in a different direction: *Thirty Are Better Than One* marks a new moment in the age(s) of mechanical reproducibility, a vision of modernity that is, as Warhol would have it, significantly "better." Warhol's ironic nod to a system of valuation (good, better, best) of Art forces a reconsideration of value—that long-since trumped concern of humanism. In the wake of Warhol, art carries with it the echoes and traces of past art and history, mediating the role of the everyday and the question of banality. To highlight repetition is to bring us both back to, and away from, the certainty of anything, including the notion of the original.

Warhol's technique of the photographic silkscreen in the *Mona Lisa* and *Marilyn* series is a radical insistence that the origin of the artwork lies in the found objects of mass culture (*Mona Lisa* in its reproduced states, Jackie O, Imelda Marcos) ripped off from high art. Yet it is also important to note that many of these images gain their force by the absence, and sometimes literal death, of the referent. Warhol's own statements about death echo, oddly, Eichmann's deluded "I shall never forget them." In his *Philosophy of Andy Warhol: From A to B and Back Again*, Warhol writes the following about death: "I don't believe in it because you're not around to know it's happened. I can't say anything about it because I'm not prepared for it."[106] A Hal Foster essay on Warhol's work stresses the break in subjectivity marked by what he calls Warhol's "demurral" on death, arguing that the passage is the linguistic marker of a Lacanian "missed encounter" that suggests shock and trauma.[107] Reading against the grain of Warhol criticism, Foster dispenses with the obvious opposition between referent and simulacrum in Warhol's work to focus instead on what he terms the "traumatic realism" that marks Warhol as artist and suggests that repetition in Warhol "is not reproduction in the sense of representation (of a referent) or simulation (of a pure image, a detached signifier). Rather, repetition serves to screen the real understood as traumatic. But this very need points to the real, and it is at this point that the real ruptures the screen of repetition."[108] Stressing the difference between *wiederholen* and *reproduzieren* (repetition and reproduction) for Freud and Lacan, Foster reads Warhol's "Death in America" texts as both "referential and simulacral, connected and disconnected, affective and affectless, critical and complacent." Warhol's encounter with and elaboration of death as media spectacle (plane crashes, car crashes, etc.) and as cultural event (Marilyn Monroe) results in the repetition of images that are not just reproductions based in mourning, but offer instead, in their repetition, visual proof of the impossibility of mastery over death: a sustained melancholic fixation on the lost object.

Warhol's most famous pop images can be read, in this account, as commentary on mass consumption and the elevation of the banal to art (thus dissolving more definitively than earlier avant-garde movements the distinction between high art and low). More significantly, however, they can be seen as traumatic reenactments of moments of cultural loss. Huyssen notes how pop art's reception in West Germany coincided with the student movement and the general cultural critique of bourgeois aesthetics, notably in the work of Marcuse and Adorno. While this certainly "explains" the place that pop art could occupy without much trouble in German culture in the 1960s, it keeps the discussion on pop centered on the question of whether the movement affirmed or critiqued consumerism and bourgeois values. Yet it is precisely the reproduction and repetition—the excess of repetition—of these series (Mona Lisa, Marilyn Monroe, Campbell soup cans, Brillo soap boxes) that link them to the relationship between repetition and trauma. The trauma that lies at the center of the repetition of images moves the debate about pop art, and its possible link to the idea of postmemory, beyond the impasse on the uses and abuses of the culture industry.

This is, then, the dilemma facing our reading of the work of Rose Ausländer: whether to recuperate banality as an instance of the necessity for and the impossibility of working-through, or to challenge the aesthetic limitations of any representation of the Holocaust. By marking these repetitions of loss as the "banality of grief" (and the grief of banality), we are confronted with a new way of thinking about tropes of repetition and circulation, and the echoes of grief and mourning that mark remembrance of the Shoah in Germany today (and that circulate between the

United States and Germany). We also hear the echo of earlier texts on grieving and banality.

The centrality of translation as trope and as practice in contemporary critical discourse has significant consequences for the translation of Jewish memory in Czernowitz and in east-central Europe, but also in Germany. Translating Czernowitz and reading the work of Rose Ausländer through the prism of the network of translated texts is one layer in the palimpsest of memory texts. In thus rethinking the status of Czernowitz as Jewish city and Rose Ausländer as Czernowitz Jewish writer, I hope to make space for new notions of text, rooted not in the relationship between language and place or language and national origin, but rather between language in its multiple forms and the non-place defined by this proliferation of textuality.

Epilogue

In September 2016, after having written about Czernowitz as imaginary literary space, I finally made a trip there. While touring the city and its many sites of Jewish literary commemoration, I visited the house of Paul Celan. However, the house that is marked as Celan's house—vulytsya Saksahans'koho 5, complete with elaborately renovated Jugendstil facade and a commemorative plaque to the city's best-known poet—is not the actual house. The house where Celan was born and lived as a boy is next door, vulytsya Saksahans'koho 3, a modest building that remains unmarked. I like to think of the two houses—the one renovated for tourist consumption, the other more modest and unmarked—as another signpost to the complex interplay between the real and the literary. To visit Czernowitz today is to grapple with this very collision between real and imaginary literary spaces, and also to consider the reengagement of Jewish memory in contemporary east-central Europe.

It is this collision and my insistence on the mutability of textuality and of Jewishness that are at the very heart of *The Translated Jew*. This book's insistence on the capaciousness of Jewish text—its very nature as polysemic and polylingual—is present throughout the preceding chapters. One mode of this reengagement was to tackle the thorny issue of banality in the work of Czernowitz's second most celebrated poet, Rose Ausländer, and to attempt to read her work through the lens of serialism and pop art. Yet as a major German-language Jewish poet who moved between German and English, between Czernowitz and New York, Rose

Ausländer is recast as emblematic for the translated Jews who make up this book.

To translate Jewish memory in Germany is to listen to the shouts and murmurs that characterize the circulation of memory, postmemory, and text that exceed the referent of "German" or "Jewish." *The Translated Jew* locates these abrasions, marks, and echoes of "the Jewish" that are always present as trace within German text. In the ruin, literal and symbolic, of German (and German Jewish) history, the "Jewish" is the sign that is always implicit, present in its absence; in this way, German writing is always already "Jewish." It is precisely this Jewishness that I have sought to uncover and "translate," moving from the particular instance of German Jewish text to think about a new way of "doing" Jewish studies.

In *The Translated Jew*, I have tried to add to the burgeoning discourse in the fields of German studies and Jewish studies, and literary studies more generally, on transnational Jewish cultures in the European context by addressing several significant gaps in existing scholarship. First, this book challenges the primacy of any national literature or culture as it insists, throughout, on the notion of translation as a way to displace models of national, religious, or ethnic origin. Second, it deliberately privileges a comparative model of literary and cultural study that brings together writers and artists from literary and artistic traditions that are traditionally regarded as disparate.

Finally, the focus on artists and writers who are not usually brought together challenges the rigid orthodoxies of national literatures that are still somewhat surprisingly intact. The complex intertextual reworking found in the poems and installations of conceptual poets and artists such as Anne Blonstein, Ulrike Mohr, Alan Sondheim, and Daniel Blaufuks are but one example of this attempt to move outside the margins not only of German Jewish literature, but of the borderlines between art and poem. For instance, although Alan Sondheim's work is known in the admittedly small circle of cyberpoetics and experimental poetry, he is virtually unknown in German studies. Similarly, the work of the visual and media artist Daniel Blaufuks, which engages in important ways with the novels of Georges Perec and W. G. Sebald, has up to now been relatively obscure in Anglo-American circles. The extended discussions in *The Translated Jew* of the work of the experimental poet Anne Blonstein and conceptual artist Ulrike Mohr also help to delineate new art practices of German Jewish cultures "outside the margins."

The Translated Jew: German Jewish Culture outside the Margins begins with a retelling of the joke my mother would tell again and again
of the cannibal on the Air France plane. My mother's anxious retelling
of this racist joke reflects, in many respects, the complex intertwining of
French Jewish cultures with the legacies of French colonialism that Hélène Cixous similarly returns to again and again in her memoir writings,
as she obsessively writes about the impossibility and also the necessity of
"speaking the J." If my mother's cannibal joke, and Cixous's insistence on
thinking and writing "the Jewish" beyond the margins, was my starting
place in thinking about the vicissitudes of translation and "the Jewish,"
the chapters that followed gave new ways to imagine the spaces created
when the German Jewish moves outside and can inhabit the margins. In
the first chapter, I highlight a provisional art space near the former Berlin
wall, the Sculpture Park, which no longer exists. Similarly, my turn to
the simultaneously visible and invisible, legible and illegible lines that
demarcate the *eruv* serves as a blueprint for the multidirectionality and
polysemy of Jewish spaces and cultural spheres that are central to this
project. The *eruv* is more than a metaphor, though: this type of space
is real, as are Ulrike Mohr's trees that had grown randomly on the roof
of the East Berlin Palace of the Republic before being transplanted to
the Sculpture Park. Mohr's project with ruins and exiled trees enables a
creative reimagining of Jewish and German spaces.

In the second chapter, drawing on Dan Miron's idea of Jewish literary historiography as a series of "tangential" or "contiguous" readings, I
juxtapose a disparate set of writers who foreground, in various ways, the
process of translation. In the work of both the postwar German writer
W. G. Sebald and the bilingual French-American writer Raymond
Federman, the role of author/translator (and, in Federman's case, self-
translator) is paramount. The American Jewish writer Alfred Kazin and
Federman create complex works that mediate between the United States
and Europe, and the work of the German-Jewish Portuguese artist Daniel
Blaufuks reflects on Sebald and Georges Perec. Finally, Sebald, Federman, Kazin, and Blaufuks all open up a space for thinking about the
relationship between text and image. In bringing together writers who
do not usually occupy the same critical spaces—reading in the mode
that Dan Miron has called "tangential" or "contiguous"—I suggest the
multidirectional movement among the J and the Jew and the Jude and
the Juif. In other words, I read these three writers tangentially, as part of

a multidirectional matrix, as one more way of thinking about the complex relationship between Jewish writing and translation.

The third chapter expands the relationship between writing and translation to include contemporary experimental digital media, performance, and conceptual poets who all inhabit the border zone, "outside the margins," among Jewish, Holocaust, and German texts. At the center of this chapter is a discussion of the British Jewish poet Anne Blonstein; her 2010 project *correspondence with nobody* uses the rabbinic exegetical tradition of *notarikon*, in which each letter of a word is expanded to its own word. Blonstein creates a *notarikon* translation of Paul Celan's translations into German of Shakespeare's sonnets. This breathtaking work breaks the frame of national literatures, poetic forms, and the frame that has served to define Jewishness. In Blonstein's *notarikon* translation of Celan's translations of Shakespeare's sonnets, Shakespeare is then read through the prism of multiple translations, becoming perhaps even yet another "translated Jew."

The diverse set of literary and visual artworks that I discuss in this book's chapters all grapple with the aftermath of what Max Weber famously termed the *Entzauberung der Welt* (disenchantment of modern life). It is this very sense of disenchantment that opens the possibility of poetic renewal, of reimagining German Jewish culture that I set out as my task.

The original working title of this book was *The Translated Jew:* [. . .] *Outside the Margins*. My collapsing and erasing the very existence of the category of German Jewish by placing it in brackets, with an ellipsis, was to imagine—however institutionally impossible such a title would be—a title which is part and parcel of that same *Entzauberung*. To reimagine German Jewish culture outside the margins is, in the end, an attempt to reinvest, or to "re-enchant" a certain cultural space. It is the reimagining and the displacement of a cultural category—what we might want to call the German Jewish—that is at stake in this book.

NOTES

Introduction

1. Hélène Cixous, *Stigmata*, trans. Eric Prenowitz (New York: Routledge, 1998), 209. It is interesting that Cixous uses the most quintessential Christian bodily image—the stigmata—to explore her ideas about the cut, the mark of language. The stigmata are the marks on the body that are without language as such; however, no other cultural or historical event has produced more visual or textual artistic afterlives than the crucifixion of Christ.

2. This only works in French, with the echoes of Cixous's dialogue on language-as-rupture with Derrida, the "young Jewish saint" Cixous anoints in her *Portrait of Jacques Derrida as a Young Jewish Saint*. The title of Cixous's book is an (almost) direct citation of James Joyce's *A Portrait of the Artist as a Young Man*, minus the indefinite article at the beginning. Interestingly, the French translation of Joyce's novel omits the article *(Portrait d'un artiste)*, as does Cixous's original French title *(Portrait de Jacques Derrida en jeune saint juif)*, thus creating the English translation that omits the article *(Portrait of Jacques Derrida as a Young Jewish Saint)*. The elided "a" of the French translation of Joyce, which is continued into Cixous's book on Derrida and its translation into English, serves as another node in the network of translation and failed translations across languages and cultures.

3. See Todd Samuel Presner, *Mobile Modernity: Germans, Jews, Trains* (New York: Columbia University Press, 2007), 7.

4. Cixous, *Stigmata*, xii.

5. Hélène Cixous, *Portrait of Jacques Derrida as a Young Jewish Saint*, trans. Beverley Bie Brahic (New York: Columbia University Press, 2004), 3. For Cixous, with her family history "held between a double contradictory memory" of Germany and France and Algeria, German was the "idealizable" language of her dead relatives in Germany; she "asserts" but does not "believe" that her mother tongue was German, but she does this "to ward off the primacy of French." In 1954 she left Algeria for France, a country she goes to but where, in her words, she never "arrives": "it was by 'arriving' in France without finding my way or my self that I discovered: the chance of my genealogy and history arranged things in such a way that I would *stay passing*; in an originary way for me I am always passing by, in *passance*." Cixous, *Stigmata*, 227.

6. "I like the progressive form and the words that end in *–ance*. So much so that if I went toward *France* without mistrust, it is perhaps because of this ending which gives the present participle its lucky chance." Cixous, *Stigmata*, 227. See also Emily Apter's discussion of Cixous's "Algeriance" in *The Translation Zone* (Princeton, N.J.: Princeton University Press, 2006), 105.

7. See Gilles Deleuze and Felix Guattari, *Kafka: Toward a Minor Literature*, trans. Dana Polan (Minneapolis: University of Minnesota Press, 1986).

8. Deleuze and Guattari, *Kafka*, 26.

9. Deleuze and Guattari, *Kafka*, 19.

10. Deleuze and Guattari, *Kafka*, 26.

11. I am grateful to the thoughtful suggestion raised by one of the anonymous readers for Northwestern University Press about my omission of any discussion of German-Hebrew literary relations. As that reader noted, this lies outside my area of expertise; if I could work in any significant way with modern Hebrew, I would have incorporated the work of Yoel Hoffmann, an experimental poet whom I admire greatly. It is important as well to recognize the scholarship that has opened up the discussion about German culture and modern Israel in significant ways. See, in particular, Na'ama Rokem, *Prosaic Conditions: Heinrich Heine and the Spaces of Zionist Literature* (Evanston, Ill.: Northwestern University Press, 2013); Rachel Seelig, *Strangers in Berlin: Modern Jewish Literature between East and West, 1919–1933* (Ann Arbor: University of Michigan Press, 2016); and the work of Amir Eschel, Maya Barzilai, and Galili Shahar, among others.

12. See Jonathan Freedman, *Klezmer America: Jewishness, Ethnicity, Modernity* (New York: Columbia University Press, 2008), 38, where he articulates his notion of the "klezmerical" as the "syncretic, hybridizing engagement" of Jews with the majority culture.

13. Naomi Seidman, *Faithful Renderings: Jewish-Christian Difference and the Politics of Translation* (Chicago: University of Chicago Press, 2006), 8.

14. Seidman, *Faithful Renderings*, 8.

15. "Translation cannot be separated from the material, political, cultural, or historical circumstances of its production, . . . it in fact represents an unfolding of these conditions." Seidman, *Faithful Renderings*, 9.

16. Seidman, *Faithful Renderings*, 10.

17. See Talal Asad, *Formations of the Secular: Christianity, Islam, Modernity* (Stanford, Calif.: Stanford University Press, 2003). See also my discussion of the porousness between religious and secular cultures in Leslie Morris, "Placing and Displacing Jewish Studies: Notes on the Future of a Field," *PMLA* 125, no. 3 (2010): 764–73.

18. Jonathan Boyarin, *Thinking in Jewish* (Chicago: University of Chicago Press, 1996), 1.

19. Boyarin, *Thinking in Jewish*, 3.

20. Boyarin, *Thinking in Jewish*, 3.

21. Freedman, *Klezmer America*, 38.

22. See Hana Wirth-Nesher, *Call It English: The Languages of Jewish American Literature* (Princeton, N.J.: Princeton University Press, 2006), xii.

23. Dan Miron, *From Continuity to Contiguity: Toward a New Jewish Literary Thinking* (Stanford, Calif.: Stanford University Press, 2010).

24. Miron, *From Continuity to Contiguity*, 306–7.

25. Miron, *From Continuity to Contiguity*, 308.

26. Wirth-Nesher, *Call It English*.

27. Although Roth's place of birth is always mentioned in critical work on the author, he is nonetheless always approached as an American writer.

28. Raymond Federman, "A Voice within a Voice," in *Critifiction: Postmodern Essays* (Albany: SUNY Press, 1993), 76–84, 79.

29. Federman, "A Voice," 79.

30. Federman, "A Voice," 81.

31. Federman, "A Voice," 84.

32. Charles Bernstein, "Preface," in *Federman's Fictions: Innovation, Theory, and the Holocaust*, ed. Jeffrey R. Di Leo (Albany: SUNY Press, 2011), xii.

33. Bernstein, "Preface," xii.

34. Susan Suleiman has coined the term "1.5" generation to describe those—such as Perec and Federman—who survived as children. Suleiman uses the decimal point to "provoke" and create discomfort and defamiliarize the now-familiar term of "child survivor," asking, "What is a generation? What is a child? Are there in fact generations of the Holocaust, and in particular a generation of child survivors?" Susan Rubin Suleiman, "The 1.5 Generation: Thinking about Child Survivors and the Holocaust," *American Imago* 59, no. 3 (2002): 278.

35. Raymond Federman, "The Necessity and Impossibility of Being a Jewish Writer," 2004, http://www.federman.com/rfsrcr5.htm.

36. Federman, "Necessity."

37. Benjamin Schreier, *The Impossible Jew: Identity and the Reconstruction of Jewish American Literary History* (New York: New York University Press, 2015), 3.

38. Schreier, *The Impossible Jew*, 1.

39. Robert Alter, "What Jewish Studies Can Do," *Commentary*, October 1974, 71–76.

40. See, for instance, Jonathan Boyarin, *Thinking in Jewish* (Chicago: University of Chicago Press, 1996); and Vivian Liska, "Man kann verjuden," in *Against the Grain: Jewish Intellectuals in Hard Times*, ed. Ezra Mendelsohn, Stefani Hoffman, and Richard I. Cohen (New York: Berghahn, 2014), 198–212.

41. See Marc Shell and Werner Sollors, *The Anthology of Multilingual American Literature* (New York: New York University Press, 2000).

42. See Yasmin Yildiz, *Beyond the Mother Tongue: The Postmonolingual Condition* (New York: Fordham University Press, 2011).

43. The most noteworthy example of this kind of linguistic and cultural crossing is the figure of Yoko Tawada, a Japanese-born German writer who writes in both Japanese and German. For a beautiful self-reflexive work in which she explores the way in which language, place, and translation are inseparable from mobility and migration, see Yoko Tawada, *Überseezungen* (Tübingen: Konkursbuchverlag Claudia Gehrke, 2002).

44. Reflecting on how we all live "under the sign of Walter Benjamin" (not to mention under the sign of Susan Sontag), in particular his text *Theses on the Philosophy of History*, Jonathan Boyarin notes Daniel Boyarin's suggestion that the *Theses* be transformed into an oratorio and adds his own idea that they be written onto parchment by a scribe and chanted, like the Torah, each Saturday morning, thesis by thesis. Boyarin, *Thinking in Jewish*, 164.

45. Boyarin, *Thinking in Jewish*, 164.

46. Walter Benjamin. *The Arcades Project*, trans. Howard Eiland and Kevin McLaughlin (Cambridge, Mass.: Belknap, 1999), 456.

47. See Sigrid Weigel, "The Flash of Knowledge and the Temporality of Images: Walter Benjamin's Image-Based Epistemology and Its Preconditions in Visual Arts and Media History," *Critical Inquiry* 41 (Winter 2015): 347. Weigel draws on this aphorism to argue for the primacy of the visual in Benjamin's work.

48. See Rainer Nägele, *Echoes of Translation: Reading between Texts* (Baltimore, Md.: Johns Hopkins University Press), 1997.

49. Sigmund Freud, "Analysis Terminable and Interminable," *International Journal of Psychoanalysis* 18 (1937): 373–405.

50. Yosef Haim Yerushalmi, *Freud's Moses: Judaism Terminable and Interminable* (New Haven, Conn.: Yale University Press, 1993), 31.

51. Yerushalmi, *Freud's Moses*, 31.

52. See Amir Eshel, *Futurity: Contemporary Literature and the Quest for the Past* (Chicago: University of Chicago Press, 2013), 5.

53. Jack Zipes, "Oskar Panizza: The Operated German as Operated Jew," *New German Critique* 21 (1980): 61. See also Jack Zipes, *The Operated Jew: Two Tales of Anti-Semitism* (New York: Routledge, 1991).

54. Cited by Vivian Liska, "'Man kann verjuden': Paradoxes of Exemplarity," in *Against the Grain: Jewish Intellectuals in Hard Times*, ed. Ezra Mendelsohn, Stefani Hoffman, and Richard I. Cohen (New York: Berghahn, 2014), 205.

55. For a productive parsing of this often-cited epigraph, see Liska, "Man kann verjuden." Liska unpacks the complex debates about universality and particularity sparked not only by Celan's citation of Tsvetayeva, but also by the inclusion, in the preliminary notes to the *Meridian* speech, of the lines "Man kann zum Juden werden, wie man zum Menschen werden kann; Man kann verjuden . . ." Liska writes: "Celan links the process of *Verjudung* explicitly to the effect of poetry, its unsettling of common discourse, its power to transform the one it addresses, and its own openness to being transformed by the addressee through his or her experiences, language, situation, and individual reading. Celan enlists the power of poetic language in order to invert a murderous trope directed against the stranger into a metaphor of a positive self-estrangement performed by poetry itself." Liska, "Man kann verjuden," 207. Liska also has an insightful reading of the untranslatability of the word "verjuden": "Just as 'verjuden' ultimately cannot be translated without losing its concrete reference to the German myth reconstructed by Aschheim, so too, the only way in which the opening words of Celan's notes (where 'becoming Jewish' is identified with '*zum Menschen werden*') makes sense is if the universal 'Mensch' is understood in its particular Yiddish signification as an 'ethical human being.' Similarly, the German and uniquely German word '*verjuden*' is untranslatable and, at the same time, designates the very act, the ideal of translation: the becoming other while remaining 'unshakably itself.'" Liska, "Man kann verjuden," 207. See also Amir Eshel, "Paul Celan's Other: History, Poetics, and Ethics," *New German Critique* 91 (2004): 57–77.

Chapter 1

1. The Herrnfeld Theater was located in the Kommandantenstrasse 55–59; Kurt Singer used that same building, starting in 1935 with the premiere of Hebbel's *Judith*, until 1939 for a theater and concert space for his Jüdischer Kulturbund.

2. http://www.skulpturenpark.org. Skulpturenpark Berlin_Zentrum.

3. Sander Gilman, "Why and How I Study the German," *German Quarterly* 62 (1989): 192–207.

4. The so-called new Memory District that spans the Jewish Museum, Holocaust Memorial, and Topography of Terror contains within it, of course, the traces of Jewish memory and history that are inseparable from the urban fabric of the city of Berlin.

Yet, significantly, Karen Till's *The New Berlin: Memory, Politics, Place* (Minneapolis: University of Minnesota Press, 2006), which is meticulously researched and well argued, in the end presents a cityscape in which Jewish history, a vital trace in the layered staging and restaging of nationalism and modernity (Till, 5), becomes thinned—a part, certainly, of German history, but with the national structures of historical and cultural memory more prominent than the shakier edifices that constitute the encounters and mis-encounters of German Jewish history and memory.

5. See, in particular, Till, *The New Berlin*; James Young, *The Texture of Memory* (New Haven, Conn.: Yale University Press, 1993); and James Young, *At Memory's Edge: After-Images of the Holocaust in Contemporary Art and Architecture* (New Haven, Conn.: Yale University Press, 2000).

6. See Janet Wolff, *The Aesthetics of Uncertainty* (New York: Columbia University Press, 2008).

7. Marc Augé, *Non-Places: Introduction to an Anthropology of Supermodernity*, trans. John Howe (London: Verso, 1992).

8. Augé, *Non-Places*, 77–78.

9. Augé, *Non-Places*, 78.

10. Lutz Koepnick, "Forget Berlin," in "Sites of Memory," special issue, *German Quarterly* 74, no. 4 (Fall 2001): 345.

11. Fredric Jameson, "Hans Haacke and the Cultural Logic of Postmodernism," in *Hans Haacke: Unfinished Business*, ed. Brian Wallis (Cambridge, Mass.: MIT Press, 1986), 47.

12. One need only think of André Breton's erasure of Picabia's work in chalk in front of an audience in Paris in 1920, as well as Rauschenberg's erasure of De Kooning's work in 1953.

13. Thomas Crow, *Modern Art in the Common Culture* (New Haven, Conn.: Yale University Press, 1996), 135.

14. Alan Liu, "The Future Literary: Literature and the Culture of Information," in *Time and the Literary*, ed. Karen Newman, Jay Clayton, and Marianne Hirsch (New York: Routledge, 2002), 63.

15. Liu, "Future Literary," 69.

16. Liu, "Future Literary," 69.

17. It also cites, whether intentionally or not, Chris Marker's still photograph of the destroyed Arc de Triomphe in Paris in his postapocalyptic film *La Jetée* (1962).

18. See Rolf Goebel, "Berlin's Architectural Citations: Reconstruction, Simulation, and the Problem of Historical Authenticity," *PMLA* 118, no. 5 (Oct 2003): 1268–89.

19. See, for instance, the work of Karen Till and James Young cited earlier.

20. Wodiczko cited in Steve Rogers, "Territories 2: Superimposing the City," *Performance Magazine*, August 9, 1985.

21. Wodiczko cited in Leah Olman, "At the Galleries," *Los Angeles Times*, January 28, 1988.

22. Rosalind Krauss, *Passages in Modern Sculpture* (Cambridge, Mass.: MIT Press, 1977).

23. Wodiczko cited in Roger Gilroy, "Projection as Intervention," *New Art Examiner*, February 16, 1989.

24. Krzysztof Wodiczko, "Strategies of Public Address: Which Media, Which Publics?" in *Discussions in Contemporary Culture 1*, ed. Hal Foster (Seattle: Bay, 1987), 41.

25. See Berel Lang, "Second Sight: Shimon Attie's Recollection," in *Image and Remembrance: Representation and the Holocaust*, ed. Shelley Hornstein and Florence Jacobowitz (Bloomington: Indiana University Press, 2003), 27.

26. Andreas Huyssen, *Present Pasts: Urban Palimpsests and the Politics of Memory* (Stanford, Calif.: Stanford University Press, 2003), 81.

27. Miwon Kwon, "One Place after Another: Notes on Site Specificity," in *Space Site Intervention: Situating Installation Art*, ed. Erika Suderburg (Minneapolis: University of Minnesota Press, 2000), 38.

28. Rosalind Krauss, "Sculpture in the Expanded Field," in *The Anti-Aesthetic: Essays on Postmodern Culture*, ed. Hal Foster (Port Townsend, Wash.: Bay, 1983), 35.

29. Krauss, "Sculpture in the Expanded Field," 35.

30. Krauss, "Sculpture in the Expanded Field," 36.

31. Jennifer Cousineau, "Rabbinic Urbanism in London: Rituals and Material Culture of the Sabbath," *Jewish Social Studies* 11, no. 3 (2005): 37.

32. Debates about Jewish space have often centered on the question of Israel as real or imagined geopolitical space. The reimagining of the spaces of eastern Europe has much to do with the shifting means of Israel/Palestine as a transnational polity.

33. Charlotte Elisheva Fonrobert, "The Political Symbolism of the Eruv," *Jewish Social Studies* 11, no. 3 (2005): 29. Fonrobert here reverses Arjun Appadurai's notion of the nation-state as embodying a "sovereignty without territoriality."

34. The *eruv* in Germany was largely a rural phenomenon. In Galicia, only Krakow had an *eruv*; Lvov did not, nor did Prague, Vienna, or Budapest. The controversies surrounding the Frankfurt and Hamburg *eruvin* point to the tensions between neo-Orthodoxy and liberal Judaism after Emancipation and after the waves of Jewish migration from the country to the city in the second half of the nineteenth century.

35. The plans for building the *eruv* in Berlin have now been abandoned. In part, the gentrification of that part of former East Berlin has shifted the demographics, as young Jewish families—the people who would use an *eruv* in the first place—have been moving to less expensive neighborhoods to the north of Prenzlauerberg.

36. Clifford Geertz, *The Interpretation of Culture* (New York: Basic Books, 1973), 14.

37. Manuel Herz, "Institutionalized Experiment: The Politics of 'Jewish Architecture,'" *Jewish Social Studies* 11, no. 3 (2005): 64. For a similar article, see also Manuel Herz, "Eruv Urbanism: Towards an Alternative 'Jewish Architecture' in Germany," in *Jewish Topographies: Visions of Space, Traditions of Place*, ed. Julia Brauch, Anna Lipphardt, and Alexandra Nocke (London: Routledge, 2008), 43–62.

38. "'The architect as court's fool is given a 'small space to play anarchy in, where the architects cannot damage and disturb anything essential but achieve good effect as a decorative embellishment.'" Herz, "Institutionalized Experiment," 64.

39. Herz, "Institutionalized Experiment," 58.

40. Herz, "Institutionalized Experiment," 58.

41. Herz, "Institutionalized Experiment," 64.

42. Herz, "Institutionalized Experiment," 65.

43. Tom Gunning has argued for a more expanded notion of the indexical than the narrow sense of trace or imprint found in much recent work on film, new media, and photography; furthermore, he cautions against the overuse of index as trace or imprint. See Gunning, "Moving Away from the Index," *Differences* 18, no. 1 (2007): 30.

44. Doane, Krauss, and others interested in rethinking the status of the indexical are doing so to widen the frame of discourse about the role of photography.

45. www.dziga.com/eruv/. Website of Elliott Malkin.

46. http://rhizome.org/editorial/2007/aug/14/interview-with-elliott-malkin/. Rhizome.

47. http://thejewishmuseum.org/exhibitions/susan-hiller-the-j-street-project. Jewish Museum (New York).

48. Susan Hiller and Jörg Heiser, *The J. Street Project, 2002–2005* (Warwickshire, Eng.: Compton Verney and Berlin Artists-in-Residence Programme/DAAD, 2005), 7.

49. For an interesting reading of Hiller's project and her larger body of work, see Jörg Heiser's afterword in Hiller and Heiser, *The J. Street Project*, 619.

50. Hiller and Heiser, *The J. Street Project*, 7.

51. W. J. T. Mitchell, *What Do Pictures Want?* (Chicago: University of Chicago Press, 2004), 250–51.

52. Tim Edensor, *Industrial Ruins: Space, Aesthetics, and Materiality* (Oxford: Berg Books, 2005), 125.

53. As they state in the online catalog: "Buildings erected, buildings destroyed; density increase, populations devastated. It was a place for a community, a Wall, a parking lot, and an urban wasteland. Today, the site sits in restless anticipation as real estate values grow and interest accumulates. At the same time, bushes, grass, and small trees break through the asphalt and city foundations. Seasonal vegetation grows and covers the ground." http://www.skulpturenpark.org/exhibit/parcella/kalt.html. Skulpturenpark Berlin_Zentrum.

54. "On April 4, 2006, I was able to halt the demolition work for one day, with the help of the gardeners and construction workers, and to save all five of the trees that had been growing spontaneously. It is in fact impossible to replant wild growth or so-called 'pioneer trees,' since they had developed roots that ran for meters, geometrically, throughout the concrete slab. But the trees survived, were categorized botanically and labeled, and on February 17, 2008, were planted in the Sculpture Park Berlin in the former wall zone. There they grew in the same constellation as on the roof of the Palace." Ulrike Mohr, unpublished artist brochure, my translation.

55. Mohr, unpublished artist brochure.

56. An earlier installation on the former Russian military parade ground in Wünsdorf, *750 Kiefern in militärischer Anordnung Konversionsgelände Wünsdorf* (2003), consisted of the replanting of wild plants on the military parade ground; the trees are inspected and measured and placed according to height, in the combat position of a battalion. Eventually, the growth of the trees was intended to disrupt the military order.

57. "I plan to bring the trees into exile and to give them a sort of 'identification papers,' to produce a genetic fingerprint. As unique as they are, they should be re-planted into a natural setting and continue to grow." Ulrike Mohr, unpublished artist brochure, my translation.

58. In the course of contemplating the fate of these exiled trees, Mohr conceptualized *Area of Expertise*, an artistic exploration of what she describes as "the migration movements of wild plants that spread on roofs, in fallow land (gaps and fissures of buildings), and in empty spaces. *Area of Expertise* is conceived as a theoretical platform and should consist of texts, sketches, and research material in the form of a small publication." Ulrike Mohr, unpublished artist brochure, my translation.

59. "Self-sufficient boxes, in which the trees were supplied with water, light, and a consistent temperature for the duration of the trip. The measurement of the travel crates followed the specific growth pattern of the trees. The trees were on average roughly ten years old; however, they were much smaller than if they had been able to grow in dirt. In collaboration with professionals, modules were developed with the necessary materials such as wood, Styrofoam, and water container electricity." Ulrike Mohr, unpublished artist brochure, my translation.

Chapter 2

1. Dan Miron, *From Continuity to Contiguity: Toward a New Jewish Literary Thinking* (New York: Columbia University Press, 2010), 308.

2. Raymond Federman, "The Necessity and Impossibility of Being a Jewish Writer," http://www.federman.com/rfsrcr5.htm.

3. To be sure, some of the issues I raise about Sebald would apply to any writer on the Holocaust or on Jewish themes, in any language, who was not Jewish, but I will be trying to make the case that it is the interplay between German and Jew that makes Sebald's case particularly interesting.

4. The question, "How Jewish is it" echoes the 1980 novel by Walter Abish, *How German Is It*. Abish's novel, which won the 1981 PEN/Faulkner Award for best fiction, is an interesting point of comparison to many of Sebald's texts, since it raises the question of a fundamental "Germanness" (and Jewishness). As a Viennese-born Jew who emigrated to the United States after the war, Abish as author is also an interesting counterpart to Sebald.

5. A key formulation of this impasse is Sarah Kofman's axiomatic questions, "How can it not be said? And how can it be said?" Sarah Kofman, *Smothered Words*, trans. Madeleine Dobie (Evanston, Ill.: Northwestern University Press, 1998), 9.

6. Roland Barthes, "The Death of the Author," in *Norton Anthology of Theory and Criticism*, ed. Vincent B. Leitch (New York: Norton, 2001), 1466.

7. My reference to Benjamin's angel of history underscores the ways in which German Jewish discourse on history, landscape, and memory grew out of critical encounters with Benjamin's notions of ruin in baroque allegory (in the *Origin of German Tragic Drama*), his concept of language as "Bruchstücke" comprised of original and translation, and his reflections on the materiality of memory. For a discussion of Benjamin's insistence on memory as medium, see Karen Remmler's article "'On the Natural History of Destruction' and Cultural Memory: W. G. Sebald," *German Politics & Society* 23, no. 3 (2005): 42–64. For a reading of *The Emigrants* as a text about traumatic loss, see Katja Garloff, "The Emigrant as Witness: W. G. Sebald's *Die Ausgewanderten*," *German Quarterly* 77, no. 1 (2004): 76–94. There are, of course, other contemporary novels, such as Peter Nadas's *A Book of Memories*, that are even more complex, that create narrative ruin and theorize memory in an even more elusive manner. Peter Nadas, *A Book of Memories*, trans. Ivan Sanders with Imre Goldstein (New York: Farrar, Straus and Giroux, 1997). Sebald's work, similar and yet markedly different in its American reception from Nadas, Kertesz, Manea, and other major contemporary voices grappling with (a largely eastern) European past, can be read as a mediation between Germany and other geographical spaces through his foregrounding of the transmission of language.

8. See Rüdiger Görner, "Im Allgäu, Grafschaft Norfolk: Über W. G. Sebald in England," *Text + Kritik* 158 (2003): 27.

9. See Martin Swales, "Theoretical Reflections on the Work of W. G. Sebald," in *W. G. Sebald—A Critical Companion*, ed. J. J. Long and Anne Whitehead (Seattle: University of Washington Press, 2004), 23–28.

10. John Zilcosky, "Sebald's Uncanny Travels: The Impossibility of Getting Lost," in *W. G. Sebald—A Critical Companion*, ed. J. J. Long and Anne Whitehead (Seattle: University of Washington Press, 2004), 102–20.

11. Thomas Mann and, in a different medium, Bertolt Brecht might be the earlier analogous figures whose work had an impact on the Anglo-American world.

12. In thinking about intentional lacunae between language and place, a pivotal case is Marc Shell's encyclopedic project of redefining American literature as work produced *in* America, regardless of the original language of the text. See Marc Shell and Werner Sollors, eds., *The Multilingual Anthology of American Literature: A Reader of Original Texts with English Translations* (New York: New York University Press, 2000).

13. Beginning in 1985 with President Ronald Reagan's visit to the military cemetery of Bitburg but his refusal to visit a concentration camp, a series of events unfolded in West Germany that galvanized public discourse about Jewish memory and the Holocaust. Bitburg was followed in 1986 by the Historians' Debate, sparked by an exchange between the philosopher Jürgen Habermas and the conservative historian Ernst Nolte. In 1995, the publication of Wilkomirski's book *Fragments* (*Bruchstücke*) unleashed public debate about the validity and viability of Holocaust memory, as the uncertainty of Wilkomirski's origins surfaced soon after the book's translation into English. Each of these events—Bitburg, the Historians' Debate, the Wilkomirski Affair—were heavily covered in the media and created a new public debate on issues of history and memory in Germany. There were a number of other similar events in Germany and Austria, but these remain the pivotal ones.

14. One small point that bears mentioning: the German edition of Grass's *Krebsgang* calls it a novella; by the time it appeared in English, it was super-sized to a novel. We can speculate about this, of course, and while the reason undoubtedly has to do with marketing, it is also clear that the weight of the novel swelled, with the accumulated debate, by the time it appeared in English. Similarly, Sebald's texts have increased in significance, through public debate and in particular through translation.

15. See Berel Lang, *Act and Idea in the Nazi Genocide* (Chicago: University of Chicago Press, 1990); Saul Friedlander, ed., *Probing the Limits of Representation* (Cambridge, Mass.: Harvard University Press, 1992); James E. Young, *Writing and Rewriting the Holocaust* (Bloomington: Indiana University Press, 1988); Dominick LaCapra, *Representing the Holocaust: History, Theory, Trauma* (Ithaca, N.Y.: Cornell University Press, 1996); and Cathy Caruth, *Trauma: Explorations in Memory* (Baltimore, Md.: Johns Hopkins University Press, 1995).

16. For an incisive discussion of tropes of rubble and translated language as Derridean trace in Bachmann's short story "Simultan," see Siobhan S. Craig, "The Collapse of Language and the Trace of History in Ingeborg Bachmann's 'Simultan,'" *Women in German Yearbook* 16 (2000): 39–60.

17. For an excellent discussion of Sebald and translation, see Lynn L. Wolff, *W. G. Sebald's Hybrid Poetics: Literature as Historiography* (Berlin: Walter de Gruyter, 2014).

18. See Taryn L. Okuma, *Literary Non-Combatants: Contemporary British Fiction and the New War Novel* (Madison: University of Wisconsin Press, 2008). In the conclusion to the book Okuma argues for reading Sebald as a post-imperial British novelist.

"'People Nowadays Hardly Have Any Idea': Post-Imperial British Memory and W. G. Sebald's *The Rings of Saturn*," paper presented at the Center for German and European Studies Symposium, University of Wisconsin–Madison, April 29, 2004.

19. W. G. Sebald, *The Rings of Saturn*, trans. Michael Hulse (New York: New Directions, 1998), 3–4.

20. Sebald, *The Rings of Saturn*, 89.

21. Sebald, *The Rings of Saturn*, 89.

22. See Pico Iyer, *The Global Soul: Jet Lag, Shopping Malls, and the Search for Home* (New York: Vintage, 2000), 67.

23. Walter Benjamin, "The Storyteller: Observations on the Works of Nikolai Leskov," in *Walter Benjamin: Selected Writings, Volume 3, 1935–1938*, ed. Howard Eiland and Michael W. Jennings (Cambridge, Mass.: Belknap Press of Harvard University Press, 2002), 145.

24. Benjamin, "The Storyteller," 149.

25. Carol Jacobs, "The Monstrosity of Translation: Walter Benjamin's 'The Task of the Translator,'" in *Telling Time: Lévi-Strauss, Ford, Lessing, Benjamin, de Man, Wordsworth, Rilke* (Baltimore, Md.: Johns Hopkins University Press, 1993), 129.

26. For an insightful reading of this Benjamin fragment and the larger question of translation and film adaptation, see Fatima Naqvi, "A Melancholy Labor of Love, or Film Adaptation as Translation: Michael Haneke's *Drei Wege zum See*," *The Germanic Review: Literature, Culture, Theory* 81, no. 4 (2010): 291–316.

27. Benjamin, *Selected Writings*, 249. In the notes to the German edition, the editors stress the uncertain origin of this fragment that was found in the Benjamin *Nachlass*. In 1935 or 1936 Benjamin and Günther Anders held a conversation, intended for radio broadcast, about philosophical problems of translation. It is possible, although not certain, that the fragment reprinted in the collected works is the same as the one Anders refers to.

28. Walter Benjamin, *Gesammelte Schriften VI*, ed. Rolf Tiedemann and Hermann Schweppenhäuser (Frankfurt am Main: Suhrkamp, 1985), 158.

29. Sebald's concern with the transmission and translation of conversations recalls as well the pivotal relationship between testimony and memory for Jewish writing after the Shoah. It also calls to mind Giorgio Agamben's reworking of Primo Levi's turn to Coleridge's "Rime of the Ancient Mariner," where Agamben's (re)citation of the Coleridge poem, through Levi's evocation of it, serves to remind us of the urgency of narration.

30. See the interview with Chris Daniels in *Jacket*, Chris Daniels and Kent Johnson, "My Motto Is: 'Translation Fights Cultural Narcissism,'" *Jacket2* 29 (April 2006), http://jacketmagazine.com/29/kent-iv-daniels.html. Daniels goes on to explain that in addition to the seventy-two heteronyms in Pessoa's work, there is also the "orthonym, a fictional writer named Fernando Pessoa who is not actually Fernando Pessoa, but an invented writer with the author's name. Often enough, it is impossible to know exactly which is the 'real' Fernando Pessoa. But overall, it is quite simple. The confusion does not come from Pessoa, really, but from his readers."

31. Bill Freind, "Deferral of the Author: Impossible Witness and the Yasusada Poems," *Poetics Today* 25, no. 1 (2004): 139.

32. Roland Barthes, *Roland Barthes*, trans. Richard Howard (New York: Hill and Wang, 1977), 56.

33. Fernando Pessoa, *The Selected Prose of Fernando Pessoa*, trans. and ed. Richard Zenith (New York: Grove, 2001), 222.

34. Marjorie Perloff, "In Search of the Authentic Other: The Poetry of Araki Yasusada," http://www.epc.buffalo.edu/authors/perloff/boston.html.

35. Fernando Pessoa, *The Book of Disquiet*, trans. and ed. Richard Zenith (New York: Penguin, 2003).

36. Pessoa, *Selected Prose*, 254.

37. Pessoa, *Selected Prose*, 262.

38. Pessoa, *Book of Disquiet*, 286.

39. Pessoa, *Book of Disquiet*, 286.

40. See Susan Rubin Suleiman, "When Postmodern Play Meets Survivor Testimony: Federman and Holocaust Literature," in *Federman's Fictions: Innovation, Theory, and the Holocaust*, ed. Jeffrey R. Di Leo (Albany: SUNY Press, 2011), 215–27.

41. Raymond Federman, *Double or Nothing* (Boulder, Colo.: Fiction Collective Two, 1998), 0.

42. Georges Perec, *W, or The Memory of Childhood* (New York: David Godine), 77.

43. Suleiman, "Postmodern Play," 220.

44. Suleiman, "Postmodern Play," 221.

45. Raymond Federman, *SHHH: The Story of a Childhood* (Buffalo, N.Y.: Starcherone Books, 2010), introduction by Davis Schneiderman.

46. Raymond Federman, *SHHH*, 7.

47. Federman, *SHHH*, 5.

48. Federman, *SHHH*, 3.

49. Federman, *SHHH*, 19.

50. Federman, *SHHH*, 53.

51. Federman, *SHHH*, 53.

52. Giorgio Agamben, *Remnants of Auschwitz: The Witness and the Archive*, trans. Daniel Heller-Roazen (Cambridge, Mass.: MIT Press, 1998), 119.

53. While I will use the name "Ferber," from the English translation, I want to stress that the English is not a replacement for the name "Aurach" from the original German, but rather carries the traces of that name.

54. W. G. Sebald, *The Emigrants*, trans. Michael Hulse (New York: New Directions, 1996), 149.

55. Sebald, *Emigrants*, 230.

56. Sebald, *Emigrants*, 230–31.

57. For an excellent discussion of the link between trauma and language in Sebald, see Garloff, "Emigrant as Witness."

58. Sebald, *Emigrants*, 182.

59. Frank Auerbach's biography is, perhaps, the Jewish version of Sebald's own: born in Berlin in 1930, he was sent with the *Kindertransport* to England in 1937, where he then became a British citizen in 1947. Eric Santner has pointed out the affinity between Auerbach's style of painting, which consists of multiple erasures, with the narrator's method of crossing out, deleting, and correcting his text. Santner also points out that there is an image of a sketch by Auerbach in the German edition of *The Emigrants*. See Eric Santner, *On Creaturely Life: Rilke, Benjamin, Sebald* (Chicago: University of Chicago Press, 2006), 165.

60. It also evokes Benjamin's notion of the aura and the "auricular." The name

"Aurach" is a homophone, interestingly, for the aurochs, a primitive race of cattle and the ancestor of all the bovids, that survived until the Bronze Age in Britain and then in Europe. The last auroch died in 1627 in a Polish park, but two German zoologists in the 1970s worked to re-create the species. Ur-ox, the primeval cow, cow as ruin, extinct in Britain but re-created through German science and wandering the Scottish highlands, is an example, perhaps, of Sebald's ironic twist on his own natural history of destruction.

61. I am indebted to Ann Klefstad for pointing out that the name "Ferber" also evokes IG Farben, the aniline dye company that became an industrial giant of the Nazi era and was the first producer of synthetic colors. See also Carol Jacobs, *Sebald's Vision* (New York: Columbia University Press, 2015), for a helpful discussion of Sebald and IG Farben.

62. Sebald, *Emigrants*, 181.

63. Sebald, *Emigrants*, 181.

64. Sebald, *Emigrants*, 233.

65. Alfred Kazin, *New York Jew* (New York: Alfred A. Knopf, 1978), 91–92.

66. Dorothy Norman, *Alfred Stieglitz: An American Seer* (New York: Random House, 1973), 75–76.

67. Stieglitz cited in Katherine Hoffman, *Stieglitz: A Beginning Light* (New Haven, Conn.: Yale University Press, 2004), 237.

68. Kazin, *New York Jew*, 92.

69. Alfred Kazin, *A Walker in the City* (New York: Grove, 1958), 171.

70. For an interesting analysis of the formative role Whitman played in the emergence of Yiddish modernist poets in New York, see Rachel Rubinstein, "Going Native, Becoming Modern: American Indians, Walt Whitman, and the Yiddish Poet," *American Quarterly* 58, no. 2 (2006): 431–53. Rubenstein also explores the complex way in which Jews and American Indians were linked in the Western imagination. Although Rubenstein does not discuss Kazin, it would be interesting to reflect on Kazin's adoption of the term "native" to describe his assertion of Americanness in "On Native Grounds."

71. Kazin, *New York Jew*, 148–49.

72. Kazin, *New York Jew*, 44.

73. Robert Towers, "Tales of Manhattan," review of *New York Jew*, by Alfred Kazin, *New York Review of Books* 25, no. 8 (May 18, 1978).

74. *Alfred Kazin's Journals*, ed. Richard M. Cook (New Haven, Conn.: Yale University Press, 2011), 44.

75. Kazin, *New York Jew*, 97.

76. Alfred Kazin, *A Lifetime Burning in Every Moment: From the Journals of Alfred Kazin* (New York: HarperCollins, 1996), 147.

77. Kazin, *A Lifetime Burning*, 149.

78. Kazin, *A Lifetime Burning*, 147.

79. See Hasia R. Diner, *We Remember with Reverence and Love: American Jews and the Myth of Silence after the Holocaust, 1945–1962* (New York: New York University Press, 2009).

80. Irving Howe, *Selected Writings, 1950–1990* (San Diego, Calif.: Harcourt Brace Jovanovich, 1990), 241.

81. Howe, *Selected Writings*, 241.

82. Kazin, *Walker in the City*, 51–52.

83. Julian Levinson, *Exiles on Main Street: Jewish American Writers and American Literary Culture* (Bloomington: Indiana University Press, 2008), 157.

84. Levinson, *Exiles*, 157.

85. Levinson, *Exiles*, 157.

86. Levinson acknowledges the brokenness, however, of Jewish liturgy as Kazin creates the pastiche of the prayer book.

87. For an excellent exposition of the affinities between Roth's novel and Kazin's work, see Levinson, *Exiles*.

88. Kazin, *Walker in the City*, 100.

89. Kazin, *Walker in the City*, 103.

90. Kazin, *Walker in the City*, 100.

91. The Singer siddur was compiled and translated by Simeon Singer, rabbi of London's West End Synagogue, in 1889 and was considered a liturgical and literary masterpiece. Singer's siddur was published as *The Authorised Daily Prayer Book of the United Hebrew Congregations of the British Empire*. Within eighteen years it had gone through eight editions, was to be found in nearly every Jewish home in England, and was the siddur found in most Orthodox synagogues in America, where a subsidy from the Montefiore family had enabled a pocket-sized edition to be sold for twenty-five cents.

92. For an insightful discussion of this passage, see Levinson, *Exiles*, 160–61. Levinson points out that the first passage comes from Psalm 95, part of the Friday night service, and is then followed by a prayer that comes after the Shema.

93. Kazin, *Walker in the City*, 101.

94. Kazin, *Walker in the City*, 101.

95. Kazin, *Walker in the City*, 100–101.

96. Kazin, *Walker in the City*, 103.

97. Kazin, *Walker in the City*, 103.

98. Kazin, *Walker in the City*, 103.

99. Kazin, *Walker in the City*, 104.

100. Daniel Blaufuks, "A Conversation between Rémi Coignet and Daniel Blaufuks, in *Toda a Memória do Mundo, parte um / All the Memory of the World, Part One* (Lisbon: Museu Nacional de Arte Contemporanea—Museu do Chiado Imprensa Nacional-Casa da Moeda, Winckler: Série Foto, 2014), 201.

101. See Mary Cosgrove, "Sebald for Our Time: The Politics of Melancholy and the Critique of Capitalism in His Work," in *W. G. Sebald and the Writing of History*, ed. Anne Fuchs and Jonathan James Long (Würzburg: Königshausen & Neumann, 2007), 91–110.

102. Daniel Blaufuks, *Works on Memory: Selected Writings and Images* (Cardiff, Wales: Ffotogallery, 2012), 25.

103. Blaufuks, *Toda a Memória do Mundo* 214.

104. Blaufuks, *Works on Memory*, 26.

105. W. G. Sebald, *Austerlitz*, trans. Anthea Bell (New York: Random House, 2001), 261.

106. Sebald, *Austerlitz*, 261.

107. Sebald, *Austerlitz*, 261.

108. Sebald, *Austerlitz*, 233.

109. See Leslie Morris, "Reading H. G. Adler (Tangentially)," in *H. G. Adler: Life*,

Literature, Legacy, ed. Julia Creet, Sara Horowitz, and Amira Dan (Evanston, Ill.: Northwestern University Press, 2016). In this essay, I focus on the work of H. G. Adler with the aim of suggesting how Adler's work, through Sebald's text and Blaufuks's project, continues to shape the complex re-patternings of German Jewish textuality.

110. J. J. Long, *W. G. Sebald: Image, Archive, Modernity* (New York: Columbia University Press, 2007), 81.

111. I am grateful to Meagan Tripp for the suggestion of the parallel between the glass of the camera and the glass preventing Blaufuks from entering the room.

112. Greil Marcus as cited in Ulrich Baer, *Spectral Evidence: The Photography of Trauma* (Cambridge, Mass.: MIT Press, 2002), 67.

113. Daniel Blaufuks, *Terezin* (Göttingen: Steidl, 2010).

114. Sebald, *Austerlitz*, 90.

115. Vilém Flusser, "The Photographic Universe," in *Towards a Philosophy of Photography*, trans. Anthony Mathews (London: Reaktion Books, 2000), 65.

Chapter 3

1. See Kaja Silverman, *Male Subjectivity at the Margins* (New York: Routledge, 1992).

2. See Sander Gilman, *Jewish Self Hatred: Anti-Semitism and the Hidden Language of the Jews* (Baltimore, Md.: Johns Hopkins University Press, 1986); Daniel Boyarin, *Unheroic Conduct: The Rise of Heterosexuality and the Invention of the Jewish Man* (Berkeley: University of California Press, 1997); Daniel Boyarin, Daniel Itzkovitz, and Ann Pellegrini, eds., *Queer Theory and the Jewish Question* (New York: Columbia University Press, 2003); Daniel Boyarin and Jonathan Boyarin, eds., *Jews and Other Differences: The New Jewish Cultural Studies* (Minneapolis: University of Minnesota Press, 2008).

3. See Leslie Morris, "Placing and Displacing Jewish Studies: Notes on the Future of the Field," *PMLA* 125, no. 3 (2010): 764–73.

4. Marjorie Perloff, "Towards a Conceptual Lyric: From Content to Context," *Jacket2*, July 28, 2011, http://jacket2.org/article/towards-conceptual-lyric.

5. The work of conceptual poetry has come under fire lately by critics who see it as a poetic "in group" that speaks largely to itself, as part of a privileged white male bastion of rarefied discourse. The recent incident at Brown University, in which one of the main spokespeople for conceptual writing, Kenneth Goldsmith, read the autopsy report of Michael Brown, has only served to intensify the debate about the political meaning of appropriating texts of the "other."

6. For instance, "Flarf," which is defined by the American Academy of Poets as "the work of a community of poets dedicated to exploration of 'flarfiness.' Heavy usage of Google search results in the creation of poems, plays, etc., though not exclusively Google-based. Community in the sense that one example leads to another's reply—is, in some part, contingent upon community interaction of this sort. Poems created, revised, changed by others, incorporated, plagiarized, etc., in semi-public." Gary Sullivan, "A Brief Guide to Flarf Poetry," http://www.poets.org/poetsorg/text/brief-guide -flarf-poetry.

Maria Damon describes Flarf (positioning herself as a true Flarfy) as an "aesthetic of goofiness" (220) in which "silliness is raised to the level of an aesthetic, and at the same time it is obviously a form of abjection, a dramatic departure from the self-contained dignity of either the 'real man' or 'real poetry,' but recuperable through its display of superior intelligence." Maria Damon, *Postliterary America: From Bagel Shop Jazz to Micropoetries* (Iowa City: University of Iowa Press, 2011), 223.

7. Heather McHugh, *Broken English: Poetry and Partiality* (Middletown, Conn.: Wesleyan University Press, 1993), 1.

8. Blaufuks, *Works on Memory*, 57–58.

9. Blaufuks, *Works on Memory*, 57.

10. Blaufuks, *Works on Memory*, 57.

11. Godard created with *Breathless* the first extended use of the jump cut. By erasing all scenes with Belmondo, Blaufuks has created an even more radical series of jump cuts, and a radical interruption of the function of the jump cut. Finally, the history of the film production of *Breathless* is important, since there are multiple erasures present in Godard's film to begin with: the fact that he needed to erase thirty minutes of it to bring it to production; the multiple stories (some fictive no doubt) about the filming, the legendary tales that are all a part of this.

12. Jen Bervin, *Nets* (Brooklyn, N.Y.: Ugly Duckling, 2004), 152.

13. Rita Raley has raised the interesting question of whether or not this sort of "machine language" will, in the end, be institutionalized as "foreign languages" within the humanities in universities. Rita Raley, "Interferences: [Net.Writing] and the Practice of Codework," *Electronic Book Review*, September 8, 2002, http://www.electronicbook review.com/thread/electropoetics/net.writing.

14. Quoted in Maria Damon, "Simultaneously Reading/WritingUnder/Destroyed My Life," *Electronic Book Review*, October 5, 2013, http://www.electronicbookreview .com/thread/wuc/simultaneous.

15. Alan Sondheim, "After Auschwitz," 2003, http://www.alansondheim.org/nd.txt.

16. Sondheim, "After Auschwitz."

17. Sondheim, "After Auschwitz."

18. McHugh, *Broken English: Poetry and Partiality*, 2.

19. Damon, "Simultaneously Reading/WritingUnder/Destroyed My Life."

20. Damon, "Simultaneously Reading/WritingUnder/Destroyed My Life."

21. The word "writing" is from the Old English "writan," which means to score or form letters by carving; "writhing" is derived from the Old English verb "writhan," meaning to make coils or plait.

22. Damon, "Simultaneously Reading/WritingUnder/Destroyed My Life."

23. Patrick Greaney, "Next to Nothing: Poetic Information in Robert Fitterman and Vilém Flusser," *English Language Notes* 50, no. 1 (2012): 227–30, 228.

24. Robert Fitterman, *Holocaust Museum* (Denver, Colo.: Counterpath, 2013).

25. Robert Fitterman, *Rob the Plagiarist* (New York: Roof Books, 2009), 16.

26. Robert Fitterman, *Rob the Plagiarist*, 18, 17.

27. Susan Sontag, *Regarding the Pain of Others* (New York: Picador, 2004), 45.

28. See Sontag, *Regarding the Pain of Others*: "To remember is, more and more, not to recall a story but to call up a picture . . . narratives can make us understand. Photographs do something else: they haunt us" (89).

29. Roland Barthes, *Camera Lucida*, trans. Richard Howard (New York: Hill and Wang, 1981), 73.

30. Barthes, *Camera Lucida*, 26–27.

31. For a different reading of the "punctum" in Fitterman's work, see Martin Glaz

Serup, "Captions without Images: On Robert Fitterman's 'Holocaust Museum,'" *Jacket2*, January 26, 2015, http://jacket2.org/article/captions-without-images.

32. Of course, the history of "erasures" in modernist art and poetics, from Dada to Rauschenberg, attests to the very modernist project of showing that the creation of art is simultaneous with its undoing. As the poet (and erasure poet) Mary Ruefle notes, erasures are not unique to written text—she cites Bill Morrison's *Decasia* as a film erasure, and William Basinski's musical work, *The Disintegration Loop*. Mary Ruefle, "On Erasure," *Quarter after Eight: A Journal of Innovative Writing*, 16, http://quarter aftereight.org/ruefle.html.

33. McHugh, *Broken English: Poetry and Partiality*, 75.

34. Charles Bernstein, "This Picture Intentionally Left Blank: Rob Fitterman's 'Holocaust Museum,' Heimrad Bäcker's 'Transcript,' Christian Boltanski's 'To Be a Jew in Paris in 1939,' and the Documentary Poetics of Raul Hilberg," *Jacket2*, February 23, 2012, https://jacket2.org/commentary/picture-intentionally-left-blank.

35. Serup, "Captions without Images."

36. Patrick Greaney, "Afterword to the English Edition," in Heimrad Bäcker, *transcript*, trans. Patrick Greaney and Vincent Kling (Champaign, Ill.: Dalkey Archive Books, 2010), 151. In an article published in the *New German Critique*, Greaney states furthermore: "The blanks are 'striking' because of how they function in different, even contradictory ways in Bäcker's text: as full of other possible quotations and as a blankness that simultaneously contributes to and undercuts the text's harmony and identity with itself." Patrick Greaney, "Aestheticization and the Shoah: Heimrad Bäcker's *transcript*," *New German Critique* 37, no. 1 (2010): 27–51, 50.

37. Greaney, "Aestheticization and the Shoah," 131. See Patrick Greaney's reading of the notes not as a source to document and illuminate *transcript*, but rather as another textual vacuum: "Far from filling in the gaps left by quotation and montage, the note *incompletes* the text, and this incompleteness becomes a central formal element in Bäcker's works." Greaney, "Aestheticization and the Shoah," 45.

38. Bäcker, *transcript*, 131. See also Greaney, "Aestheticization and the Shoah," for an illuminating parsing of Bäcker's use of "gibberish" (*Kauderwelsch*) in his statement that precedes the notes and bibliography to *transcript*. Significantly, what Greaney translates as "deadly gibberish" is, in the original, "*ein Leben kostendes Kauderwelsch*," a formulation that suggests, in the extended adjectival modifier "*ein Leben kostendes*," a drawing out of language and the agency inherent in the process of killing.

39. I focus here on one of two categories of *notarikon* within Jewish textual tradition in which every letter in a particular word is interpreted as the abbreviation of a whole word. Although there is an opinion that the hermeneutic law of *notarikon* has biblical authority, the Talmud does not use it for halakhic interpretations. *Notarikon* was also widely used in medieval homiletic and kabbalistic writings.

40. Cixous, *Stigmata*, xii.

41. Cixous, *Stigmata*, xii.

42. In an email correspondence with Anne Blonstein from March 2, 2011 (one month before her death), she wrote the following to me: "I like the way you imply that the parenthetical texts I insert into 'correspondence with nobody' texts might be read as scars. For reasons I'm not fully able to explain, I often visualized these citations as sheets of glass-like text cutting into my notarikon, thus indeed wounding it but also,

hopefully, sometimes tearing the reader out of my writing to explore others'. A sort of Benjaminian act in a way."

43. William Shakespeare, *Einundzwanzig Sonette*, trans. Paul Celan (Frankfurt am Main: Insel, 1967), 40–41.

44. Anne Blonstein, *correspondence with nobody* (Basel: Ellectrique, 2008), 74.

45. Blonstein, *correspondence with nobody*, 71.

46. Blonstein, *correspondence with nobody*, 73.

47. Blonstein, *correspondence with nobody*, 73.

48. Tom Gunning has recently argued for a more expanded notion of the indexical than the narrow sense of trace or imprint found in much recent work on film, new media, and photography; furthermore, he cautions against the overuse of index as trace or imprint. See Tom Gunning, "Moving Away from the Index," *Differences* 18, no. 1 (2007): 30.

49. In part, I propose to think of a way out of the circularity of the debates about the role of gender in the Holocaust, or even what I see as the vexed question of gender and the Holocaust, which has largely centered on whether the "experience" of women eclipses the category of Jews more generally.

50. Silverman, *Male Subjectivity at the Margins*, 35.

51. Cixous, *Stigmata*, xi.

52. Dora Appel, *Memory Effects: The Holocaust and the Art of Secondary Witnessing* (New Brunswick, N.J.: Rutgers University Press, 2002), 177.

53. Amelia Jones, *Body Art/Performing the Subject* (Minneapolis: University of Minnesota Press, 1998), 10.

54. See Dora Appel, "The Tattooed Jew," in *Visual Culture and the Holocaust*. Ed. Barbie Zelizer (New Brunswick, N.J.: Rutgers University Press, 2000), 300. Appel cites Joshua Burgin's claim that "for me to take the Star of David as a Jewish mark of identity and mark myself permanently with it makes me feel more Jewish than I ever felt before."

55. We talk about "reading" people as a metaphor, but with tattoos this "reading" is no longer metaphor but rather a literalization.

56. Appel, *Memory Effects*, 181.

57. Appel, *Memory Effects*, 185.

58. Michael Kimmelman, "Art Review: Tattoo Moves from Fringes to Fashion. But Is It Art?" *New York Times*, September 15, 1995.

59. Mark Taylor, *Pierced Hearts and True Love: A Century of Drawings for Tattoos*, ed. Don Ed Hardy (New York: Drawing Center, 1994), 39.

60. In "Jews with Hogs," Frederic Brenner consciously plays with the marginalized status of both the Jew and the Hell's Angels, as he places emblematically macho bikers outside a synagogue, with the bearded quasi-rabbinic/quasi–outlaw biker in the center. Appel points out the dual reading of the biker's beard as simultaneously "modern cultural rebellion and traditional observant Jew" (Appel, *Memory Effects*, 181).

61. For an important analysis of the history and cultural meanings of "disgust," see Winfried Menninghaus, *Disgust: The Theory and History of a Strong Sensation*, trans. Howard Eiland and Joel Golb (Albany: SUNY Press, 2003).

62. http://ineradicablestain.com/skin-call.html. The website lists as a subtitle for *Skin* the following: "A Story Published on the Skin of 2095 volunteers." The website also

has a "progress report," dated April 20, 2010, stating that 1,875 out of 2,095 have been provisionally accepted.

63. On the website for the project, one of the participants suggested that each "word" tattoo the word on one of their children, thus ensuring a "second edition" of the text.

64. Cixous, *Stigmata*, xii.

65. http://ineradicablestain.com/skin-call.html.

66. Simon Morley, *Writing on the Wall: Word and Image in Modern Art* (Berkeley: University of California Press, 2003), 17.

67. Damon, *Postliterary America*, 219.

68. Email correspondence with Adeena Karasick, February 4, 2010.

69. "Art invites us to intellectual consideration, and that not for the purpose of creating art again, but for knowing philosophically what art is." Hegel quoted in Arthur C. Danto, *After the End of Art: Contemporary Art and the Pale of History* (Princeton, N.J.: Princeton University Press, 1998), 31.

70. Danto, *After the End of Art*, 33.

71. Danto, *After the End of Art*, 31.

72. "To claim that art has come to an end means that criticism of this sort is no longer licit. No art is any longer historically mandated as against any other art. Nothing is any more true as art than anything else, nothing especially more historically false than anything else. So at the very least the belief that art has come to an end entails the kind of critic one cannot be, if one is going to be a critic at all." Danto, *After the End of Art*, 27–28.

73. Danto, *After the End of Art*, 18.

74. The exhibition *Not Prepared* took place in 2004, as part of Molgan's graduate work in art at Beit Berl College in Israel. In 2005–6 the exhibition showed in the United States at Wesleyan University's Davison Art Center. For an excellent overview of Molgan's work, see Paula J. Birnbaum, "Modern Orthodox Feminism: Art, Jewish Law, and the Quest for Equality," in *Contemporary Israel: New Insights and Scholarship*, ed. Frederick E. Greenspahn (New York: New York University Press, 2016), 131–65.

75. See Sander Gilman, *The Jew's Body* (London: Routledge, 1991), for a full discussion of the medicalized discourse about the nose and the history of the nose job. According to Gilman, the first nose job was performed in Berlin by Jacques Joseph, a German Jewish surgeon who began to do the surgery in the 1890s.

76. A scandal in the Orthodox community a decade ago demonstrates the complexity of these issues. Wigs that had been made from the hair of Hindu women, who had cut their hair as part of a religious ritual at the Tirupati temple in India, were contested by Israeli rabbinic authorities because the hair was part of an idolatrous worship ritual. The question of Orthodox Jewish wigs ties into the larger issue present in Europe of the debates about head-covering overall in Muslim (and by extension, Jewish) culture.

Chapter 4

1. "No poet cracks open the possibilities for translation more than Paul Celan. With Celan, translation is not a supplemental activity but a hermeneutic necessity." Charles Bernstein, "Celan's Folds and Veils," *Textual Practice* 18, no. 2 (2004): 199.

2. "One might say Celan's own written German is a kind of translation from German's linguistic norms, and that reading even the German text requires a task of translation." Shira Wolosky, "On (Mis-)translating Paul Celan," in *Poetik der Transformation:*

Paul Celan—Übersetzer und Übersetzt, ed. Alfred Bodenheimer and Shimon Sand-bank (Berlin: De Gruyter, 1999), 146.

3. Bernstein, "Celan's Folds," 200.

4. Bernstein, "Celan's Folds," 200.

5. Bernstein, "Celan's Folds," 201.

6. For an excellent discussion of Celan's poem and the complex relationship between Czernowitz and Sadagora, see Katja Garloff, *Words from Abroad: Trauma and Displacement in Postwar German Jewish Writers* (Detroit, Mich.: Wayne State University Press, 2005), 136–47. Garloff points out not only that Celan's mother was from Sadagora, but also that Sadagora was reviled by the more cosmopolitan Jewish citizens of Czernowitz as a place of criminality.

7. What is also interesting are the many variations on the name of Sadagora in the region. In German, it is Sadagora, but in Romanian it is Sadagura, in Ukrainian Sadhora, in Russian Sadgora, and in Yiddish Sadagera. The many slippages of the name suggest a place that is linguistically impossible to locate.

8. "Czernowitz gibt es wirklich, nicht bloß als Topos einer literarischen Welt." Win-fried Menninghaus, "Czernowitz/Bukowina als Topos deutsch-jüdischer Geschichte," *Merkur* 3/4 (1999): 345. For a lengthy exploration of Czernowitz as topos, see Andrei Corbea-Hoisie, *Czernowitz* (Frankfurt am Main, 1998); and Marianne Hirsch and Leo Spitzer, *Ghosts of Home: The Afterlife of Czernowitz in Jewish Memory* (Berkeley: University of California Press, 2011). Also, note that all translations are mine unless otherwise stated.

9. The *Meridian* speech was written on the occasion of Paul Celan receiving the Georg Büchner Prize in Darmstadt, October 22, 1960. It has had a significant influence on contemporary poetics and poetic theory not only in Germany, but also in Francophone and Anglophone literary circles. It stands as the axiomatic text about place and the poetic text in its exploration of the absence that now marks the spaces of east-central Europe. The term "non-place" is drawn from Marc Augé.

10. Similarly, Wolfgang Koepp's 1999 documentary film *Herr Zwilling und Frau Zuckermann* highlights the difficulties of representing a vanished, vanquished place such as Czernowitz. On the one hand, the various attempts to move into the spaces of eastern Europe have been critical in reshaping the geographical contours of memory, addressing head-on the absence of Jewish culture in what were once its thriving capitals. On the other hand, this has resulted, perhaps inevitably, in a fetishization of the absent culture, replacing the critical discourse about absence with Jewish tourism.

11. Italo Calvino, *Invisible Cites*, trans. William Weaver (New York: Harvest, 1974), 19.

12. In 1910 the population of Czernowitz was 30 percent Jewish; in 1930, it was more than 35 percent.

13. Menninghaus, "Czernowitz/Bukowina," 348.

14. Menninghaus, "Czernowitz/Bukowina," 345. Menninghaus stresses the history of the Bukovina as a misreading that is simultaneously a repression of the rise (or rather return) of antisemitism that accompanied the disintegration of the Habsburg monarchy, as the Jews became vilified by the Romanians, the ethnic Germans from Schwaben, and the Ukrainians.

15. The shifting role of eastern European Jewish cities has been complicated over the past decade or so by the phenomenon of Jewish American synagogue youth tours to Israel that now make a requisite stop in Poland to visit the camps. Thus the students

are given a narrative in which Europe is the killing field of the genocide of Europe's Jews, which is then put in opposition to a narrative of the state of Israel as the place of redemption and freedom. Leaving aside the enormously problematic reading of Israeli history and culture that this forced narrative suggests (and which is beyond the scope of this project), let me comment simply on the ways in which the spaces of eastern Europe are then configured in the American Jewish imaginary. An important corrective to this is the work of Barbara Kirchenblatt-Gimblett, whose newly opened Polin Museum of the History of Polish Jews in Warsaw is devoted to conveying the full range of historical and cultural encounters between Poles and Polish Jews, and their ongoing resonance in the shaping of American Jewish life.

16. In *Inventing Eastern Europe: The Map of the Civilization on the Mind of the Enlightenment* (Stanford, Calif.: Stanford University Press, 1994), Larry Wolff develops the notion of eastern Europe as "idea," arguing that the "shadow" of the "Iron Curtain" persists, despite its absence, because the *idea* of eastern Europe remains. This is particularly interesting when considering the substantive differences between Czernowitz and cities such as Prague and Krakow that have now become Jewish tourist destination sites.

17. "Schwarze Milch der Frühe" is the first line of Celan's poem "Todesfuge," and is generally thought to have come from a poem in Rose Ausländer's first volume of poetry, *Der Regenbogen*, published in Czernowitz in 1939. See Helmut Braun, *Rose Ausländer: Materialien zu Leben und Werk* (Frankfurt am Main: Fischer Taschenbuch Verlag, 1991), 98. Although John Felstiner acknowledges that the image of "black milk" occurs in Ausländer's 1939 volume, he states that "there's no way of knowing" where Celan came up with the image of "schwarze Milch," and also suggests as possible source a passage from the book of Lamentations. John Felstiner, *Paul Celan: Poet, Survivor, Jew* (New Haven, Conn.: Yale University Press, 1995), 34.

18. See Leslie Morris, afterword in Rose Ausländer, *The Forbidden Tree: Englische Gedichte* (Frankfurt: Suhrkamp Verlag, 1995).

19. "Ich suche den toten Freund / im Traum /Das Schreiben /tut weh." Rose Ausländer, *Gesammelte Werke*, vol. 6: *Wieder ein Tag aus Glut und Wind: Gedichte 1980–1982* (Frankfurt: S. Fischer Verlag, 1986), 67.

20. "Diese harten Tage / Vergeblich leuchten / die Anemonen." Ausländer, *Gesammelte Werke*, vol. 6: 67.

21. See Jacques Derrida, *The Work of Mourning* (Chicago: University of Chicago Press, 2001).

22. Marc Augé, *Non-Places: An Introduction to Supermodernity* (New York: Verso, 2009), 96.

23. Augé, *Non-Places*, 78.

24. Walter Benjamin, *Gesammelte Schriften*, vol. 5: 570.

25. Benjamin, *Illuminations* (New York: Houghton Mifflin Harcourt, 1968), 75.

26. Ausländer, *Forbidden Tree*, 97.

27. Judah Halevi's poem "libi ba'mizrach" begins: "My heart is in the east and I am at the edge of the west." *The Penguin Book of Hebrew Verse*, ed. T. Carmi (London: Penguin, 1981), 347. The longing for Zion expressed in the poem, and the formulations of east and west, have become absorbed into the poetic vocabulary of Jewish poetry. Ausländer's formulations of the relationship between home and exile draw on this dialogue in this and other poems.

28. See Rose Ausländer, *Gesammelte Werke*, vol. 4: *Im Aschenregen die Spur deines Namens: Gedichte und Prosa 1976* (S. Fischer Verlag, 1984), 77.

29. "schwingt Jerusalem herüber zu mir." Ausländer, *Gesammelte Werke*, vol. 4: 77.

30. A similarly dialogic, reciprocal relationship between Israel and the I is found in the poem "Israel 11": "Zurück / ins zukünftige / Meinland Deinland" "Back / to the future / My Land Your Land." Rose Ausländer, *Gesammelte Werke*, vol. 3: *Hügel aus Äther unwiderruflich: Gedichte und Prosa 1966–1975* (Frankfurt: S. Fischer Verlag, 1984), 244. Maria Klanska argues that Ausländer exhibits an identificatory impulse not only with Jews, but with Israelis, citing the line in which the poetic I "swings" her "blue-white scarf" — the national colors of the state of Israel — to the east. Maria Klanska, "Zur Identitätsproblematik im Schaffen Rose Ausländers," in *Nationale Identität aus germanistischer Perspektive*, ed. Maria Katarzyna Lasatowicz and Jurgen Joachimsthaler (Opole, 1998), 154.

31. "Friedliche Hügelstadt / von Buchenwäldern umschlossen / . . . Vier Sprachen / verständigen sich / verwöhnen die Luft / Bis Bomben fielen /atmete Glücklich / die Stadt." Ausländer, *Gesammelte Werke*, vol. 6: 348.

32. "Vier Sprachen / Viersprachenlieder / Menschen / die sich verstehen." Ausländer, *Gesammelte Werke*, vol. 4: 130.

33. "Landschaft die mich / erfand / wasserarmig / waldhaarig." Ausländer, *Gesammelte Werke*, vol. 4: 72.

34. "Warum ich schreibe? Vielleicht weil ich in Czernowitz zur Welt kam, weil die Welt in Czernowitz zu mir kam. Jene besondere Landschaft. Die besonderen Menschen. Märchen und Mythen lagen in der Luft, man atmete sie ein. Die viersprachige Czernowitz war eine musische Stadt, die viele Künstler, Dichter, Kunst-, Literatur- und Philosophieliebhaber beherbergte." Ausländer, *Gesammelte Werke*, vol. 3: 285.

35. "Auch ich verlor / meinen Namen / unter Namenlosen // Auch ich / fragte das Nichts / nach dem Sein." Ausländer, *Gesammelte Werke*, vol. 3: 135.

36. I borrow the term "postmemory" from the work of Marianne Hirsch and Andrea Liss. For the elegiac dimension of postmemory, see also Leslie Morris, "Postmemory, Postmemoir," in *Unlikely History: The Changing German-Jewish Symbiosis 1945–2000*, ed. Leslie Morris and Jack Zipes (New York: Palgrave/St. Martin's, 2002).

37. "Auch mir / blühten duftige Mutterworte / auch ich wuchs auf / unter phantastischen Legenden." Ausländer, *Gesammelte Werke*, vol. 3: 135.

38. "entwurzeltes Wort / verschollene Vöge." Ausländer, *Gesammelte Werke*, vol. 3: 224.

39. "Denk ich an Deutschland in der Nacht /dann bin ich aus dem Schlaf gebracht." *Heinrich Heine: The Complete Poems of Heinrich Heine*, trans. Hal Draper (Boston: Suhrkamp/Insel, 1982), 407.

40. There are countless references to angels throughout Ausländer's work. Not all of these references have biblical origins. For instance, in the poem "The Angel in You" ("Der Engel in dir") the topos of the angel is completely severed from its biblical context, whereas her well-known poems "Die Tauben" and "Hunger" are replete with biblical imagery.

41. It is also dedicated to her friend H. A. P. Grieshaber, an artist who did a number of woodcuts of Benjamin's Angel of History. Ausländer's first line about the "Angel of History" cites not only Benjamin but also a series of woodcuts by Grieshaber, who founded an art magazine in 1964 with the title *Engel der Geschichte*.

42. "'Engel der Geschichte' / Rose und Schwert / im Gefieder." Ausländer, *Gesammelte Werke*, vol. 6: 146.

43. Ausländer, *Gesammelte Werke*, vol. 5: 203.

44. "Ich rede . . . / vom gelben Stern /auf dem wir / stündlich starben / in der Galgenzeit /nicht über Rosen /red ich." Ausländer, *Gesammelte Werke*, vol. 4: 212.

45. "Mit meinem Volk in /die Wüste gegangen / ich betete nicht / zum Schlangen- und / Sandgott." Ausländer, *Gesammelte Werke*, vol. 4: 101.

46. Celan's poem begins, "No More Sand Art, no sand book, no masters" ("Keine Sandkunst mehr, kein Sandbuch, keine Meister"). Paul Celan, *Selected Poems and Prose of Paul Celan*, trans. John Felstiner (New York: Norton, 2001), 250–51.

47. "Vielhundert Jahre gewandert / von Wort zu Wort." Ausländer, *Gesammelte Werke*, vol. 4: 101.

48. Rose Ausländer Nachlass, Rose Ausländer-Gesellschaft e. V. Cologne. I am grateful to the support of Helmut Braun for giving me access to Ausländer's papers in the Nachlass.

49. See, most importantly, the poems entitled "Bukowina I" (volume 2: 21); "Bukowina II" (volume 4: 72); "Bukowina III" (volume 4: 130); and "Bukowina IV" (volume 6: 347).

50. Isaac Leib Peretz, *The Three Great Classic Writers of Modern Yiddish Literature*, vol. 3: *Selected Works of I. L. Peretz*, ed. Marvin S. Zuckerman and Marion Herbst (Malibu, Calif.: Joseph Simon/Pangloss, 1996), 386.

51. Peretz, *Three Great Classic Writers*, 386.

52. Peretz, *Three Great Classic Writers*, 387.

53. "eine Landschaft, die mich / erfand." Ausländer, *Gesammelte Werke*, vol. 4: 72.

54. "Mein Vaterland ist tot / sie haben es begraben / im Feuer." Ausländer, *Gesammelte Werke*, vol. 5: *Ich höre das Herz des Oleanders: Gedichte 1977–1979* (Frankfurt: S. Fischer Verlag, 1984), 98.

55. Itsik Manger, *The World According to Itzik: Selected Poetry and Prose*, trans. and ed. Leonard Wolf (New Haven, Conn.: Yale University Press, 2002), 106. "ikh hob zikh yorn gevalgert in der fremd, / itzt for ikh zikh valgern in der haym. / mit ayn por shikh, ayn hemd oyfn leyb, / in der hand dem shtekl. Vi ken ikh zayn on dem?"

56. "ikh vel nisht kushn dayn shtoyb vi jener groyser poet, / chatch mayn hartz iz oykh ful mit gezang un geweyn. / vos heyst kushn dayn shtoyb? ikh bin dayn shtoyb. / un ver kusht es, ikh bet aykh, zikh aleyn?" Manger, *The World According to Itzik*, 106.

57. Margul-Sperber's translation into German: "Lächeln beim Schein vom weißen Brot / Die Kinder und sterben den sanften Tod" and Rose Ausländer's "Lächeln, umleuchtet vom weißen Brot, / die Kinder und träumen sanft in den Tod." In Ausländer's version of the poem, the children smile not, as in Margul-Sperber's translation, at the appearance of the white bread, but rather are "illuminated" by the bread, they dream "into death," gently. That Rose Ausländer inserts the verb "to dream" (*träumen*), although it is not present in Margul-Sperber's translation, can be read as a distancing device.

58. Ausländer's translation of these lines into German: "Stehen Mütter in Lumpen gehüllt / auf dunklen Schwellen im Abendwind."

59. All versions of the Manger poem are found in the Rose Ausländer Nachlass, Cologne.

60. Marianne Moore, *Complete Poems* (New York: Penguin, 1994), 262.

61. Rose Ausländer, "The Poet in Two Worlds," Rose Ausländer Nachlass, Cologne.

62. Ausländer, *Gesammelte Werke*, vol. 5: 122.

63. Ausländer, *Forbidden Tree*, 105.

64. Rose Ausländer Nachlass, Cologne.

65. Rose Ausländer Nachlass, Cologne.

66. Rose Ausländer Nachlass, Cologne.

67. Rose Ausländer Nachlass, Cologne.

68. Rose Ausländer Nachlass, Cologne.

69. Ausländer, *Forbidden Tree*, 152.

70. Moore, *Complete Poems*, 85.

71. For an insightful reading of Ausländer's poetry in English, see Matthias Bauer, "Trauma oder Rettung: Rose Ausländer und die englische Sprache," in *Blumenworte Welken: Identität und Fremdheit in Rose Ausländers Lyrik*, ed. Jens Birkmeyer (Bielefeld: Aisthesis Verlag, 2008), 201–22.

72. Rose Ausländer Nachlass, Cologne.

73. Rose Ausländer Nachlass, Cologne.

74. Raymond Federman, "The Writer as Self-Translator," in *Beckett Translating/ Translating Beckett*, ed. Alan Warren Friedman (Philadelphia: Pennsylvania University Press, 1987), 14.

75. A review in *The Forward* of the exhibit on Nelly Sachs at the Jewish Museum in Berlin two years ago described Sachs as "the utterly humorless and genuinely deranged Marianne Moore." Benjamin Ivry, "Wait 'Till the Sun Shines, Nelly Sachs," *The Forward*, June 21, 2010, http://forward.com/the-assimilator/128874/wait-till-the-sun-shines-nelly-sachs/.

76. Moore, *Complete Poems*, 36.

77. See Aris Fioretos, *Nelly Sachs: Flight and Metamorphosis* (Stanford, Calif.: Stanford University Press, 2012), 147. The biography of Sachs by Fioretos is more than a biography. It brings together the work of Nelly Sachs with the collected scraps of cultural and historical texts, weaving a complex web of a poet/story/text/archive/poem. Fioretos turns a sharply critical and nuanced eye to Sachs as both poet and literary figure. Yet his assessment of her poetry acknowledges that what struck a chord in her contemporary readers is precisely what makes us "squirm" today: "That is, their tone. The poems' persona speaks with utter earnestness and without avoiding symbols which today, after sixty years of (over)use, easily come across as hackneyed. Marching boots, crying children, and murdering hands . . . If a poet were to use such imagery today, he would risk counteracting its purpose. The diagnosis would be evident: Holocaust kitsch."

78. See Klaus Neumann, *Shifting Memories: The Nazi Past in the New Germany* (Ann Arbor: University of Michigan Press, 2000), 89.

79. Fioretos, *Nelly Sachs*, 145.

80. Nelly Sachs, *Briefe der Nelly Sachs*, ed. Ruth Dinesen and Helmut Müssener (Frankfurt: Suhrkamp, 1984), 54.

81. It also entails reading her as a translator of Swedish poetry into German.

82. "von der ehemaligen Gnaden wurde sie zur schlechthinnigen Jüdin." From the correspondence of Paul Celan and Gisèle Lastrange, cited in Liska, *When Kafka Says We: Uncommon Communities in German-Jewish Literature* (Bloomington: Indiana University Press, 2009), 137.

83. For an insightful discussion of the correspondence between Celan and Sachs, see Celan, *Selected Poems and Prose of Paul Celan*, trans. Felstiner, 136.

84. Liska, *When Kafka Says We*, 131.

85. Celan, *Selected Poems and Prose of Paul Celan*, trans. Felstiner, 141.

86. Celan, *Selected Poems and Prose of Paul Celan*, trans. Felstiner, 141.

87. Paul Celan and Nelly Sachs, *Correspondence*, trans. Christopher Clark (Riverdale-on-Hudson, N.Y.: Sheep Meadow, 1995), 7.

88. Celan and Sachs, *Correspondence*, 33.

89. "so lest uns wie verkehrte Schrift / im Spiegel/ Erst totes Ding und dann der / Menschenstaub." Translation by Esther Kinsky of Sachs poem cited in Liska, *When Kafka Says We*, 127.

90. Liska, *When Kafka Says We*, 128.

91. Emily Dickinson, *The Complete Poems of Emily Dickinson*, ed. Thomas A. Johnson (Boston: Little, Brown, 1976), 657.

92. Ingeborg Bachmann, *Songs in Flight: The Collected Poems of Ingeborg Bachmann*, trans. Peter Filkins (New York: Marislio, 1995), 305. It is interesting that Filkins translates the second occurrence of the German neologism "Sterbenswort" as "syllable" instead of "dying words" of the previous line.

93. Arendt first captured the essence of banality in *Eichmann in Jerusalem* in her observation about the "grotesque silliness" of Eichmann's final words: "After a short while, gentlemen, *we shall all meet again*. Such is the fate of all men. Long live Germany, long live Argentina, long live Austria. *I shall not forget them*." Hannah Arendt, *Eichmann in Jerusalem: A Report on the Banality of Evil* (New York: Penguin, 1963), 250. Arendt's parsing contains the legendary and much misquoted term the "banality of evil."

94. It is also significant that this is expressed in a German twisted by Eichmann's "heroic struggle with the German language" that in Arendt's text is never enacted or performed, just "reported" on.

95. In her critique of Arendt's *Eichmann in Jerusalem*, Shoshana Felman posits on the one hand the law (embodied in the Eichmann trial) as a discourse about limits and the limits of Holocaust historiography. At the same time, she suggests that art has the potential to embody limitlessness, bringing the Holocaust closer in that it participates in what she terms the "language of infinity." In this paradigm, banality inhabits the realm of law and limits and stands in opposition to art. Oddly, Felman does not ground the term "banal" etymologically, but it would serve her argument well, as the word "banal" comes from the old French *ban*, which designates a precinct of the court. See Shoshana Felman, "Theaters of Justice: Arendt in Jerusalem, the Eichmann Trial, and the Redefinition of Legal Meaning in the Wake of the Holocaust," *Critical Inquiry* 27, no. 2 (2001): 201–38.

96. "I've been quoted a lot as saying, 'I like boring things.' Well, I said it and I meant it. But that doesn't mean I'm not bored by them. Of course, what I think is boring must not be the same as what other people think is . . . Apparently, most people love watching the same basic thing, as long as the details are different. But I'm just the opposite." Andy Warhol and Pat Hackett, *POPism: The Warhol 60s* (New York: Harcourt Brace Jovanovich, 1980), 50.

97. "Pop Art proper exists in Germany only in the world of its epigones . . . Pop is a product of the megalopolis, and since the loss of Berlin, Germany has no super-cities to inspire it." John Anthony Thwaites, as quoted in Lucy R. Lippard, *Pop Art* (London: Thames and Hudson, 1966), 192.

98. Andreas Huyssen, "The Cultural Politics of Pop: Reception and Critique of US Pop Art in the Federal Republic of Germany," *New German Critique* 4 (Winter 1975): 77–97.

99. See Janet Wolff, *The Aesthetics of Uncertainty* (New York: Columbia University Press, 2008).

100. Roland Barthes, "That Old Thing, Art . . . ," in *Post-Pop Art*, ed. Paul Taylor (Cambridge, Mass.: MIT Press, 1989), 25.

101. Barthes, "That Old Thing, Art . . . ," 24.

102. 1963 was the year that Arendt published *Eichmann in Jerusalem*, and it was also the year in which a number of key works by Andy Warhol were done: his series of *Disaster* paintings (*Ambulance Disaster, Tuna Fish Disaster, White Burning Car III, White Car Crash Nineteen Times, 129 Die in Plane Crash*) and the *Marilyn Monroe* and *Mona Lisa* silkscreens (*Thirty Are Better Than One*). A synchronic reading of the year 1963 would also include not only Kennedy's assassination but the Berlin premiere of Rolf Hochhuth's controversial play *The Deputy*, and the publication of Gunther Grass's *The Tin Drum*.

103. Benjamin Buchloh, "Andy Warhol's One-Dimensional Art, 1956–1966," in *Andy Warhol: A Retrospective*, ed. K. McShine (New York: Museum of Modern Art, 1989), 50.

104. Lisa Saltzman, "'Avant-Garde and Kitsch' Revisited: On the Ethics of Representation," in *Mirroring Evil: Nazi Imagery/Recent Art*, ed. Norman L. Kleeblatt (New York: Jewish Museum/New York and Rutgers University Press, 2002), 53–64, 54.

105. See Hal Foster, "Death in America," *October* 75 (Winter 1996): 38–39.

106. Andy Warhol, *The Philosophy of Andy Warhol (From A to B and Back Again)* (New York: Harvest, 1975), 123.

107. Foster, "Death in America," 37.

108. Foster, "Death in America," 42.

INDEX

absence: of "artfulness" in banality,
189 (*see also* banality); in counter-
monuments, 37; of European culture,
182; of "the Jewish," 22, 51, 69, 73,
150–51, 198; of Jewish life in east-central
Europe, 156–58, 163, 166, 169, 173,
219nn9–10, 220n16 (*see* non-place); of
Jewish life in Germany, 41, 45, 50–52;
"La Disparition," 81, 115–16; in post-
Holocaust art and poetry, 82, 116, 120–
21, 124, 129, 190, 194. *See also* elegies;
erasure
Acconci, Vito, 135, 140
Adler, H. G., 159; in Sebald's text, 105–9,
213–14n109; *Theresienstadt: The Face
of a Coerced Community* (1955), 104,
122
Adorno, Theodor: on bourgeois art, 190, 195;
"poetry after Auschwitz," 72, 116–18,
121, 171
aesthetics, post-Holocaust, 7, 18, 67, 71, 73,
102, 155–56, 189, 193–95; of body art,
136, 140, 147, 149, 151; of destruction,
36, 53; of uncertainty, 33–34, 43, 55,
190–91
Agamben, Giorgio, 78, 210n29
age of authorial disintegration, 7, 67, 69.
See also authorship; subjectivity
Airwar and Literature, 71. *See also* Sebald,
W. G.
Alter, Robert, 15–16, 171
American Jews: immigration to the United
States, 89–91, 94, 96–99, 174, 212n70;
literature, 11–16, 19–20, 65–66, 90–98,
209n12; poets, 112, 128, 153 (*see also*
poetry, American); postwar American
Jewish culture, 93, 138, 150, 219–20n15;
in postwar Germany, 27, 30–32, 44,
101–2; translations between Europe and

America, 6, 19–20, 30–32, 44, 51–52,
62, 65–67, 73, 88–102, 136, 190, 199
(*see* Anglo-American literary circles;
Kazin, Alfred); Yiddish-speaking, 98 (*see*
Yiddish)
Anglo-American literary circles, 20, 69–70,
93, 98–99, 154, 198, 209n11; theory, 8,
140
Antin, Eleanor, 149
Appel, Dora, 134, 136, 217n54, 217n60
Appelfeld, Aharon, 162, 178
appropriation, 78, 114, 119, 123, 193, 214n5.
See also authorship
Arbeit macht frei (1997), 38–39. *See also* Ho-
heisel, Horst
archival impulse, 104–7, 109
Arendt, Hannah: Blonstein's citation of, 125;
debates on culture, 190; *Eichmann in
Jerusalem*, 189, 224nn93–95, 225n102;
walk with Alfred Kazin (1952), 92–93, 95
Attie, Shimon: *Writing on the Wall*, 40–42,
48, 52
Augé, Marc, 33, 158, 161–62, 219n9
Auschwitz: Jewish tourism, 44, 158; post-
Holocaust art and writing ("after Ausch-
witz"), 72, 78, 116–18, 121, 163, 170–71,
192; as referent, 20, 33, 38, 47–48, 63,
82, 131–32, 135, 141, 155 (*see* referent:
beyond Auschwitz)
Ausländer, Rose, 20–21, 25, 197–98, 220n17,
221n30, 221nn40–41, 222n57; banality
of grief, 188–91, 195; correspondence
with Marianne Moore, 178–83; as
Czernowitz Jewish writer, 153–91, 196;
"The Inheritance," 168–69; "Janus
Angel," 171; "Jerusalem," 163–66; and
Nelly Sachs, 183–88; translations of Itsik
Manger, 172–78; *Without a Visa*, 167.
See also Czernowitz

Austerlitz (2001), 67–68, 76, 104–8, 111, 122. *See also* Sebald, W. G.

authenticity: of Jewishness, 25, 53, 63, 78, 138; of original text, 86, 142, 189, 192; of writing subject, 7, 79. *See also* appropriation; banality

authorship: coauthorship, 24; Jewish, 69–70, 78–80, 210n30. *See also* age of authorial disintegration; narrator

Bachmann, Ingeborg, 72, 178, 184, 187

Bäcker, Heimrad: conceptual poetry, 20, 25, 113–14, 152, 216nn36–38; *nachschrift*, 122–25

banality: in art, 21, 138, 154, 191–94; of evil, 224n93, 224n95; of grief, 37, 188–90, 195–96. *See also* Ausländer, Rose; Warhol, Andy

Barthes, Roland, 7, 69, 78–80, 120, 191

Beckett, Samuel, 14–15, 67, 80, 83

Bellow, Saul (*The Victim*), 96

Belmondo, Jean-Paul (*Breathless*), 115–16, 215n11

Benjamin, Walter: Angel of History, 171, 208n7, 221n41; influence of, 4, 17–18, 73, 154, 194, 216–17n42; reflections on memory, 55, 69; reflections on translation, 9, 25, 76–77, 86, 99, 163, 210n27

Berlin: absence/presence of Jewish spaces in, 19, 25, 45–47, 51–53, 204–5n4, 206n35; Brandenburg Gate, 32–38; Israeli artists in, 6; "Palace Tree Refugees" in, 58–63; and pop art, 43, 52, 224n97; Scheunenviertel, 40–41, 44; Sculpture Park, 18, 27–31, 53–57, 199, 207n54; *Trabihenge* (Stonehenge), 42–44. *See also* Berlin Wall

Berlin Gateless, 37. *See also* Hoheisel, Horst

Berlin Wall: fall of, 40–42, 58; former zone, 27, 62; Sculpture Park, 53, 56, 199, 207nn53–54. *See also* Mohr, Ulrike

Bernstein, Charles, 15, 121, 153–54

Bildung, 86, 158–59, 170. *See also Kultur*

Blake, William, 91–92

Blaufuks, Daniel: *An Absence*, 115–16, 215n11; *All the Memory of the World, Part One (Toda a Memória do Mundo, parte um)*, 102–4; legibility of Jewishness, 25, 113, 152; "memento mori" book, 114; relationship between text and image, 19, 66–67, 122, 156, 198–

99, 213–14n109 (*see* Sebald, W. G.); *Terezin*, 105–12

Blonstein, Anne: conceptual poetry and Jewishness, 25, 113, 152, 198; *correspondence with nobody*, 20, 125–30, 143, 200, 216n39, 216n42. See *notarikon*

Bobrowski, Johannes, 184

body, gendered, 132–33, 136, 148–51, 217n49. *See also* body art; purity laws

body art, Jewish, 20, 131–52. *See also* body, gendered

Book of Disquiet, 78–80. *See* Pessoa, Fernando

Borges, Jorge Luis, 15, 24, 72, 104

Boyarin, Daniel, 9, 113

Boyarin, Jonathan, 10–11, 17, 113

Bukovina: Buchenland, 168–69; memory of, 161, 165–68, 172–75; poets from, 155, 178; as site of Jewish population, 157, 162, 219n14. *See also* Czernowitz

Burgin, Joshua (*Tattoo Jew*), 137–39, 217n54

Butler, Judith, 135, 143, 150

Call It Sleep (1934), 13–14, 98. *See also* Roth, Henry

Calvino, Italo, 15, 72; *Invisible Cities*, 157–58

Carnesky, Marisa: *Jewess Tattooess*, 137, 145

Caruth, Cathy, 71

Celan, Paul, 15, 18, 170; Czernowitz (*Meridian* speech), 21, 153, 155–57, 159, 162–63, 197, 204n55, 219n6, 219n9; readings of, 170, 183–87; *Sandkunst*, 172; Shakespeare's sonnets, 20, 125–30, 200; *Todesfuge*, 220n17; translations by, 24–25, 218nn1–2; translations of, 73

Certeau, Michel de, 33

Chicago, Judy, 149

Christianity: imagery, 201n1; translational relationship with Judaism, 8–9

Cixous, Hélène: language, 201n2, 201n5; marker of the "J," 4–6, 8–9, 18, 25, 52, 199; scarriness of literature, 4, 113, 125, 131, 133, 141–42, 201n1. *See* laceration, cultural; stigmatext

codework, 20, 116–18, 122, 124, 215n13. *See also* Sondheim, Alan

Cold War, 27–28. *See also* Berlin Wall; Germany, East; Germany, West

correspondence with nobody, 20, 125–30, 143, 200, 216n39, 216n42. *See also* Blonstein, Anne

Cousineau, Jennifer, 44

Crane, Hart, 93
cultural transmission, 7–8, 21, 73, 208n7
Cummings, E. E., 129, 160, 175, 178
cyberpoetics, 144, 198
Czernowitz: as birthplace, 20, 153–55, 159, 162, 170, 174–75, 178–79, 182; contemporary, 197, 220n16; as Habsburg Jewish city, 17, 156–59, 173, 219n6 (*see* Habsburg Empire); as non-place, 21, 25, 156–58, 161–62, 165–69, 172, 188, 196, 219n10. *See also* Bukovina; east-central Europe

Damon, Maria, 116, 118, 144, 214–15n6
Danto, Arthur: *The Abuse of Beauty*, 140; the end of art, 145–47. *See* Hegel
Deleuze, Gilles, and Felix Guattari, 6, 116
Demidenko controversy (Demidenko, Helen), 79
Derrida, Jacques, 4, 18, 160, 201n2
destruction, aesthetics of: in literature, 72, 74–75, 93, 185, 211–12n60; site-specific public art, 32–33, 35–38, 40, 42, 52. *See also* Haacke, Hans; Hoheisel, Horst; Sebald, W. G.; Wodiczko, Krzysztof
desubjectification, 84. *See also* authorship; narrator
diaspora: exile poet, 175; of Jewish body, 132–33, 136, 138; of Jewish spaces, 30, 45–46; poetics of, 68–69, 73–74, 102, 143–44, 154, 162, 165; represented in art, 65; of texts, 9
Dickinson, Emily, translations of, 126, 154, 162, 187. *See also* Celan, Paul
Diner, Hasia, 96
Domin, Hilde, 184
Double or Nothing (1998), 81–82. *See also* Federman, Raymond
Drawing Center of New York's *Pierced Hearts and True Love* exhibit (1995), 138–39. *See also* body art, Jewish

east-central Europe: Jewish memory and spaces in, 21, 158, 161, 165, 168–69, 196–97, 219n9; Jews of, 154, 156–57
Eastern Europe: Jewish tourism in, 44, 156, 158, 219n15; reimagining spaces in, 88, 161, 173, 206n32, 219n10, 220n16. *See also* east-central Europe; *Ostjude*
Eco, Umberto, 72
Eichmann, Adolf, 189, 194, 224nn93–95. *See also* Arendt, Hannah

Eisenman, Peter (Memorial to the Murdered Jews of Europe), 44, 47
elegies: to Czernowitz, 153, 155–62, 166–69, 173–74, 196–97; to German past, 37, 69, 183, 197; to Holocaust, 121, 189–90, 192–93; to lost Jewish spaces, 8, 30–31, 41–42, 48, 52, 156, 158, 162; nature of translation, 8, 76; to personal loss, 128, 160; re-creations, 42, 48, 158, 161, 166. *See* memory: elegiac
Emerson, Ralph Waldo, 93
Emigrants, The, 75–76, 84–87, 211n59. *See also* Sebald, W. G.
emptiness, 32, 166, 177–78, 207n58. *See also* non-place; nothingness
en passance, 6, 9, 130, 201n5. *See also* Cixous, Hélène
Ensler, Eve, 149
Enzensberger, Hans Magnus, 184, 190
erasure: of image, 82, 89, 115–16, 205n12, 215n11; of minority cultures, 52; of the past, 51; of place, 42, 55, 158; of tattoos, 142, 148–49; of text, 85–86, 105, 115, 120–22, 124, 172, 178, 211n59, 216n32; vanished Jews/Jewish culture, 89, 115, 153, 157–58, 162, 168–69, 219n10; of writing subject, 80. *See also* absence
eruv (*eruvin*): concept of, 19, 25, 43–47, 52–53, 55, 63, 199, 206nn34–35; as digital space, 48–50, 62, 65. *See* Hiller, Susan (*The J. Street Project*); Malkin, Elliott
exile: "Palace Tree Refugees" in, 60–62, 199, 207n57, 220n27; poet in, 172, 174–76, 178–79, 183, 188; in sculpture, 54; writing, 65, 68, 144, 159. *See also* Heimat

Federman, Raymond: circulation of Jewishness between Europe and America, 19, 102; *Double or Nothing*, 81–82; 1.5 generation child survivor, 15, 102, 203n34; post-Holocaust literary aesthetic, 25, 67, 72, 156; self-translation, 14, 20, 66, 80–84, 88, 183, 199; *SHHH: The Story of a Childhood* (2010), 83
Felman, Shoshana, 224n95
Felstiner, John, 153, 220n17
Finley, Karen, 149
Fitterman, Robert: conceptual poetry, 20, 25, 112–13, 152, 156; *Holocaust Museum*, 118–24

183, 202n11, 221n30; third-generation
Israelis, 146
Iyer, Pico, 74–75

Jackson, Shelley: legibility of Jewish female
body, 132; *Skin: A Mortal Work of Art*,
141–45, 148. *See also* body art, Jewish
Jacob, Carol, 76
"Janus Angel," 171. *See also* Ausländer, Rose
Jerusalem: in Ausländer's poem, 163–66; in
Manger's poem, 175
"Jerusalem" (1953), 163–66. *See also* Ausländer, Rose
"jewished englished," 125, 129–30
Jewish Museum (Berlin), 37, 46, 204n4,
223n75
Jewish Museum (New York), 50–51, 193
Jewishness: absence of, 157, 161, 164, 169;
defining, 4–9, 11–12, 15–19, 198, 200,
208n4; geography of, 32, 41, 45–48, 52–
53, 62–63; hiding, 3, 89; markers of, 68–
70, 73–74, 78, 89–90, 92–93, 96–101;
performing, 32, 150, 152, 170; textuality
and, 21–26, 184–85, 197; transgressive,
113, 131–33, 136, 138–39
Judesein ("Jew in the world"), literary, 12–13,
66. *See* Miron, Dan

Kafka, Franz, 6, 17, 67, 70, 75, 93, 171
Kant, Immanuel, 140–41, 147
Karasick, Adeena, 25; *Genrecide*, 144–45
Kazin, Alfred: Jewishness, 19, 25, 90, 92–
101; mediation between America and
Europe, 19–20, 66, 88–101, 199; *New
York Jew* (1978), 88, 92, 94; *On Native
Grounds* (1942), 93–94, 212n70; post-
Holocaust aesthetics, 67, 102; *Walker
in the City* (1951), 88, 90–92, 97, 99,
101
Kimmelman, Michael, 138, 146–47
kitsch, 136, 190, 193; Holocaust kitsch, 184,
223n77. *See also* Warhol, Andy
Kittner, Alfred, 162, 174
Klüger, Ruth, 159
Koepnick, Lutz, 34
Krauss, Rosalind: indexical power of the
image, 47, 132, 207n44; on modern
sculpture, 39, 42–43
Kultur, 93, 158. *See also Bildung*

Lacan, Jacques, 194–95
LaCapra, Dominic, 71

laceration, cultural, 4. *See also* Cixous,
Hélène
laceration, textual, 118
La Disparition (A Void), 81, 115–16. *See also*
Perec, Georges
Landscape Monumentalists (*Landschaftsmonumentalisten*), 42
Lang, Berel, 71
legibility/illegibility: of gendered Jewish body,
132–36, 144, 149–50, 152; of Jewishness,
15, 69, 169; in post-Holocaust poetry,
155, 162, 190; of spatial lines, 19, 28, 45,
53, 199; of text and image, 72, 77, 105,
111, 117, 123–24. *See also* translation
Levinson, Julian, 97–98
literature: American, 13, 16, 20, 92–94, 96,
98, 209n12 (*see also* Anglo-American
literary circles); challenging national
categories, 6, 10, 16, 65–66, 70, 73–74,
198, 200; Jewish, 7–8, 11–13, 23, 174;
post-Holocaust, 8, 38, 67, 71; scarriness
of, 4, 125, 131 (*see also* Cixous, Hélène).
See also German-Jewish: text
Lodz (Litzmanstadt), 87, 158
Lui, Alan, 36–37

Magritte, René, 81, 143
Malkin, Elliott, 48–49, 62, 65. See also *eruv*
Manger, Itsik, 162, 172–78. *See also* Ausländer, Rose; Czernowitz
Marcus, Greil, 109
Marcuse, Herbert, 190, 195
marginality: authors on/outside the margins,
67, 126, 154, 182, 198; Jewish body,
19, 133, 138–39, 143; Jewish writing,
7, 10, 116, 128–29, 131, 200; marginally known art, 31, 42; place, 153, 156;
sexuality, 113, 132–33; social groups,
137, 139; status of the Jew, 4, 22, 26,
199, 217n60
Margul-Sperber, Alfred, 159, 162, 176,
222n57
Matta-Clark, Gordon, 35–36, 52
Mayer, Hans, 159
McHugh, Heather, 114, 118, 120
Méc, Miklós, 55
Melville, Herman, 93
memory: acoustic, 71, 76, 85–86, 116; archival, 104–7, 121–23 (*see also* archival
impulse); childhood, 81–82, 97, 102,
155 (*see* trauma: childhood); circulating
between Britain and Germany, 70, 74–

reflections on, 66–67, 102, 104, 109–
10, 114–15, 198–99; *La Disparition (A
Void)*, 81, 115; 1.5 generation writer, 81,
102, 203n34 (*see* 1.5 generation); *W, or
the Memory of Childhood* (1975), 81,
83, 102
Peretz, I. L.., 173–74. *See* Yiddish
Perloff, Marjorie, 79, 114
Pessoa, Fernando: *Book of Disquiet*, 78–80;
heteronyms, 78–80, 83–84, 210n30
(*see* heteronymity); Jewishness, 25, 72;
self-translation, 15; translated by Celan,
154, 162
poetry, American, 153–54, 160, 175, 178–79,
182. *See also* Anglo-American literary
circles; modernism
poetry, erasure, 82, 115, 120–22, 124, 216n32
poetry, Holocaust, 154, 169, 171, 183–84.
See also aesthetics, post-Holocaust
pop art, influence of: on body art, 148; in
Germany, 43, 52, 190, 195, 224n97; on
post-Holocaust art and poetry, 191–95,
197 (*see* Warhol, Andy)
postcolonial theory, 8, 74
postmemory, 69; in Germany, 21–22, 31, 73,
198; reinscribed onto body, 134–36; reproduction and translations in, 155, 168,
191–92, 195. *See also* memory; trauma
postmodernism, 33, 70, 193
postwar period: culture, 21, 31, 44, 92, 96,
116, 138, 150; works and criticism produced in, 66, 70, 72, 109, 123, 153, 159,
184, 186, 199
Prague: Jewish tourism, 44, 158, 220n16;
Kafka in, 17; in Sebald's *Austerlitz*, 106,
111–12, 206n34
Presner, Todd, 4–5
Price, Derrick, 114
Proust, Marcel, 70
purity laws (*niddah*), 148–49. *See also* Molgan, Hagit

Rahv, Philip, 93
Raley, Rita, 215n13. *See also* codework
referent: beyond Auschwitz, 20, 33, 47, 117
(*see also* Auschwitz); carnal, 131, 135–
36, 139; "German" and "Jewish," 22, 52,
69, 198; status of, 35–36, 38, 40, 43, 79,
121–22, 169, 181, 191, 193–95
Reinartz, Dirk, *Deathly Stills: Pictures of
Former Concentration Camps*, 105,
109–11

remembrance, Holocaust, 37–38, 48, 50, 190,
192. *See also* memory
Resnais, Alain, *Toute la memoire du monde*
(1956), 104
Rilke, Rainer Maria, 70, 120
Rings of Saturn (1995; trans. 1998), 73–74,
102. *See also* Sebald, W. G.
Roth, Henry, 89, 94, 202n27; *Call It Sleep*
(1934), 13–14, 98
Roth, Philip, 150
rubble, figurative, 66, 69, 72, 85, 109,
209n16; of history, 68, 186–87. *See also*
ruins
ruins: historical, 22, 53, 63, 66, 68, 92, 109,
198; of memory, 77; narrative, 69, 72–
74, 78, 86, 96, 158, 169, 172, 208n7,
211–12n60; spatial, 28, 32, 37, 41, 53,
55, 87, 158, 199. *See also* destruction,
aesthetics of

Sachs, Nelly, 178, 183–88, 223n75, 223n77
Samsa, Gregor, 74
Sandkunst, 172, 222n46. *See also* Celan, Paul
Scheunenviertel (Jewish quarter), 40–41, 44–
45. *See also* Berlin
Schlögel, Karl, 156
Schneemann, Carolee, 135, 149
Scholem, Gershom, 171
Schreier, Benjamin, 15
Sebald, W. G.: *Airwar and Literature*, 71;
Austerlitz, 67–68, 76, 104–8, 111, 122;
Daniel Blaufuks's reflections on, 66–
67, 101–2, 104–12, 122, 198–99; *The
Emigrants*, 75–76, 84–87, 211n59;
Jewishness, 19, 25, 68–70, 73–74, 78, 84,
208nn3–4; narrative ruin, 68–69, 72–73,
77–78, 86–87, 208n7, 211–12n60 (*see*
ruins); narrative techniques, 76–81, 84–
88; reception of, 209n14, 209–10n18;
rethinking post-Holocaust aesthetics, 67,
71–73, 122, 156, 198–99, 210n29; *Rings
of Saturn* (1995; trans. 1998), 73–74,
102; self-translation, 15, 20
secondary witness: through body art, 134, 146
secularism, 10, 126, 149, 170, 171
Seidman, Naomi, 8–9, 126
Shakespeare: elegiac impulse, 160; sonnets,
20, 115, 125–30, 162, 200. *See also*
Blonstein, Anne; Celan, Paul
Shell, Marc and Werner Sollors (*Multilingual
Anthology of American Literature*), 16–
17, 209n12. *See also* multilingualism

SHHH: *The Story of a Childhood* (2010), 83.
    See also Federman, Raymond
Shoah: post-Shoah literature, 8, 69, 210n29;
    remembrance in Germany, 37, 53, 184,
    190, 195; representation of, 85, 136.
    See also Holocaust
siddur, Singer, 98–99, 101, 213n91
Silverman, Kaja (*Male Subjectivity at the
    Margins*), 113, 132
Six-Day War, 96
Skin: A Mortal Work of Art, 141–45, 148.
    See also Jackson, Shelley
Soja, Edward, 158
Sondheim, Alan: boundaries of Jewishness,
    25, 113–14, 152, 198; codework, 20,
    116–18, 122, 124; post-Holocaust aes-
    thetics, 156
Sontag, Susan, 119–21, 203n44
spaces, Jewish: on body, 132, 136; in Israel,
    206n32; literary, 5, 8, 13, 29, 68, 71–75,
    88, 101, 106–7, 123–25, 156, 190–91,
    197; memory, 18–19, 30–35, 37, 39–
    41, 43, 87, 132, 208n7, 219nn9–10;
    re-creation of, 25, 40; reimagined,
    156–64, 169, 199, 206n32, 219–20n15;
    transnational geography, 31, 45 (*see also*
    geography, Jewish); urban, 7, 25, 30, 43–
    53, 55, 61–63, 158; vanished, 153, 157–
    58, 162, 219n10. See also *eruv*; memory;
    non-space
Speer, Albert, 122
Spiegelman, Art, 135
Starnberg, Elieser, 162
Stevens, Wallace, 160, 178, 180
Stieglitz, Alfred: *The Steerage* (1907), 88–92,
    101
stigmatext, 4, 113, 133, 141–42, 149. *See also*
    Cixous, Hélène
Stih, Renata and Frieder Schnock, 31, 38, 52
subject: division between object and, 146;
    poetic, 164–65, 171, 178; unified, 8,
    132, 135–36; writing, 7, 24, 69, 79–80.
    See also subjectivity
subjectivity: anti-subjectivity, 80; break in,
    128, 194; German Jewish, 7, 66, 75,
    79, 109; Jewish, 4, 21–22, 132–35, 138;
    representing the Holocaust, 119, 192.
    See also age of authorial disintegration
Suleiman, Susan, 82, 203n34

Tattoo Jew, 137–39. *See also* Burgin, Joshua
Taylor, Mark, 139, 148

textuality: boundaries of, 19–20, 26, 67, 113,
    123, 162; intertextuality, 191; mutability
    of, 6–7, 187, 196–97
Theresienstadt (camp), 44, 104–8, 110.
    See also Adler, H. G.
*Theresienstadt: The Face of a Coerced Com-
    munity* (1955), 104–8, 122. *See also*
    Adler, H. G.
Timm, Uwe, 72, 74
Todesfuge, 220n17. *See also* Celan, Paul
tourism, Jewish, 30–31, 40–42, 44–45, 156,
    158, 197, 219n10, 220n16
translation: body as site of, 131–32, 137, 147,
    150 (*see also* body art); between Euro-
    pean and American culture, 19, 32, 51,
    65–67, 73; examples of translated Jews,
    15, 69, 170, 198, 200; failed, 10, 201n2;
    Jewish-Christian, 8–9 (*see also* Christianity);
    of Jewish memory, 67, 70, 72–73,
    76–78, 196, 198, 209n13, 210n29; of
    Jewishness, 3–8, 10, 22, 25–26, 65,
    68–70, 72–73, 78, 113, 131, 164–66,
    169–70, 198–99; through mobility and
    migration, 19, 66, 68, 70, 73, 203n43;
    multilingual, 13–14, 83, 163–64, 173–
    79, 181, 218nn1–2; *notarikon*, 125–30,
    200 (*see also* Blonstein, Anne); between
    original and translated text, 15, 20, 77–
    81, 84–86, 98–101, 155, 163, 181, 191,
    208n7, 209n14; partial, 10, 124; philo-
    sophical problems of, 210n27; of place,
    21, 28–29, 32, 42, 155, 161–66, 169, 196
    (*see also* Czernowitz); of poems, 120,
    125–30, 153–54, 162–70, 173, 176–79,
    181, 187–88, 200; self-translation, 5, 14,
    20, 66, 80, 83, 153–54, 162, 179, 181–
    83, 199 (*see also* Federman, Raymond);
    between text and image, 65, 105, 110,
    113, 116, 122, 124; trans-Jewish, 21, 26
    (*see also* cultural transmission); "turn to
    translation," 73; untranslatability, 8, 25,
    126, 162, 204n55; from/into Yiddish, 14,
    130, 153, 162, 172–74, 176–78 (*see also*
    Yiddish). *See also* Jewishness
trauma: in art, 34, 52, 120; childhood, 82–83,
    85, 102; historical, 38, 51, 118; loss of
    language, 8, 85, 159; postmemory, 134,
    136, 139; reenactments of, 188–91, 194–
    95; in writing, 65, 67, 69, 71–72, 75,
    95–96, 98, 102, 170, 174, 183. *See also*
    memory; postmemory
Trilling, Lionel, 93

Ungaretti, Giuseppe, 162
U.S. Holocaust Memorial Museum
   (USHMM), 20, 118–21

Vainshtein, Marina, 132–37, 141, 145, 147.
   See also body art

W, or the Memory of Childhood (1975), 81,
   102. *See also* Perec, Georges
Walker in the City (1951), 88, 90–92, 97, 99,
   101. *See also* Kazin, Alfred
Warhol, Andy: banality in art, 21, 188–95,
   224n96, 225n102; connections with
   post-Holocaust art, 25, 52, 147. *See also*
   banality
Weber, Max, 200
Weil, Simone, 93, 125
Weimar era, 27–28, 30, 34, 41
Weiner, Lawrence, 52
Weiss, Peter, 72
Wharton, Edith, 93
White, Hayden, 71
Whitman, Walt, 89, 91, 212n70
Wilke, Hannah, 135
Wilkomirski Affair (Wilkomirski, Binjiman),
   71, 79, 209n13
Williams, William Carlos, 89, 91–92

Wirth-Nesher, Hana, 11, 13
Wissenschaft des Judentums, 16, 22
Without a Visa (1974), 167. *See also* Auslän-
   der, Rose
Wodiczko, Krzysztof, 39–40, 52
Wolf, Christa, 72
Wolf, Uljana, 120
World War II: aftermath of, 27, 51, 59
   (*see also* postwar period); emigration
   after, 3, 95, 97, 160, 208n4; Jewish life
   before, 157, 163, 166; reflections on, 94,
   96; survival of, 159, 170, 175
Writing on the Wall, 40–42, 48, 52

Yasusada controversy (Yasusada, Araki), 79
Yerushalmi, Yosef Haim, 22–23
Yiddish: "jewished englished," 130; as part
   of multilingual world, 13–14, 21, 98;
   poetry, 13, 153, 162, 172, 174–78,
   212n70; theater, 27; "thinking in Jewish," 10–11; translated from, 176–78,
   204n55; Yiddish conference (1908), 157,
   173–74 (*see* Peretz, I. L.)
Young, James, 32, 35, 71

Ziegelboim, Shmuel (Ziegelboim suicide),
   94, 97